THE

Rise and Fall

OF

MODERN AMERICAN

CONSERVATISM

THE

Rise and Fall

OF

MODERN AMERICAN
CONSERVATISM

A SHORT HISTORY

DAVID FARBER

PRINCETON UNIVERSITY PRESS
PRINCETON AND OXFORD

COPYRIGHT © 2010 BY PRINCETON UNIVERSITY PRESS

Published by Princeton University Press,

41 William Street, Princeton, New Jersey 08540

In the United Kingdom: Princeton University Press,

6 Oxford Street, Woodstock, Oxfordshire OX20 1TW

press.princeton.edu

Library of Congress Cataloging-in-Publication Data

Farber, David R.

The rise and fall of modern American conservatism : a short history / David Farber.

   p.   cm.

Includes bibliographical references and index.

ISBN 978-0-691-12915-0 (hardcover : alk. paper)   1. Conservatism—United
States—History. I. Title.

  JC573.2.U6F34   2010

  320.520973—dc22

2009050142

British Library Cataloging-in-Publication Data is available

This book has been composed in Minion Pro with Künstler Script
and Copperplate Gothic display

Printed on acid-free paper. ∞

Printed in the United States of America

1 3 5 7 9 10 8 6 4 2

CONTENTS

ILLUSTRATIONS

CHAPTER ONE, PAGE 9: From his election to the United States Senate in 1938 until his untimely death in 1953, Robert A. Taft refused to bow to the New Deal juggernaut. Here Taft is surrounded by fellow Ohioans as he gears up to run for the 1952 Republican Party presidential nomination. (Courtesy of the Ohio Historical Society.)

CHAPTER TWO, PAGE 39: William Buckley established himself as conservatives' greatest modern publicist while still in his twenties. Buckley first lambasted liberalism in print at Yale University, where he served as chairman of the student newspaper, the *Yale Daily News*. (Courtesy of Manuscripts and Archives, Yale University Library.)

CHAPTER THREE, PAGE 77: Arizona Senator Barry Goldwater brought a bare-knuckles style to political conservatism; his 1964 presidential run helped to inspire a new conservative movement in the United States. (Courtesy of the Arizona Historical Society.)

CHAPTER FOUR, PAGE 119: Phyllis Schlafly supported Senator Taft; shared William Buckley's hatred of communism; championed Goldwater's candidacy with her blockbuster best seller, *A Choice, Not an Echo*; and then made her greatest contribution to the conservative ascendency by successfully mobilizing a grassroots movement that defeated the women's Equal Rights Amendment. (Courtesy of Phyllis Schlafly.)

CHAPTER FIVE, PAGE 159: Ronald Reagan became the conservative movement's greatest icon. At a time when many Americans believed that liberals had run out of answers to the nation's problems, Reagan offered movie-star looks, a ready wit, and a few carefully thought-out conservative principles to the American electorate. In 1980, those voters made him president. (Courtesy of the Ronald Reagan Library.)

CHAPTER SIX, PAGE 209: George W. Bush reflected the conservative movement's powerful religious base. Bush's firm faith in Christianity, economic liberty, and the righteous power of American military might would not be enough to keep the conservative movement from crashing in the first years of the twenty-first century. (Photo by Eric Draper; courtesy of the George W. Bush Presidential Library.)

ACKNOWLEDGMENTS

WHEN I WAS FIFTEEN YEARS OLD, I went door to door canvassing for George McGovern. The regular Democratic precinct captain had decided to sit out the presidential election. A good many of my Chicago neighbors took pity on me and tried to explain to me why I was an idiot. I've been thinking about what they told me ever since. So, first of all, thanks to the good people of Chicago who were willing to talk politics with an unformed youth; this book provides a few of the snappy answers I wished I had back in the day.

A more immediate thanks to friends and colleagues around the world with whom I have discussed American conservatism. I am particularly grateful to Professor Jun Furuya, director of the Center for Pacific and American Studies at the University of Tokyo, who invited me several times to Japan, where I was able to try out aspects of this book before a very generous crew of international scholars. I met Desmond King at one of Professor Furuya's Tokyo seminars, and between beers he allowed that I might not be completely wrong about American conservatism. My thanks for his continued and generous support.

Like political conservatives (and liberals), historians have an institutional culture that allows them to work out their projects in a collegial, yet cutthroat, fashion. I gave talks on the subject of this book at many venues; particular thanks for allowing me to hold forth to the Modern America Workshop at Princeton University, the Huntington Library and Roy Ritchie, the Université Lyon II, IEP de Lyon and Vincent Michelot, the Teaching American History federal grant program, the Pacific Coast Branch of the American Historical Association, the American Historical Association, the Policy History Conference (with special thanks to the dean of conservative historians, Don Critchlow), and the Organization of American Historians. For help in getting this project off the ground and supporting me in the process I am grateful to Bruce Schulman and Rick Perlstein. Fulbright scholar and friend Masaru Nishikawa made critical contributions to the success of this project; I am in his debt. Without Brigitta van Rheinberg, editor-in-chief at Princeton University Press, this book would not have existed; she inspired the project and guided it over the years. She is an extraordinary reader and critic, and her support and encouragement were essential to my work. Thanks, as well, to editor Clara Platter and the entire editorial and production team at Princeton University Press.

Several colleagues read all or part of the manuscript. Will Hitchcock, who can write like an avenging angel, gave generously of his time and tried to save me from fuzzy thinking. Todd Shepard shared his extraordinary knowledge of modern politics and helped me think through the narrative arc as we hung out at Bottle Beach and Had Khom. Michelle Nickerson, whose own work on conservatism inspired me, sharpened my analysis and kept readers from seeing a few of my blind spots. Jeff Roche, whose work on cowboy conservatives influenced this work, signed off on key sections. I am indebted to my dear friend Richard Immerman for his careful reading of the manuscript. He is a man of extraordinary energy and intellectual depth. The publisher arranged for a couple of expert anonymous reviewers. One gave me a genial kick in the pants and the other provided a brilliant and detailed critique; I am fairly sure I know who they are, but the rules of the game require that I simply say: well played and thank you. Thanks, too, to my many students who have heard versions of this material in diverse forms; based on your reactions, I tried to keep the boring parts to a minimum.

Beth Bailey once again read the daily word count, and then each draft of each chapter, and then each draft of the entire manuscript. Here we sit, writing away, thirty feet apart in a refurbished shoe factory overlooking Pearl Street, which is an elegant name for a messed-up alley. How wonderfully predictable.

THE

Rise and Fall

OF

MODERN AMERICAN

CONSERVATISM

INTRODUCTION

In early 1936, Robert A. Taft, a president's son and almost always the smartest person in any room, thought that he was a liberal. Then he heard President Franklin Roosevelt explain to the American people that he and his administration were redefining liberalism. In 1776, the president said, liberals had "sought freedom from the tyranny of a political autocracy." Now, Roosevelt continued, liberals demanded not freedom from political tyranny but "against economic tyranny"— and in this fight, "the American citizen could appeal only to the organized power of government."[1]

"The President has sought to appropriate to the New Deal," Taft fumed, "all the ideals of liberalism, and to brand his opponents as Tories, and tools of entrenched greed."[2] Taft clung for a brief period to the L-word, but by 1938, running for the Senate, he used, for the first time, another word to describe his politics: *conservative*. (The term had been used episodically before, but never regularly by American politicians of note.) Taft, modern conservatism's first major figure, understood that the New Deal had forced a new divide in American politics, one that pushed the politically minded to ponder two new disciplinary political orders, master categories that would for decades transcend party or region. In the late 1930s, politicians and their constituents began to sort themselves out as liberals or conservatives. What follows is a short history of political conservatives' evolving and contingent disciplinary order and the constituencies who embraced it, from the time of Robert Taft through the presidency of George W. Bush.

My central argument is that modern American conservatism is a disciplinary order generated by hostility to market restraints and fueled by religious faith, devotion to social order, and an individualized conception of political liberty. New Deal liberalism, in its most enduring form, insisted that the state needed to discipline the capitalist system in order to ensure that working people (broadly defined) and their families could maintain their dignity and their buying power. It was, Franklin Roosevelt memorably said, the "hazards and vicissitudes" of the market economy from which the New Deal would protect the American people.[3] Political conservatives responded to liberal claims by arguing that it was not the market that needed disciplining but individuals.

In the 1930s and 1940s, conservatives looked for that discipline primarily in the workings of capitalism, which they argued rewarded the worthy and punished the unworthy. They believed that government protection robbed individuals of their self-respect and autonomy. They also saw a moral hazard in liberal schemes to protect individuals from the discipline of the market: if irresponsible behavior carried no risk, too many people would behave irresponsibly. Many of these economically minded disciplinarians, including Taft, knew very well that a market-based economic system was a harsh master. Thus they argued that a certain kind of religious faith, a respect for enduring and thus tested social hierarchies, and a trust in cultural orthodoxy were necessary to enable individuals—as well as their families, communities, and the nation—to stay strong and to maintain a salutary moral stability in the face of the economic challenges and cultural risks a market economy would surely bring. These early conservatives did not clearly articulate all aspects of this emergent political field, nor did they all agree on the relationship between economic success, religious faith, and respect for long-standing social forms. Others would spell out those connections in the following decades, though not without serious disagreements and always in response to changing circumstances, their own particular talents, political opportunities, and the shifting political stands of their liberal opponents.

Over time, post–New Deal liberals insisted that market relations—as well as other major institutional structures in American life—needed further disciplining to promote not only economic equity but social and political equality as well. In embracing policies and positions that challenged traditional racial and gender inequalities, they also argued that cultural heterodoxy and social innovation were beneficial to the United States. Conservatives continued to insist that economic liberty was the bedrock on which American prosperity, individual rights, and morality were based. Most conservatives, however, in claiming to protect economic liberty for individuals, proved willing to sacrifice civil liberties and to restrain rights-claims in order to maintain religious, moral, and social order. As William Buckley wrote, the liberal is "bewitched . . . with the value of [social] innovation," whereas a conservative "urges conformity [to] 'institutions' of society."[4] Without such conformity, Buckley and many other conservatives believed, society becomes vulnerable to the undisciplined forces of consumer desire, modernist (atheistic) cultural relativism, and foreign threats to the American way of life. From the 1930s forward, liberals and conservatives reframed issues of equality and liberty within their respective disciplinary orders. Their efforts were most intense as they struggled with the challenges of civil rights, national security, and national identity.

In making this argument, I emphasize both the contingent nature of change and the role of individuals. I also feature the major role conservatives have played in politicizing civil society in behalf of their cause. Characteristically working outside the political party system, conservatives have been dedicated to forging new institutions capable of spreading their political message, organizing activists, and mobilizing voters. Liberals have worked a similar democratic vein but in part because conservatives for so long—even into contemporary times—have believed themselves to be shut out of mainstream institutions such as the mass media and universities, they have been particularly invested and inventive in creating a politically potent counterpublic.

I am also emphasizing, in a fashion rare among American historians, the centrality of the search for order in American politics. While an older generation of American historians used this rubric to explore the age of industrialization and progressivism, the notion that the desire for order and security have played a vital role in American political life, generally, has fallen out of fashion, at least among American historians. Instead, American historians have framed the national narrative most specifically around the struggle for equality. I agree that the struggle for equality is central to American history. But to understand the power and pull of political conservatism, I argue, a counternarrative built on many Americans'—liberals and moderates, as well as conservatives—desire for order and stability needs to be constructed, as well. As I will relate, the struggle for equality and economic equity often stands in direct counterpoint to conservative or conservative-leaning Americans' political demand for order and stability. Americans' belief, half-hearted and conflicted as it often is, in equality; their ambivalent faith in individual economic liberty; and their desire for order, security, and stability create an inexorable political tension. The conservative politicians, social activists, and intellectuals I write about in this book have struggled to master those sometime contradictory desires. These heroes of the conservative order have done their best to convince Americans that conservatism provides the American people with a just and tested way to keep their families safe, their dreams alive, and their nation strong.

Each of the following six chapters is anchored by a well-known conservative actor: Robert Taft, William Buckley, Barry Goldwater, Phyllis Schlafly, Ronald Reagan, and George W. Bush. I use each figure to emphasize a particular theme in the development of modern conservatism and to explain how and why conservatives crafted a disciplinary order that captured a segment of the American political imagination by claiming moral superiority, critiquing economic egalitarianism, relishing bellicosity, and embracing cultural nationalism.

This work differs from other recent interpretations of modern political conservatism because I link economic conservatives and social conservatives into the larger disciplinary political order I have sketched above. Rather than arguing that a majority of conservatives act in irrational opposition to their own best economic interest, or defining conservatism as a highly intellectual enterprise led by a small band of erudite figures, I am offering another explanation built on a larger, historically contingent framework. In so doing, I have the advantage of learning from the many dissertations and monographs produced in the past few years that effectively connect conservative grassroots political organizing to national political developments.

In chapter 1, I present the estimable Senator Robert A. Taft, whose historical legacy has only grown since his death in 1953. While giving Taft his due as a progenitor of modern conservatism, this chapter

also traces the formation of modern liberalism. My claim throughout the book is that conservatives define themselves in relationship
to liberalism. Taft set the conservative political agenda for a generation and anchored labor-intensive industries, free market enthusi-
asts, and many small-business owners to the conservative cause. Taft
feared that liberals did not understand what made America great.
"Before our system can claim success," he wrote, "it must not only
create a people with a higher standard of living, but a people with a
higher standard of character—character that must include religious
faith, morality, educated intelligence, self-restraint, and an ingrained
demand for justice and unselfishness."[5] Taft, a man before his time,
set conservatism on its virtue-claiming course.

In chapter 2, I introduce the wit and wisdom of William Buckley.
Through Buckley I explore the creation of a conservative counterpublic in the 1950s. Buckley created that counterpublic by linking
intellectually oriented, devoutly religious Americans to the conservative political cause. He explicitly targeted liberals for opprobrium and
articulated an overarching liberal-conservative divide in American
political culture. In politics, individuals matter, and Buckley personified a new sort of American conservative: he was witty, free of conspiratorial zealotry, and always ready to joust with any liberal brave
enough to engage him intellectually. Buckley made political conservatism fun, dashing, and intellectually respectable, even as he built
the movement's political culture around ideas of religious faith and
deference to capitalist success and white men.

Chapter 3 brings us to Senator Barry Goldwater and his brand
of cowboy conservatism. Here, I use Goldwater's road to the 1964
Republican presidential nomination to explain how the senator
taught millions of Americans—white southern voters, in particular—how and why they were conservative Republicans. Further, I
examine how the Goldwater campaign produced movement conservatives who would become so central to the conservative takeover
of the Republican Party and the institutionalization of conservatism in American public life. The Goldwater network, built from a
multitude of single-issue organizations, nonpartisan conservative
groups, and populist grassroots activists, became the "other" sixties
movement.

In chapter 4, I explain how Phyllis Schlafly expanded the conservative movement by building new, activist cadres and linking religious traditionalists both to the conservative cause and to the Republican Party. Building on a loose network of grassroots conservative women who had been active in the anticommunist cause, the antiprogressive education movement, and the National Federation of Republican Women, Schlafly organized conservatives' attack on feminism, in general, and the Equal Rights Amendment, in particular. Put bluntly, Schlafly gave new life to a flagging conservative movement in the early 1970s by energizing a new base of activists: women who disapproved of the feminist agenda. These antifeminist women activists emboldened politicians who were worried about a "gender gap" to make "traditional values" (understood as keeping the "traditional" family safe from feminism and homosexuality) a key component of the conservative movement of the late twentieth and early twenty-first centuries.

Chapter 5 focuses on the singular contributions of Ronald Reagan to modern American conservatism. Reagan made conservatism popular and conservatives nationally electable. In the face of sixties leftist activists and then the hard times of the late 1970s, Reagan convincingly portrayed conservatism as a forward-looking, optimistic faith in the American way of life (as he defined it). His sunny, good-natured faith infuriated liberals who believed Reagan to be either a mean-spirited cynic or a dunderheaded fool who did not know what he did not know. But Americans made him the first two-term president since Eisenhower. By 1988, at the end of his second term, for the first time since such polling data existed, more Americans identified themselves as conservatives than as liberals.

Chapter 6, the story of George W. Bush, marks the end of the conservative ascendency. Bush took power backed by a strong and diverse conservative political movement. As political candidate and then president, George Bush, the Christian Texas businessman who was saved from his Ivy League "sixties lifestyle" when he found his personal savior, embodied the contradictions and the vibrancy of modern political conservatives. His administration, in its zealous war on "evildoers," its tax cuts for the wealthy, its embrace of a "culture of life," and its disregard for ecological stewardship, offered Americans a vision in which success was measured by dominion on earth and heavenly salvation. Bush's muscular use of state power marked the apogee of conservatism as practical politics but its failure, in his hands, as a governing ideology.

The rise and fall of modern American conservatism does not run along a straight line. Robert Taft rejected free trade and the aggressive use of American military power abroad; later conservatives insisted on the centrality of free trade to their cause and the necessity of using American might to make the world more secure and more just. William Buckley worried that some economic conservatives failed to pay obeisance to the Christian verities, whereas Barry Goldwater was uncomfortable mixing religion and politics. Ronald Reagan insisted that the federal government needed to be systemically dismantled but did not seem to have the will or, finally, the inclination, to actually take on the power of the state. A dozen and more years later, Phyllis Schlafly and other prominent conservatives were sometimes mortified by President George Bush's vigorous use of state power both at home and abroad. And in the aftermath of the economic meltdown of 2008 and the presidential victory of Barack Obama, some conservatives even seemed uncertain about their absolutist faith in the free market.

Still, over the course of some seventy-five years, conservatives have adhered to a consistent belief in the need for a disciplined, well-ordered society. While liberals have insisted on the primacy of equality in the pursuit of justice and continue to argue that economic liberty and the free market must be restrained in order to assure that equality, conservatives have argued that a disciplined, well-ordered society can and must be built on the proven economic power of the free market, a firmly resolved patriotism, traditional religious faith, and long-standing cultural precepts. To repeat, in stark terms, what I have argued above: liberals believe in disciplining the free market; conservatives believe in disciplining the individual. American conservatives have done their best to win elections and strengthen American society by offering the American people that core political vision. In the historical account that follows, I trace the rise and fall of that conservative political order.

ONE

ROBERT TAFT

*The Gray Men of Modern Conservatism
and the Rights of Property*

THE EARLY YEARS OF MODERN AMERICAN CONSERVATISM are often portrayed, at least by sympathizers and advocates, as a heroic and idiosyncratic tale of marginal intellectuals and writers hammering against an iron cage of liberal folly that had captured the American mass mind. In the face of New Deal certitudes about the moral necessity of government planning led by hordes of government bureaucrats, a cast of iconoclasts, we are told, began a guerrilla war of ideas that would eventually break the bars of conventional wisdom and bend the social order to their truths: for example, Friedrich von Hayek, the solitary Austrian émigré economist, in *The Road to Serfdom* taught those with the good sense to listen that collectivism, however it is garbed, is an attack against both the human spirit and economic growth; and Ayn Rand, the best-selling Russian émigré novelist, romanced the young and the idealistic with stories of supremely talented individualists who would rather destroy society than participate in its pathetic, government-sponsored attempts to give succor to the downtrodden, the ineffectual, and the weak.

Godfrey Hodgson, the marvelous British chronicler of modern America, goes so far in his witty history of conservatism as to portray Albert Jay Nock, a cranky, misanthropic intellectual who dismissed the masses as an uneducable bunch of cretins, as a cornerstone of the rising conservative countermovement that would eventually conquer the American polity through the force of its ideas. Intellectual history, especially for those of us who still find stimulation in books and ideas, is never unwelcome. But as the scholar Clinton Rossiter wrote in a 1953 review of Russell Kirk's *The Conservative Mind*, "The historian of ideas has a deep obligation not to put too much faith in the power of ideas."[1] Intellectual history is not the most direct approach to explaining the power of conservatism in America.

Not surprisingly, conservative politics and policies in the 1930s and 1940s were championed by conservative politicians who were supported by conservative constituencies. Men of good fortune—rich, privileged, and often enough talented and accomplished—dominated the conservative cause as the age of Roosevelt ended. The political Hector of this corps at the dawn of the post–New Deal era was Senator Robert Alphonso Taft, son of President and Supreme Court Justice William Howard Taft and nephew of the Cincinnati business tycoon Charles P. Taft. During the Great Depression and World War II, Taft castigated the New Deal for its big-government, welfare-state, market-regulating ways. Economic liberty, he insisted, was Americans' constitutional birthright. Strong men, not a strong state, made American great.

At first, the people, by and large, did not listen. They voted again and again for Franklin Roosevelt, who promised to use the power of government to safeguard them from the vicissitudes of the capitalist system and to fight against America's enemies abroad. But after the war, with Americans anxious to rebuild their lives after years of economic travail and national sacrifice, Taft found his moment in the political sun. As labor unions launched thousands of disruptive strikes that embroiled the American people in class conflict, Taft called for social order and unity. He insisted that the free enterprise system and a self-disciplined, moral citizenry provided the United States with the tools needed to achieve prosperity, maintain liberty, assure domestic tranquillity, and pursue national greatness. Taft fought successfully against a slew of state-sponsored and collectivist solutions to Americans' political and economic challenges. In the years right after World War II, he led the effort to stop the expansion of the New Deal state and to forge a forthrightly conservative, antiliberal Republican Party.

Senator Taft was no eccentric (though he was his own man) and no intellectual (though he was very smart). He was a cold, confident man of tested views who had marched through the institutions of the American establishment. Like the Tafts before him, he was educated at Yale, where he had been tapped for Skull and Bones (grandfather Alphonso Taft had helped establish the secret society for Yale's favorite sons in 1832). Unlike some who came to Yale as legacies of prior Yale men, Robert Taft was an extraordinarily diligent and capable student. He graduated first in his class and entered Harvard Law School on his merits; in his final year there he was named president of the *Harvard Law Review* editorial board. While such an establishment path, even when bolstered by birth to one of America's preeminently successful families, is no guarantee that an individual will emerge as a conservative defender of the system that has produced such a path and such a family, it does tilt the game board in that direction.

Taft had a rigorous mind that generally ran in straight lines and in earnest directions. At seventeen, stymied by a lack of hand-eye coordination but aware that athletics were an expected part of a manly mien, he had tried to teach himself the art of hitting a baseball by crafting his own instruction manual: "Take back with right hand.

Right hand lo[o]se, left gripped. Avoid pendulum swing. Left elbow down. Right elbow down. Left wrist straight. Grip left hand as baseball is hit. Follow thru. Pivot body. Eye on ball."[2] Here was a youthful intellect marvelously if joylessly concentrated on the task at hand. While Taft's rigor, in this case, produced poor results, his logical and disciplined approach to life's problems stayed remarkably constant throughout his life.

His father assured that he stayed that way. When Taft was offered a position as secretary to Supreme Court Justice Oliver Wendell Holmes, President Taft interceded, writing that such rarified work was not the thing for a young man who had already spent too many years in the academic sink mulling over abstractions and general principles. The time had come, the president wrote, to go back to Cincinnati, join a law firm, and get on with "the actual drudgery of the practice and procedure in Ohio."[3] Taft did as his father commanded. With skill and discipline, surrounded by men of accomplishment and assisted by his family name, he became a powerful man in his own right.

Senator Taft and the like-minded men in gray business suits who stood at the center of American conservatism in the immediate–World War II years did not need an Austrian to tell them that capitalism was good and communistic state economic planning was bad. Nor did they need a novelist to explain to them that businessmen, real estate developers, large landholders, professional men, and inventive manufacturers were the engine of the good life in a free society and therefore had earned their status and their wealth. They never thought differently, and millions of Americans agreed with them. Robert Taft conservatives were dedicated to the ordered preserve of the institutions and traditions that, they believed, made America rich, powerful, and morally sound. As much as they trusted in the corporations, limited partnerships, and sole proprietorships that structured the economic order, so too did they believe in the fraternal and spiritual organizations that gave stable form to American community life. They were united by their fight against FDR's New Deal and Truman's Fair Deal, and less passionately and consistently by their fear of the moderate, go-along to-get-along Republicanism championed by Dwight D. Eisenhower. Political conservatives in the

1940s and early 1950s were dedicated to preserving individual economic liberty. For money and for leadership, American conservatism counted on such men in the immediate postwar years. It still does. Men (and women) of good fortune are one of the bases on which American conservatism stands.

While twenty-first-century chroniclers of modern conservatism have downplayed the role of the propertied and the privileged in their accounts, preferring to portray colorful intellectual antecedents or—when they discuss its latest iterations—to focus on the voting record of white church-goers and NASCAR fans, scholars with an eye for the long view of American conservatism have not. The grand-daddy of historical revisionism, Charles A. Beard, argued in the first years of the twentieth century that the American Constitution was a conservative counterattack on the populist Articles of Confederation. According to Beard, ". . . the solid conservative interests of the country were weary of talk about the 'rights of the people' and bent upon establishing firm guarantees for the rights of property."[4] Men of property, capital, and entrepreneurial energy, he argues, crafted the constitution to create a government that protected wealth against the shifting desires of backwoodsmen, rednecked farmers, and other have-nots who clamored for economic redistribution, debt relief, and easy money. The United States government, Beard tells us (and a chorus of "original intent"–espousing, conservative constitutional law scholars echo) was born conservative.

Beard's Founding conservatives, with Alexander Hamilton standing front and center, established centralized federal power to protect and promote the good fortunes of America's economic elite. Because they overwhelmingly assumed that the national government would be directed by men of wealth and high status, essentially unchallenged by the respectful and deferential masses, they were confident that national governmental power would not be used to restrict economic elites but rather to promote economic development led by the nation's most capable citizens.

Several generations of historians have taken issue with the elegant simplicity of Beard's economic interpretation of the Constitution as a power grab by the self-interested wealthy merchant elite, noting that the pro-Constitution forces were composed of disparate elements motivated by myriad concerns. Still, his Progressive Era critique of America's foundational story has been defended, even as it has been greatly refined. A twenty-first-century Beardian, the historian Robin Einhorn, amplifies even as she revises Beard's economic interpretation, giving it a solidly southern twist. In her account of America's conservative, anti-statist tradition, *American Taxation, American Slavery* (2006), she argues that Americans in the years between the War of Independence and the Civil War, rather than being innate Lockeians, raised on a frontier alter of liberty "where virtually everyone has the mentality of an independent entrepreneur" (as the Harvard political scientists Louis Hartz wrote in his 1954 Cold War classic, *The Liberal Tradition in America*), were a people of many minds on questions relating to social provision, government services, and the protection of property. But, she writes, America's southern slaveholders were not. It is an awkward statement to make, given our understanding of slavery as a moral abomination, but the nation's most vocal proponents of slavery were among the leading conservatives of the nineteenth century.

The large-slaveholding class worked single-mindedly to keep government power and majority rule weak in order to assure that no powerful federal authority capable of exercising a national, democratic will could arise and destroy slavery, whether through outright abolition or through the indirect policy of placing burdensome taxes on slave "property." These slaveholders were well aware that, state by state, northerners had ended slavery in their region during the two decades after the Revolutionary War. And slaveholders did have a great deal to protect: in 1860 the capital value of slaves constituted 20 percent of all American wealth, which was more than the combined worth of the entire nation's railroad and manufacturing assets.[5] These anti-statist and antidemocratic slaveholders were a new kind of conservative faction. Hamilton and his allies developed the power of the national government to protect and develop America's system of credit and finance to benefit most directly the capitalist elite. In contrast, wealthy slaveholders were, so to speak, the New Right of their era. They rounded up support from their less-well-to-do white neighbors by denouncing the Hamiltonians as antidemocratic elitists, who meant to control society and government through "the pageantry of rank, the influence of money and emoluments, and the terror of military force."[6] They (a group that includes Jefferson, Madison, and later John C. Calhoun of South Carolina) championed and institutionalized anti-statist, antitaxation, and pro–property rights policies to ensure that their fundamental economic asset—enslaved people—was not taken away by the power of national authority.

This anti-statist stance became integral to American political culture and to the policy claims of a broad range of economic elites, all of whom had more to fear from an empowered democratic majority than to gain from an activist federal government. When new manufacturing and financial elites boomed in the late nineteenth century, these men deliberately built on the antebellum slaveholders' political tradition, and structural impositions, to protect their property, their wealth, and their status from feckless majorities who might use their electoral power to take them away. Ironically, these new elites used both the authority of the federal courts to keep states from passing pro-labor laws and the power of Congress and the president to raise tariffs against imported manufactured goods. Federal power in the late nineteenth century (the Gilded Age) served the antiregulatory, anti–domestic tax, pro-property needs of the well-to-do. Men of good fortune did their best to use a Hamiltonian probusiness national government and Jeffersonian anti-statist rhetoric to protect their assets and their economic prerogatives from any class-based, majoritarian political foray.[7] Self-interested as they were, it need be said that the economic policy tilt engineered by men of wealth paid off: the United States economy boomed during the Gilded Age, creating great fortunes as well as the highest wage scale in the world.

Robert Taft, like many young, well-born, and ambitious men coming of age in the early twentieth century, especially after the economic reforms of the Progressive Era had played out, inherited this political orientation. Taft would have rejected any claim that he was, politically speaking, following in the footsteps of the slaveholding class of the antebellum South. He was, after all, a Republican, and he hailed Abraham Lincoln, champion of free labor, northern manufacturers, and the North's expanding middle class—not the Confederacy's patrician slavemaster Jefferson Davis—as his personal and political hero. Slaveholding and slaveholders were anathema to him, and he saw no need for linking his principles to southern antebellum stratagems. But if the senator from Ohio rejected the Lost Cause, he did revere those constitutional principles that protected private property from the grasping hands of those who wanted something for nothing; and if it had taken rich men of all kinds, representing quite different factions, to create and preserve those principles, so what? Successful politics—liberal or conservative—depend on adding, not subtracting, constituencies.

Taft had already graduated from Yale (class of '10) when Charles Beard's *An Economic Interpretation of the Constitution* was published in 1913, and it is unlikely he ever read it. Beard's thesis, however—that the Constitution aimed above all to protect property from the machinations of economic levelers or financial manipulators—was Taft's own. In a 1938 speech before a sympathetic audience of Cleveland-area Republicans gathered at the Tippecanoe Club, made while he was running for the Senate, Taft blasted New Dealers for disregarding the Constitution in their reckless pursuit of socialistic measures: ". . . more and more the [Roosevelt] Administration has become enamored of a policy of planned economy. . . . The professors in Washington are obsessed with the belief that by passing laws and issuing thousands of regulations they can produce an automatic prosperity. For that purpose they were prepared to cast aside every constitutional principle which the Anglo-Saxon race had established in centuries of struggle. They have scant regard for individual rights to life, liberty, and property established by the Constitution."[8] Taft, here and elsewhere, spoke for many (though too few to bring any of his three bids for the Republican presidential nomination to a happy conclusion). And in his speech he did more than defend property holders against what he considered government theft. In a few short sentences he intertwined three critical themes of modern conservatism: fealty to the property-preserving original intent of the Constitution, contempt for social-experiment-loving, tradition-disregarding intellectual elites, and a reverence for the "Anglo-Saxon race" (over time conservatives would replace this racially loaded phrase with the more inclusive "Western civilization" or the religiously uplifting "Judeo-Christian tradition"). But it was the protection of economic liberty, at least on the domestic side of politics, that most moved Taft and so many other self-proclaimed conservatives during the age of Roosevelt and its immediate aftermath.

The Taftian persuasion, by the late 1930s and early 1940s, was primarily but not solely a Republican one. Both major political parties in those years were still internally debating the reach of the federal government in the American economy. But the Democrats—excepting a few old-school types, mostly from the one-party South, whom FDR had failed to purge in the memorable midterm election of 1938—had broadly agreed that Washington should play a major role in safeguarding Americans' economic security and prosperity. To do so, the liberal majority of the Democratic Party argued, taxes on the well-to-do should be raised so that an economic safety net could be woven into the fabric of the free enterprise system. And to ensure that the economic security of the majority was maintained, business owners would have to abide by a series of rules that included workers' rights to organize collective bargaining units, a national minimum wage, and government restrictions on banking and other financial practices. The capitalist free market, New Dealers averred, had to be disciplined by the federal government to protect Americans from its predations and periodic downswings.

This particular divide between Republicans and Democrats was relatively new. As late as 1928, many observers were hard pressed to discern which presidential candidate, Democrat Al Smith or Republican Herbert Hoover, was the greater protector of the perquisites of capital and capitalists. Economic conservatism in those pre–Great Depression, Roaring Twenties days had ruled both parties at the highest levels. But Roosevelt and his "professors" ended that particular consensus by inventing a new kind of political liberalism. That reinvention and the New Dealers' very claiming of the liberal tradition changed the game of American politics.

Robert Taft's first foray into national politics came hard on the heels of the invention of New Deal liberalism. When Franklin Roosevelt first ran for the presidency in 1932, his ideological orientation was unclear, even to him. In fact, Roosevelt never embraced a strong ideological position; in the middle of the New Deal years a reporter badgered him about his political "philosophy" until a bemused Roosevelt finally replied, "Philosophy? Philosophy? I am a Christian and a Democrat—that's all."[9] FDR had come of political age in the years before World War I as a progressive. But progressivism was a term that had long lost clear political meaning and purpose (in 1912, all three major candidates for the presidency—President William Howard Taft, former President Theodore Roosevelt, and soon-to-be President Woodrow Wilson—called themselves progressives, as did FDR's 1932 opponent, Herbert Hoover). Moreover, by 1932, progressivism had become too linked, for Roosevelt's taste and purpose, with the crusading spirit of individual moral reform, most extravagantly displayed in the national temperance movement that had resulted in the passage of the Eighteenth Amendment, which banned the sale and importation of alcoholic beverages. Roosevelt was not much interested in individual moral reform; at a time when the Great Depression had left 25 percent of Americans unemployed and tens of millions facing homelessness and hunger, he wanted to use public policy to bring economic security to the American people. To provide that security he was willing to reinvent the role and reach of government in the United States.

Roosevelt was, in his own heart and in the eyes of his followers, hardly a radical. He saw no need to change, let alone overthrow, Americans' constitutional principles or the capitalist system. In his first inaugural address, he would casually assure the citizenry: "Our Constitution is so simple and practical that it is possible always to meet extraordinary needs by changes in emphasis and arrangement without loss of essential form."[10] So, to explain his policies and his principles to the American people, he adapted an older language to new circumstances. He told them that he was, in accord with long-standing American tradition, a liberal. But, he stated in his acceptance speech at the June 1936 Democratic Party convention in Philadelphia, unlike liberals of an older time, who had in 1776 "sought freedom from the tyranny of a political autocracy—from the eighteenth century royalists who held special privileges from the crown," New Deal liberals would fight for Americans' economic freedom from the "economic royal-ists" who had "created a new despotism and wrapped it in the robes of legal sanction." He explained: "A small group had concentrated into their own hands an almost complete control over other people's money, other people's labor—other people's lives. For too many of us life was no longer free; liberty no longer real; men could no longer follow the pursuit of happiness." The new liberalism of the industrial age, Roosevelt argued, demanded not freedom from political tyranny but "against economic tyranny" and in this fight "the American citizen could appeal only to the organized power of government. . . . Govern-ment in a modern civilization has certain inescapable obligations to its citizens, among which are protection of the family and the home, the establishment of a democracy of opportunity, and aid to those over-taken by disaster."[11] Twentieth-century liberalism, unlike the liberal-ism of the nineteenth century, said President Franklin Roosevelt, had to confront the brutal inequities and terrifying insecurities produced not by concentrated political power but by concentrated wealth.

Robert Taft, never an easy-going fellow, was disgusted by Roos-evelt's presumption. As Taft saw it, Roosevelt had stolen liberalism from the real liberals. In an April 30, 1936, speech to the Women's Republican Club of New Hampshire, made just before the forty-six-year-old stepped forward as Ohio's "favorite son" candidate for the Republican Party presidential nomination, Taft let loose at FDR. "The President has sought to appropriate to the New Deal," Taft fumed, "all the ideals of liberalism. . . . But the general ideal expressed by the President, that every worker may be able to live a better and more prosperous life," he continued, "is not one from which anyone wishes to dissent. . . . [T]he question is whether the methods of the New Deal are attaining those ideals, or destroying all opportunity. . . . [T]he truly liberal platform will be that platform which proposes pol-icies which in the light of experience and common sense will attain that result."[12] Liberalism, as Taft understood it, was a political phi-losophy that championed individual liberty, and he and his followers were the rightful guardians of that Anglo-American tradition.

When Taft spoke of liberty, he did not mean libertarianism or any other sort of individualistic permissiveness. He was a practical man not given to abstract flights of fancy; ergo, the phrase "in the light of experience and common sense." He simply meant that government should give broad freedom to individuals, whether worker or employer, to pursue their economic interests so that they *might* become more prosperous if they were *able* enough to take advantage of free market opportunities. Taft did not believe that individuals' right to pursue economic opportunity should be understood to mean that the government had the duty to assure that everyone was treated equally in the job market.

So, even as Taft publicly argued that African Americans, too, should be able to enjoy the American dream, he consistently fought against government enforcement of equal employment practices. In 1939, he told a black audience composed of Howard University graduates—men and women struggling against an entrenched, legally sanctioned racism that had systemically denied them employment opportunities commensurate with their talents and achievements— that if they just tried hard enough they would reap the rewards the American way offered its citizens: "On a firm foundation of constitutional freedom, you can build an economic security. . . . [B]ut you can only do it by your own efforts, and the efforts of your group, without leaning on the white people or on the government, but with their willing assistance."[13] Be strong, Taft told his black audience; compete with fortitude and you will reap the fruits of the free market. Taft was not blind. He knew that racism restricted black Americans' opportunities. But he believed that protecting government-guaranteed individual economic liberty was more important than using government power to enforce equal opportunity. Modern liberals would argue that Taft believed that property rights trumped human rights. Taft would have insisted on a different formulation: property rights are the foundation on which human rights are built.

Taft's faith in the virtues of economic liberty and his disgust over FDR's expropriation of liberalism from the old liberals placed him in rich company. In the mid-1930s, a small group of wealthy men, joined by the Democrats' 1928 presidential candidate, Al Smith, had come together to block Roosevelt's bid for a second term. Alfred P. Sloan, the spectacularly wealthy president of General Motors, urged the men to call their group the Association Asserting the Rights of Property and to rally the American people to their cause with the slogan "Rights of Property Is the Foundation of All Social Order."[14] Another GM executive, S. M. DuBrul, not overwhelmed by his boss's political instincts, tried to explain that the Great Depression made property rights a tough sell: "[A]ny organization which was known to be directly interested primarily in the protection of established property rights would be most undesirable and largely ineffective at this juncture. . . . Our job is to rebuild an appreciation of the dangers to individual liberty which are implicit in so many of the current trends . . . [government] doles, benefits, payment, and so on."[15] DuBrul believed that electoral battles could not be won by asking Americans to respect the rights of the propertied, especially at a time when so many had so little. Americans had to be shown that the New Deal was not securing their way of life but was instead endangering it by destroying the wealth-producing system of free enterprise. Against Roosevelt's cry that "the only thing we have to fear is fear itself," DuBrul wanted to teach Americans to fear the New Deal.

Agreeing with DuBrul was another prominent member of the group, John W. Davis, the 1924 Democratic Party presidential candidate and one of the nation's most esteemed corporate counsels. The courtly Davis, a Wall Street lawyer raised by a pro-slavery Virginian, was his era's most perfect embodiment of the Hamiltonian-Jeffersonian hybrid conservative persuasion. Legal scourge of the New Deal, Davis made headlines in the 1930s (and occasionally won major court cases) castigating the expansive reach of the federal government on behalf of his clients, a who's who of corporate America. In the early 1950s, Davis would cap his brilliant career by enthusiastically defending the state of South Carolina's right to segregate its schools in the *Brown v. Board of Education* Supreme Court case. A first-rate wordsmith who could recite from memory long quotations from Shakespeare, the Bible, and even the Koran, Davis offered up a list of names for the nascent association of the rich and their supporters, including the League for American Rights, League for Constitutional Rights, and then the winner, the Liberty League. By late 1934, the American Liberty League was established to stop the New Deal.

In 1936, the league, spearheaded by many of America's corporate and financial leaders, enrolled more than 125,000 members and spent more than a million dollars trying to defeat Roosevelt.[16] Avowedly nonpartisan (that is, they were allied neither with Republicans nor Democrats; they wanted both parties to champion the rights of property holders), the league distributed millions of anti–New Deal pamphlets and at its peak had a staff almost three times the size of the national Republican Party. Key members and funders of the organization included Sloan, Pierre and Irénée du Pont, Howard Pew of Sun Oil, Sewell Avery of Montgomery Ward, Colby Chester of General Foods, financier E. F. Hutton, Frank Rand of International Shoe Company, and many other leading businessmen, a number of whom would continue to be major financial backers of conservative political causes, foundations, and institutes of all kinds in the years ahead. Their election-year offensive began with a nationally broadcast address by Al Smith, the former governor of New York and the 1928 Democratic presidential candidate. Smith went after the New Deal with everything he had. In a spectacular display of vitriolic hyperbole, he lambasted it as a communistic, class-dividing spawn of the Soviet Union. His rhetoric would become a standard conservative trope in the years ahead: "There can be only one capital, Washington or Moscow. There can be only the clear, pure, fresh air of free America, or the foul breath of communistic Russia. There can be only one flag, the Stars and Stripes, or the flag of the godless Union of the Soviets."[17]

Smith and other Liberty Leaguers, with money to burn, hit hard and hit often. But the group, as DuBrul feared, was operating in an extremely challenging political environment. Red-baiting lacked political traction in 1936, and the patrician yet folksy and churchgoing Roosevelt made for an unlikely agent of godless communism. Master politician that he was, Roosevelt turned the Liberty League's attacks to his own purposes. Just days before the 1936 election, Roosevelt stood, steel leg braces holding him up, before thousands of supporters in New York City's Madison Square Garden: "We now know that Government by organized money is just as dangerous as Government by organized mob. Never before in all our history have these forces been so united against one candidate as they stand today. They are unanimous in their hate for me—and I welcome their hatred. I should like to have it said of my first Administration that in it the forces of selfishness and of lust for power met their match. I should like to have it said of my second administration that in it these forces met their master."[18] FDR rarely focused his campaign rhetoric against his actual Republican opponent, Kansas Governor Alf Landon, a reform-minded, moderate progressive from the Theodore Roosevelt wing of the GOP (TR, in his 1912 presidential battle with Robert Taft's dad, had told a Chicago audience, "This country will not be a permanently good place for any of us to live in unless we make it a reasonably good place for all of us to live in").[19] Instead, FDR ran against Herbert Hoover (again!), the Liberty League, and all the male-factors of great wealth that had, he said, unleashed the Great Depression on the American people. Roosevelt won nearly 61 percent of the vote and every state except Maine and Vermont. Working-class white ethnics, Jews, African Americans, and southern whites, believers all (though for different reasons and with conflicting understandings) in economic security and a sense of fair play, formed the unstable base of a New Deal electoral coalition. Joining them were many farmers, small-business operators, and even a small minority of big business-people—property owners of all kinds who believed that Roosevelt, while too generous to unionists, the unemployed, and the irrespon-sible, was fighting to save the free enterprise system by reforming it. In the 1936 election, nineteenth-century liberalism went down in flames, and New Deal liberalism ruled the land.

New Deal liberals' total domination of the political landscape was short-lived. In 1938, a storm of bad economic news, Roosevelt's failed effort to purge the Democratic Party of its conservative wing (mostly southern and sometimes labeled "Jeffersonian Democrats" for their states-rights approach to governance), and his ill-advised attempt to "pack" the Supreme Court with additional appointees (to help elderly judges, FDR claimed, but really to provide a judicial majority for pro–New Deal decisions) played perfectly into the hands of liberals' political enemies. The recession of 1937 demonstrated the fragility of New Deal economic measures; the failed party purge showed poli-ticians that Roosevelt's political clout was limited; and the negative public response to FDR's manipulative court plan told conservatives that Americans were anxious about the power of unchecked big government. Many liberals, including President Roosevelt, took stock in 1938 and began to scale back and rethink their plans for further big government programs. By the end of the 1930s, many key New Deal liberals had turned away from big government policies of public jobs programs, broad-scale economic planning, and direct intervention in the affairs of business and emphasized Keynesian fiscal policy—using the government's power to tax and spend, especially deficit spending during recessions—to smooth out the free market boom-bust cycle and promote national economic growth.[20] As the Roosevelt administration regrouped, conservatives went on the offensive.

In 1938, Robert Taft, who had lost his last elected office in the Roosevelt landslide of 1932, ran for the U.S. Senate in Ohio. With major financial backing from Ohio's wealthiest families, he first defeated a moderate Republican for his party's nomination and then went on to trounce the pro–New Deal Democratic incumbent. Taft was one of eight new Senate Republicans. On the House side, the Republican minority jumped from 89 members to 169. Conservatives, mostly Republican but also well represented in the southern wing of the Democratic Party, were back in business. Robert Taft, a smart, principled conservative who began his Senate career with national name recognition, thanks to his father, was seen by pundits, party professionals, and himself as a strong contender for the 1940 Republican presidential nomination.

Despite the electoral surge, conservatives were still a decided minority at the end of 1930s. And like most out-of-power minorities, they knew best what they opposed. The New Deal remained their punching bag. While Republican moderates and most conservative Democrats accommodated themselves to the major New Deal reforms, especially Social Security and most of the economic regulations that seemed to safeguard the nation's financial system, Taft and his allies, with only a few exceptions, fought to roll back the New Deal. Throughout Taft's nearly fifteen years in the Senate, he would continue to fight liberal, big government domestic policy—though he could also be a pragmatic and sympathetic statesman who recognized that sometimes for some people private enterprise failed. So, for example, Taft actually championed public housing for the destitute; a policy position that surprised many of the senator's business supporters. Taft was principled but not dogmatic.

But immediately after taking office in January 1939, Taft—and the nation—had to face a new and very different kind of challenge: the outbreak of global war. As the Nazis swept across Europe and the Japanese slashed away at China, Taft took center stage as an articulate advocate of keeping America out of the conflagration. Taft was no defender of the Nazis, nor was he any kind of pacifist; as the Germans expanded their reach, he fought to build America's military defense. But as long as the country remained strong, Taft was certain that Germany would not attack the United States. And Japanese expansion in Asia rarely concerned him; like most of his congressional colleagues, as well as most of the American people, he paid it little heed before the events of December 7, 1941. As Taft saw it, British Prime Minister Winston Churchill was barking up the wrong tree when he urged "the New World, with all its power and might, [to] step . . . forth to the rescue and the liberation of the old."[21] The United States, Taft believed, need only look after its own defense and keep the belligerents out of the western hemisphere. Nothing had sufficiently changed to negate the wisdom of George Washington's Farewell Address: "Why quit our own to stand upon foreign ground? Why, by interweaving our destiny with that of any part of Europe, entangle our peace and prosperity in the toils of European ambition, rivalship, interest, humor, or caprice?"[22] Taft loved America and wished, above all, that its fate be tied to no other nation and no other cause.

Such a position in 1939 identified Taft as a unilateralist opposed to Wilsonian internationalism. Taft believed that the United States did not need to defend other people's freedom nor did it need to spread democracy abroad. "[W]e should not undertake to defend the ideals of democracy in foreign countries," he declared, ". . . no one has ever suggested before that a single nation should range over the world, like a knight-errant . . . and tilt, like Don Quixote, against the windmills of fascism."[23] In opposing entanglement in the war, Taft was with the vast majority of his countryfolk, and he was joined by midwestern conservatives, prairie state populists, old-school progressives, prominent socialists, and many others.[24] Taft did, however, make his specific case against Roosevelt's aggressive struggle to intervene against the Axis powers in a manner befitting his conservative political stance.

"War is the health of the State," wrote the leftist social critic Randolph Bourne in 1918, as he watched Americans, aflame with war fever, give away their liberties in the name of wartime solidarity.[25] Bourne was primarily concerned about the wartime government's destruction of freedoms of speech, press, and assembly. Taft feared what another war would do to Americans' economic liberty. American intervention in Europe's new war, he believed, would give President Roosevelt the power to turn his rapacious New Deal into an unprecedented government behemoth. Roosevelt and his warhawks, he warned, want to "give arbitrary power to the President to tell every citizen what he shall do, in manufacture, in commerce, in agriculture; to draft man power and capital; to fix all wages and prices."[26] Taft was right. As the United States went to war, government power reached deeply and profoundly into every American's life.

Taft also argued that the internationalists were wrong when they claimed that America's global economic interests mandated intervention against Germany and Japan, even if neither nation directly attacked the United States. Taft insisted that the United States could, and essentially should, go it alone economically. Fighting a global war to assure that Americans could invest and trade in Europe and Asia was too high a price to pay for such a limited and uncertain return. Like most Republicans, Taft had always strongly supported high-tariff walls against imported goods in order to keep U.S. manufacturers well-protected from foreign competition, and he expected foreigners to practice the same policy. Protectionism was economic common sense among Ohio industrialists, who were Taft's key constituents. In May 1940, the senator wrote to one of his close political supporters, "If a nation of 130,000,000 people with all the natural resources they need, can't maintain a free economy among themselves, then I don't see why they can maintain that economy any better by exporting and importing a limited amount of goods. . . . I can't think of anything more destructive to American prosperity than the abandonment of protective policy."[27] Taft, like most self-identified conservatives in the late 1930s, opposed free trade. An economic unilateralist by inclination and political consideration, he also feared that economic interdependence would force the United States into devastating foreign wars. Taft had worked under Herbert Hoover during World War I to provide food and aid to a devastated Europe, and he believed that the United States had been pushed into the horrors of the Great War by just such international economic interests.

Many big businesspeople, particularly international financiers and large exporters, found this stance backward looking. John Cowles, a Minneapolis newspaper publisher and prominent Republican, dismissed Taft's defense of protectionism, arguing that future American prosperity would depend on global trade: "It seems to me his tariff philosophy must be inherited, and he has failed to realize that policies that may have been advantageous when the United States was a debtor nation will, if continued, prove disastrous now that America is a creditor nation."[28] Roosevelt and liberal Democrats, more generally, attracted the support of a number of export-driven and international investment–oriented businesspeople and financiers (many of them located on or around Wall Street) by fighting against Republican tariff policy and pushing the United States toward a more open, reciprocal foreign trade policy. Freer trade, FDR believed, would benefit American consumers through lower prices and allow the nation's most economic and productive industries to grow by expanding their international sales and investments. Because Main Street and Wall Street were not reading from the same economic hymnal, trade policy, in the 1930s and 1940s, did not fit easily into a conservative-liberal framework.

Generally, Taft and political conservatives were stymied by the war. It took the focus off domestic politics, the area in which conservatives had strong feelings and, they believed, winning political arguments. The war also gave Roosevelt a unique opportunity to keep the power of incumbency, yet again, on the side of the liberals. Motivated at least in part by the fall of Europe to the Nazis, FDR broke the tradition set by George Washington in 1796 and ran for a third term in 1940.

Though respectful of Roosevelt's formidable political skills, Taft desperately wanted to take him on. He could, he believed, give the

American people a genuine chance to choose between more big government and a return to the older ways of limited, property-protecting
government. But it was not to be. After a heated convention battle
that forced six roll-call votes, the Republican Party cast Taft aside and
selected a more liberal, far more internationalist-leaning, New York
City–based candidate as its champion: the genial Wall Street lawyer
and utilities executive, Wendell Willkie, a man unstained by prior
elected office. The moderate, internationally oriented East Coast
Republicans had won the day. In large part, the Republicans rejected
Taft because a majority in his own party believed that his outspoken
anti-interventionist rhetoric would kill his presidential chances. Many
also believed that Taft's frontal assault on the New Deal remained
unpopular and that a more carefully couched critique of New Deal
excesses would win back the Republican majorities of the 1920s.

Taft offered another explanation. There was nothing wrong with
his message. Americans, he believed, could be convinced to accept
his fierce anti–New Deal opinions, and many still supported his outspoken, unilateralist views on the war. The problem, he wrote a col-
league, was that presidential politics had become the kind of game in
which he had too few skills. "[T]he public sentiment of the day, fostered and promoted by the newspapers, magazines and columnists,"
he bitterly noted, is "to regard politics as a show in which only an
actor can be promoted."[29] (That same year, Ronald Reagan, the man
who would become conservatives' favorite actor, appeared in one of
his greatest roles, as George Gipp in the gridiron classic *Knute Rockne
All American*.) Taft knew he lacked both charisma and a winning personality. And he understood that the growing importance of the mass
media in American national politics made cold-blooded, analytically
minded, professional politicians like himself an ever-harder sell in
the electoral marketplace, whatever their political ideology. Policies
and principles mattered, but when it came to presidential politics,
personality and packaging could easily sway a nomination and, even
more, an election. A gray man in a suit who had been first in his class
at Yale was tough to market.

Roosevelt's victory in 1940 and the subsequent entanglement of
the United States in the war left little room for conservative attacks

on the liberal state. The war was everything; as President Roosevelt himself told the press corps less than a year before the 1944 election, "Dr. New Deal" had to give way to "Dr. Win-the-War."[30] And "Dr. Win-the-War" was not going to bow out from the fight before achieving victory—Roosevelt would run again. Fighting a bitter partisan battle in the climactic days of World War II was not in the cards. Once again, the less contentious, moderate, internationalist, East Coast Republicans won the 1944 Republican presidential nomination for their man, Thomas Dewey, easily defeating Taft's candidate, Ohio governor John Bricker, who was even more fiercely anti–New Deal and anti-internationalist than even Taft himself. Dewey had a good life story: he had gained fame in the 1930s as a New York City federal prosecutor who had shrugged off death threats to go after the nation's organized crime kingpins. He had almost won the nomination in 1940 when he was just thirty-eight years old and had easily won the New York governorship in 1942.

Dewey was no New Dealer. He called for fiscal restraint and a balanced budget. But he also supported government enforcement of civil rights legislation and the Social Security safety net. Dewey, Taft wrote to a Republican fund-raiser, "has no real courage to stand up against the crowd that wants to smear any Republican who takes a forthright position against the New Deal."[31] Worse, from Taft's perspective, was that Dewey, like Willkie before him, swam in the internationalist current that carried along the Republican Party's entire East Coast contingent. Nonetheless, Taft supported Dewey, even as he assumed that the Republicans had little chance of defeating the nation's commander-in-chief during the final months of World War II. American voters, Taft observed in a rare light note, were unlikely to "take out a winning pitcher in the eighth inning."[32]

Taft fought for reelection to his Senate seat in a far less jocular mood. He had, at first, taken his Democratic opponent lightly. But by the last weeks of his campaign, he confronted a new political phenomenon that was changing politics in the United States: organized labor had forged a powerful new weapon—the political action committee—and in Ohio it was trained on Robert A. Taft. The CIO Political Action Committee had formed in 1943 to turn out a massive vote for Franklin Roosevelt's bid for an unprecedented fourth term. Its goal was to make sure working-class men and women, who had prior to 1936 been irregular voters of uncertain loyalty, cast their ballots on election day. So besides making large financial contributions to its preferred candidates, the CIO-PAC mobilized a vast network of political campaign workers, concentrated in the Northeast, Midwest, and West Coast, where its members' numbers were greatest, to get its people to the polls and to vote for liberal Democrats. The CIO mobilized hundreds of thousands of election day workers and made itself the single most vital cog in the liberal Democratic Party political coalition. Conservatives had moneyed supporters, but they had no mass activist base to identify their voters and get them to the polls. By acting outside the normal political party apparatus, the Left had outmaneuvered the Right.

The CIO Ohio Council lambasted Senator Taft. Taking a page from FDR's 1936 "economic royalist" harangue, the CIO accused Taft of waging "a systemic campaign to force America back into the 'Robber Baron' days when a few big business kings ran both the economy and the government of the country from a few offices in Wall Street." Taft's Democratic opponent, counseled and financially supported by the CIO, echoed the charges: "Taft comes from one of Ohio's wealthiest families. . . . He represents wealth and large corporations." The Democrats and the CIO made sure that Ohio voters, in the year 1944, remembered that Taft had, until the Pearl Harbor attack, dismissed the dangers of Nazi and Japanese aggression: "He Wanted to Do Business with Hitler and Hirohito—The Amazing Story of Senator Taft."[33] Taft, despite his good family name, wealthy campaign donors, the power of incumbency, a weak opponent, and overwhelming Republican partisan support in rural Ohio, barely withstood the combined fury of these attacks. He won reelection by fewer than eighteen thousand votes out of nearly two million cast. The end of 1944 was a bad time to be a conservative or a onetime "isolationist."

Between 1932 and 1944, Franklin Roosevelt had accomplished a political grand slam. He had gotten himself elected to the presidency four times. He had passed more significant legislation than any president before him. He had led the United States through world war and had proven himself an extraordinary international leader. His successes had realigned the American electorate, establishing a liberal coalition that produced massive victories for the president's beloved Democratic Party. Taft and his conservative allies could do nothing about the first three, but FDR's final accomplishment, they knew, was vulnerable to time and chance.

Franklin Roosevelt died of a cerebral hemorrhage on April 12, 1945. His death left the nation bereft. Harry Truman, untested and unimposing, was the unexpected president. When the war finally ended in the summer of 1945, people celebrated, but no one knew what would happen at home or abroad. Mainstream economists feared that without massive government military spending America would slip back into recession. Many major employers, long dependent on military contracts, began laying off workers as they prepared to convert back to the uncertainties of peacetime production. Workers feared a return to Depression-era unemployment rates even as they watched inflation shrink their buying power. As millions of men returned from the war, most Americans wondered how they would secure their future in the new, postwar world. Not readily identifiable as liberal or conservative, most Americans wanted stable, normal lives after having endured years of economic anxiety and the sacrifices of war.

Taft and his fellow conservatives saw political opportunity amid this uncertainty. Truman, Taft knew, was no Roosevelt. The new president's ability to fight his political enemies and lead the nation was limited, at best. Truman, who made it clear that he meant to use his accidental presidency to expand the New Deal, was vulnerable, and Taft went on the attack within weeks of Truman's ascent to power. Taft was confident that Americans had had enough of wartime controls of every kind. He came out swinging against any continuation of wartime price and employment controls (during the war, some seventy-five thousand people, assisted by three hundred thousand volunteers, worked for the Office of Price Administration to make sure that business owners did not take advantage of wartime shortages to raise their prices or lower their quality).[34] He demanded an end to Franklin Roosevelt's Fair Employment Practices Commission, arguing that racial discrimination was wrong but that it was not the government's job to police employers' hiring decisions. Most of all, Taft began targeting the growing, federally protected power of organized labor, the nemesis of Taft's allies in the business community and, thanks to the CIO-PAC, of all probusiness politicians.

Organized labor did not take the conservative attack lying down. Unionists, too, meant to take full advantage of the opportunities they saw in the fluid postwar world. At war's end, thanks in part to pro-labor government, about 30 percent of America's private sector workers were unionized, and organizers meant to bring millions more into the ranks of the movement. As the sympathetic labor historian Nelson Lichtenstein writes, "Unions seemed on the verge of recruiting millions of new workers in the service trades, in white-collar occupations like banking and insurance, across great stretches of the South and Southwest and even among the lower ranks of management."[35] Liberal unionists, aligned with more radical factions within organized labor, including communists, hoped to create a national workers movement that would recast American political and economic life by mandating a more equitable distribution of the nation's wealth.

Little remembered today or even much taught to students of American history, the immediate post–World War II years were rife with class warfare. In 1946, millions of men and women went on strike. Many only wanted higher wages to combat postwar inflation and the loss of overtime pay. Others sought to redraw the line that separated workers from managers and to redistribute America's wealth. United Auto Workers leader Walter Reuther led that charge. He demanded that General Motors give its striking hourly workers a 30 percent raise without increasing the cost of its automobiles. When GM's Alfred Sloan rejected the demand as financially impossible, Reuther insisted that GM opens its books to the UAW so that labor and management together could figure out what was possible and what was fair. GM then accused Reuther of being some kind of collectivizing, proletariat communist, a charge Reuther accepted: "If fighting for a more equal and equitable distribution of the wealth of this country is socialistic, I stand guilty of being a socialist."[36] Reuther hoped to ignite a radical labor movement that would drive a stake through the kind of unfettered capitalism that had ruled the United

States before the New Deal. Along the same political line, the CIO used its war chest to hire hundreds of organizers to spread the labor union cause to the Deep South in Operation Dixie. In 1946, unionists were on the offensive.

Most Americans found the workers' offensive, well, offensive. Some five thousand strikes had broken out—shutting down coal mines, lumber mills, auto plants, railroads, factories, shipping docks, and on and on. It was nerve racking. It was chaos. Food was not being shipped. Gasoline was in short supply. Prices of everyday staples like meat and bread skyrocketed (actually owing to the end of wartime price controls). After the long years of the Depression and the privations of the war, people wanted life to be orderly and affordable goods to be on the shelf. The majority of people who were not in labor unions wanted workers to work and prices to be fair so that people could buy what they needed and businesses could prosper and America could move forward. Economic security, some believed, was being waylaid by the CIO policy of strikes, demands, and class warfare and by President Truman's inability to keep the economy on an even keel.

Senator Taft did his utmost to link President Harry Truman and his fellow liberals to the labor unrest and the economic uncertainties the transition from wartime to peacetime produced. "President Truman," he told his fellow Ohio Republicans at their 1946 state convention, "has endorsed every project of the CIO PAC, and has therefore made the PAC program the official program of the Democratic party.... To please a faction, to make a supposed political issue, the President plunged the whole economic life of the nation into chaos.... Only delay, confusion and disaster can result from the continued control by a party half PAC, and the other half[,] with no program except obstruction[,] demoralized and discouraged."[37] Liberals had gained control of the federal government by blaming Herbert Hoover and the Republicans for the Great Depression. Roosevelt had promised the American people that the government would take a stick to those greedy and irresponsible capitalists who had broken the nation's banks and industries and so restore Americans' economic security. Now, Taft was turning the tables. It was liberal big government and radical big labor that were responsible for the nation's economic misery and domestic disorder. The Truman administration, he stated in his prolix fashion, "has failed to restore a stable economy here at home on which permanent progress can be based. . . . It has encouraged every move toward a managed economy with a minimum of liberty for individual and business effort. . . . Washington is a picture of confusion and indecision, interspersed with demands for arbitrary power and more money."[38] Taft lacked a silver tongue, but he had voiced a winning political message. In the early run-up to the 1946 congressional elections, the senator appeared on the cover of every leading weekly news magazine.

The 1946 election saw the return of the Republican Party to congressional control after fourteen years in the political wilderness. Republican majorities were impressive—245 to 188 in the House and 51 to 45 in the Senate. Taft was hailed by his party and by the press as the champion of this Republican takeover. Liberals' then-favorite magazine, the *New Republic*, warned its readers, "Congress . . . now consists of the House, the Senate, and Bob Taft."[39] Taft's time had come.

Despite the Republican victory, Senator Taft remained cautious and even pessimistic. Liberals had dominated American political life for so long, Taft feared, that a majority of Americans had lost the ability to understand the principles that made the country great. To a sympathetic audience of Yale alumni in early 1947, he expressed his concerns: "Programs are judged on the question of whether they give more money, more bath tubs, more automobiles and less time to work. Certainly no one can be against these economic objectives, but it is wrong to subordinate the need for greater morality, greater liberty of thought and greater liberty of action. I believe that opportunity and not security is still the goal of the American people if they think about it, but they don't think about it."[40] In his party's moment of triumph, Taft saw dark clouds: "Both liberty and justice have been forgotten. . . . The whole world has drifted toward the philosophy of totalitarian government." Wistfully, he ended his remarks—perhaps the most poignant of his political life: "It is up to our universities and our schools to see that our people never forget again the eternal principles on which true progress can only be made."[41] But such a culture war would have to wait for another champion.

Back in Washington, Taft focused his energies on turning the tide of organized labor in the United States. He was far from alone. The Republican leadership in both houses of Congress, supported by the National Association of Manufacturers, the Chamber of Commerce, and dozens of other business groups drove antiunion legislation through the House and Senate. Labor had won immense victories during the New Deal years; now economic conservatives meant to draw a line in the sand—this far and no further. Taft chose to be chairman of the Senate Labor and Public Welfare Committee so he could write the legislation that would stop organized labor's march.

Taft was a politician, not a fanatical ideologue.[42] He wanted to stop labor's leftward trajectory, not destroy unions. Rejecting the demands of some conservatives for a return to pre–New Deal labor policy, he publicly announced that he supported workers' right to organize and to engage in collective bargaining. But Taft had a clear agenda. He intended to increase the power of employers and reduce the strength of organized labor. And he meant to pass legislation that could withstand a veto by President Truman.

Taft worked hard to craft the act that would bear his name. Dozens of expert witnesses appeared before his committee, and Taft insisted that his fellow senators meet day after day, week after week, to hammer out the legislation. In his most important and long-lasting act as an elected official, Taft lived up to his own ideals—he was disciplined, intellectually rigorous, and effective. He was helped, too, by conservative businesspeople and their organizations. In the weeks leading up to passage of Taft's bill, the National Association of Manufacturers, alone, spent more than $3 million supporting the measure, buying full-page ads in 287 newspapers.[43]

The Taft-Hartley Act was, for militant unionists, death by a thousand cuts. It outlawed several potent organized labor tactics such as the secondary boycott, the closed shop, the unionizing of shop foremen, and certain forms of worksite picketing. The act gave employers increased tools to fight unionization campaigns, including the right to speak out during union certification elections and, most potently of all, the ability to work with state legislatures to pass "right-to-work" laws that would prohibit the union shop. Such legislation was quickly passed throughout the South and Southwest where unions had, and still have, little political presence. Taft-Hartley also forced unions seeking full government protection to purge all communist organizers. While Communist Party labor activists were indeed in thrall to the Soviet Union, they had also been integral to the effort to bring African Americans into the union movement, and they had long been among the fiercest in demanding expansive worker rights. Labor historian Nelson Lichtenstein argues that "[p]assage of the Taft-Hartley Act proved a milestone, not only for the actual legal restrictions the new law imposed on the trade unions, but also as a symbol of the shifting relationship between the unions, the state, and the corporations at the dawn of the postwar era."[44]

Taft hoped his popular victory over organized labor and his long service to his party would earn him the 1948 Republican presidential nomination. He toured the nation, making his case. In Chicago he laid out his political credo, blasting the "New Dealer": "He believes in a government of men. He says nothing of individual incentive or self-reliance. His whole emphasis is on a higher material average of living to be conferred upon all by a paternal state, and he says nothing of the necessity for hard work and sacrifice to reach that better standard."[45] Taft delivered his indictment of Truman with workmanlike diligence, but his campaign again could not catch fire. He was terrible at retail politics, failing to greet supporters and almost pathologically unable to smile or wave enthusiastically to bystanders at campaign stops. Republicans, desperate to win back the presidency, once more selected the moderate, East Coast internationalist Thomas Dewey—"the little man on the wedding cake," in the words of Alice Roosevelt Longworth—as their champion.[46] The conservative wing of the Republican Party had lost again, but then so did Mr. Dewey. Truman, surprising everyone but himself, won the election and brought with him the return of a Democratic Congress. American liberalism was far from dead.

Robert Taft had only five more years to live. During those years, he and the nation struggled to make sense of the Soviet threat and the internal dangers of communist subversion. Taft was out of his element in both battles. Foreign policy was never his forte, and the rush of events left him uncertain and off balance. As Senator Joseph

McCarthy took center stage and the hunt for Reds became the nation's most fearsome concern, Taft battled to stay relevant and to reshape his conservative beliefs to fit the nation's needs.

In 1952, Taft would go after his party's presidential nomination one more time. Promising conservative business interests that he would roll back the New Deal and southern segregationists that he would oppose federal intervention to end racist practices, he gained substantial support from Republican delegates to the 1952 Republican presidential nominating convention. But he lost again, embittering his conservative Republican supporters who believed, with reason, that East Coast wealthy internationalists had stolen the nomination from Taft and bestowed it on the politically moderate, internationalist war hero General Dwight D. Eisenhower.

Ironically, Eisenhower had been willing to step aside so that Taft might win the nomination. But Eisenhower, based on his experiences during World War II and his assessment of the international communist threat, believed that the United States had to commit its resources and its military might to defending its allies against the Soviet Union. As a result, in 1950 Eisenhower heeded President Truman's call to service and accepted appointment as the North Atlantic Treaty Organization's supreme commander in charge of defending western Europe against any Soviet invasion. As the 1952 election approached, Eisenhower wanted to be sure that if Taft were elected president, he would support the principle of collective security and maintain the U.S. role in NATO. The two men met and Taft hedged. Ike, with good reason, did not trust that Taft had repudiated his pre–World War II unilateralist principles. As a result, Eisenhower decided he had good cause to run against Taft for the Republican nomination for president. Eisenhower, a national war hero, had a lot of popular support; he also gained the support of the free trade, international-oriented business and financial interests who played so powerful a role in the Republican Party. Taft's nomination defeat at the hands of those big money internationalist interests would become a rallying cry for conservative GOP activists in the years ahead.

In the 1952 presidential election, General Dwight D. Eisenhower, sure-footed in the international battleground that fixated the nation and offering a moderate course domestically, won the heart of the American people. While Eisenhower cherished the same economic liberty championed by Senator Taft, the issue simply lacked the salience it had during the New Deal Era. Fighting communism at home and abroad, not saving capitalism, had become the nation's political growth business. Taft found himself increasingly on the sidelines, even as Ike's big victory made him the Senate majority leader.

A few months after Eisenhower was sworn in as president, Taft was diagnosed with cancer. Self-disciplined to the end, even as he faced great pain and the near-certainty of imminent death, Taft soldiered on, carrying out all the tasks he deemed necessary, trying whatever treatments his doctors offered, no matter how unpleasant, refusing to give in to any sense of self-pity. He died as he lived.

Robert A. Taft carried the torch for economic liberty through conservatives' darkest days. While many Republicans chose a more moderate course, accepting the New Deal as a political necessity, Taft had fought on. Even as the massive government edifice of modern liberalism took on the appearance of a permanent addition to the American way of life, Taft kept swinging his hammer, chipping away at its solid foundation. In 1952, in homage to Taft's steadfast support for the unfettered genius of the free enterprise system, Alfred P. Sloan, chairman of the board of General Motors and onetime board member of the American Liberty League, gave a large donation, one last time to Taft's bid for the presidency.[47] At the time, that contribution to the conservative cause was for naught. People of wealth and accomplishment, however, tend not to give up easily. Economic conservatives, men and women in the mold of Robert Taft, would continue to use their power, money, and intellect to promote economic liberty, fight labor union power, insist on the virtue of free market discipline, and champion those individuals for whom capitalism works best.

TWO

WILLIAM BUCKLEY

Building the Conservative Political Culture

AFTER ROBERT TAFT DIED IN 1953, no single figure in the political establishment carried the conservative torch. President Eisenhower, conservative in temperament but moderate in policy, had casually embraced the New Deal. Senator Joe McCarthy was spiraling out of control while drinking himself to death. And southern white reactionaries such as Strom Thurmond, who ran for the presidency in

1948 on the States' Rights Democratic Party ticket, had yet to find their conservative voices or credentials. Americans, especially the younger generation, seemed to be genially under the sway of a modest, anticommunist, middle-of-the road politics.

Young William Buckley was dismayed but not demoralized by the conservatives' drift. Though just twenty-eight at the time of Taft's death, Buckley was already a star in the dim conservative firmament, mainly owing to his remarkable attack on secular liberalism, *God and Man at Yale* (1951) published by the Henry Regnery Company, newly established in 1947 as a culturally and politically conservative alternative to mainstream commercial publishers. Buckley affected an intellectual demeanor—and had an abundance of IQ points—but from young adulthood onward he dedicated himself not to the life of the mind but to the conservative political cause.

Buckley is vital to the story of modern conservatism for four reasons. First, he began publicly to disengage intellectual conservatism from the embrace of elitist cranks and reactionary haters. Second, he replaced those unlovable elements with his own charming and perspicacious self, which he energetically marketed in the national media. Buckley gave conservatism a human face by becoming one of the first kings of media, with best-selling books, a nationally syndicated newspaper column, and a television show, while overseeing the Ur-text of modern conservatism, the *National Review*, for decades. Third, Buckley was an institution builder who helped create a literate, public arena in which conservative ideas and policies could be regularly pondered and conservative personalities (his own, above all) could be presented as models to the impressionable young. Fourth and most important, Buckley found ways to link devoutly religious, educated Americans to the conservative political cause even as he legitimated the intellectual character of modern conservatism.

Buckley began the *National Review* in 1955 to create a conservative movement culture, separate from political party or single cause, that could ground conservative politics in a loosely defined set of ideals based on traditional religious beliefs, anticommunism, antistatism, and freewheeling capitalism. Under Buckley's leadership, the *National Review* aimed to create conversations and debates among conservatives and to entice young readers in search of lively political discourse, rather than to lay down any narrow orthodoxy. The *National Review* was more than a magazine; it was an institutional beachhead on which conservative political activists could sort out their worldviews and organize their campaigns to take on what they perceived as an establishmentarian liberal consensus.

William Buckley was born conservative in 1925. Raised reliably Catholic in a household in which wealth was earned, honored, but not worshiped, by the time Bill had turned ten he knew the New Deal was not for him, and he was quite capable, precocious boy that he was, of explaining its deficiencies. His gentle mother and determined father (a larger-than-life character who made the family fortune in revolutionary Mexico's oil boom and drilled his numerous children in the pieties of Catholic faith and marketplace virtues) raised him right.

Buckley shocked no one who knew him by becoming the herald of a new American conservatism while still in his twenties. In 1951, fresh from Yale—where he chaired the *Yale Daily News* and was tapped for Skull and Bones, of course—Buckley leaped into the cultural wars of his time when he published *God and Man at Yale*. The book was a sensation, rushing through multiple printing runs and gaining Buckley a national stage. In it, Buckley accused his alma mater of being a witting agent of godlessness and a training ground for Reds. Under the rubric of academic freedom, Buckley reported, Yale was turning the sons of America's elites, the young men who were themselves soon to take their place in America's corridors of power, into "atheistic socialists."[1] Buckley's basic charge, that principles necessary for virtuous human conduct and faithful observance of man's place in God's universe were being willfully subverted by arrogant elites, whether aimed at professors, politicians, cultural arbiters, or leftist activists of varying colors and kind, would remain a remarkably consistent conservative theme in the decades to come.

Buckley leveled his attack from a political crouch, spending almost his entire text counterpunching, presenting himself successfully as a youthful underdog taking on the academic heavyweights, the tenured radicals of Yale. Buckley's ability to intellectually eviscerate liberals and others on the American Left with his graceful, often humorous, lightning strikes was artfully displayed. This style would, over the next several decades, give intellectually oriented conservatives a pleasure that transcended practical politics. Buckley made conservatism seem daring and clever. If Robert Taft was a Model T, ideologically functional but no fun at all, Bill Buckley was all chrome and tail fins with a big engine under the hood.

Buckley's first major public foray showed off these skills. Rather than explain his conservative views and defend them, Buckley, like the champion debater he had been at Yale, asked that readers simply accept—how could they not?—that his core beliefs, most particularly "the divinity of Christ" and "the contemporary applicability of the principal theses of Adam Smith," were "'good.'"[2] Thereafter, young Buckley took it to the Yale professoriate and their administrative enablers for teaching students to doubt their religious faith and the wisdom of the free market. Naming names throughout *God and Man at Yale*, Buckley demonstrated how many of Yale's prominent faculty members failed to teach what he was confident most Yale alumni would want their sons (Yale had no daughters until 1969) to learn.

Thankfully, Buckley did include as an appendix a draft of a speech he had prepared but not given on the 1950 Yale Alumni Day. (Yale's administration had pressured Buckley to withdraw from the event, fearing that his remarks would provoke unseemly controversy.) In the speech, he outlined, as he put it, an "educational credo" to guide learning and hiring practices at his alma mater. It really was too useful a work to be kept forever in a drawer. Yale, Buckley urged, should teach ". . . active Christianity [as] the first basis of enlightened thought and action." Second, the moral and practical superiority of democracy and capitalism should be taught, whereas "[c]ommunism, socialism, collectivism, government paternalism inimical to the dignity of the individual and the strength and prosperity of the nation" should be presented to students as dangerous and immoral ideas. To assure that professors followed these ruling principles in their teaching "the University would not *sustain* prominent members of the faculty who sought to violate the explicit purposes of the University by *preaching* doctrines against which the officials of the University had cast judgment."[3] His message, read in the McCarthyite context of the time, was blunt: apostate faculty members, like "Reds" in Hollywood and the State Department, should be fired.

Buckley's attack on the Yale professoriate as dangerous skeptics who rather enjoyed destroying their students' virtuous beliefs had a long intellectual lineage. At least since the rise of the modern research university and the diminished authority and status of the denominational college in the late nineteenth century, Americans had been waging war over how professors should and could transmit morality and knowledge to their students. The debate was not just between the proudly parochial and the avowedly cosmopolitan, though it did often take such a form (about which more later). As Bill Buckley's polemic exemplified, the battle over wherein truth lay and how it should be disseminated was a matter of intramural debate within the halls of academe, as well. In 1942, Father Robert Gannon, the Jesuit president of Fordham University, had warned Americans to beware of secular mandarins who would destroy the religious faith that made America strong and good: "We are beginning to recognize as a nation . . . that the real enemy of democracy is atheism, whether it be adorned with a black swastika, a red star, or a Ph.D."[4] Especially in the immediate postwar years, when thanks to the GI Bill, economic prosperity, and the need for a highly educated workforce, a college degree became for the first time in American history a widespread middle-class requirement (at least for men), the role and substance of higher education became fiercely contested terrain.

Liberal intellectuals, the proud majority on university campuses and in the nation's leading journals of opinion in the early 1950s, insisted that "knowledge was empirical, particular, and experimentally verifiable."[5] Professors needed to teach students, especially those young people who were to become the elite managers of American society, to test received wisdom, to be skeptical of absolutes, and to be intellectually flexible. Theologian Reinhold Niebuhr, the Cold War Protestant liberal intellectual par excellence, insisted that scientific empiricism and a pragmatic approach to knowledge were epistemologically sound and that these methodologies inoculated American youths against Marxist dogma. The Soviet Union, not the United States, hammered its people with the iron fists of dogmatic absolutism and "official theory."

Americans needed to resist the temptation of absolutism, whether it came in the form of religious indoctrination or economic orthodoxy.[6] The struggle against Soviet totalitarianism, as well as the recent victory over fascism, said liberal intellectuals, proved that open inquiry and a skepticism about the certainty of any absolute truth were vital weapons in the hands of a democratic, free people.

William Buckley scoffed at such liberal pieties. University faculty and administrators, he observed, were always in the business of disciplining the disciplines by judging what values instructors could teach their students. "I should be interested to know," he asked, "how long a person who revealed himself as a racist, who lectured about the anthropological superiority of the Aryan, would last at Yale? My prediction is that the next full moon would see him looking elsewhere for a job.... [T]hough of course they are value judgments just the same and have been upheld by various scholars not only in the past but in the present day as well."[7] Having demonstrated that university officials practiced only a limited respect for "academic freedom," he asked why institutions of higher education would tolerate classroom proponents of communism and atheism. Why were these particular immoralities protected while others were not?

Liberal orthodoxy, Buckley observed, allowed for a good deal of intellectual flexibility when it came to circumscribing allowable "value judgment" in the lecture hall. Thus, given that liberals did draw lines between acceptable and unacceptable classroom pontifications, the question became not whether one believed *in* academic freedom but what limits should be placed *on* academic freedom. Buckley wrote, "My task becomes, then, not so much to argue that limits should be *imposed* but that existing limits should be *narrowed*."[8]

Cleaning out the out-and-out communists was never the issue. Buckley made his name in the 1950s at a time when anticommunism was de rigueur on both the liberal Left and the conservative Right in the United States. In the mainstream academic world, in those early days of the Cold War, few supported the right of members of the Soviet-directed Communist Party to indoctrinate students in the ways of Stalin, and almost as few, indeed, supported the right of communists, no matter how irrelevant their politics were to their professional duties, even to hold a university position. Buckley differentiated him-self from the anticommunist mainstream, in part, through the ferocity of his disdain for the communist foe, his willingness to press the attack against any form of left-leaning belief, and with the linkages he made between atheism (or even skepticism toward Christian doctrine) and the Red enemy. Buckley helped to popularize and intellectually legiti-mate this religiopolitical cocktail among the conservatively oriented, better-educated sort. In so doing, he laid the groundwork for a politi-cal coalition little imagined by Robert Taft.

Fear and distrust of the avowedly secular and irreligious was noth-ing new in American political culture. Nor was many Americans' absolute trust in God, the power of prayer, or the moral necessity of faith. Before the 1920s, religiosity would not have been seen by most politically aware members of the citizenry to be a particularly con-servative position. Politicians across the political spectrum called on the Lord and referenced the Bible regularly to connect with their con-stituents. President Lincoln, perhaps because his personal religious views were so richly ambiguous and so tested by adversity, probably did it best, as this powerful passage from his second inaugural address attests: "Both [North and South] read the same Bible, and pray to the same God; and each invokes His aid against the other. . . . The prayers of both could not be answered; that of neither has been answered fully. The Almighty has His own purposes."[9] Many other politicians and public figures, if less movingly and with more certainty, reached out to voters by demonstrating an easy familiarity with the Bible and insisting that God was on their side.

By the 1920s, however, sophisticates of various stripes commonly used overt religiosity, especially of the more evangelical and Bible-thumping sort, as a nearly endless source of humor. H. L. Mencken, one of the Jazz Age's greatest wits, made religion and the religious his favorite target: "A man full of faith is simply one who has lost (or never had) the capacity for clear and realistic thought. He is not a mere ass, he is actually ill. Worse, he is incurable." And again: "It is often argued that religion is valuable because it makes men good, but even if that is true it would not be a proof that religion is true. . . . Santa Claus makes children good in precisely the same way. . . . The defense of religion is full of such logical imbecilities."[10] Irreligiosity, agnosticism, and a general distrust of organized religion have roots deep in the Enlightenment, and a smattering of Americans had been complaining about the prominent place and practice of religion since the nation's origins. From the 1920s onward, however, among a sector of the nation's smart set atheism, agnosticism or, at the least, a mocking distrust of organized religion was a common cultural currency.

Deeply religious Americans, especially those of a fundamentalist persuasion, took umbrage at the mockery and feared that secular intellectuals were gaining control of American life. The famous Scopes trial of 1925 demonstrated the national divide. As is well known, in the court case over the validity of the Tennessee law banning the teaching of evolution in the state's schools, Clarence Darrow put religion on the stand in the corporeal form of William Jennings Bryan, who was assisting the state of Tennessee as the acting counsel for the World Christian Fundamentals Association. Darrow, in Mencken-esque fashion, did his best to demonstrate the absurdity of a literal belief in the Bible by asking Bryan to explain a range of biblical conundrums (for example, where did Cain get his wife?). It is less well known that William Jennings Bryan, populist champion, two-time Democratic presidential nominee, antievolutionist, and proud believer in biblical inerrancy, very much held his own in the showdown. Politically, Bryan also demonstrated great prescience.

Foreshadowing William Buckley's attack on the secularists who ran elite higher education, Bryan defended the right of the people of Tennessee to set their own pedagogical standards. He asked a simple question: "Who shall control our schools?" His answer: "the people, speaking through their legislatures." He mused, "[A] teacher receiving pay in dollars on which is stamped, 'In God We Trust,' should not be permitted to teach the children that there is no God. Neither should he be allowed to accept employment in a Christian community and teach that the Bible is untrue."[11] Bryan believed that school authorities should not challenge the wisdom of the people who paid them. Parents and community members, not scientific experts or secular intellectuals, had the right to decide what local schoolchildren should learn. Bryan stood with the people in part because he was a genuine democrat but also because he believed the core wisdom of the American people, most especially their deep Christian faith, had stood the test of time in a way the hypotheses of their supposed intellectual betters did not.[12]

The patrician William Buckley and the "Great Commoner" William Jennings Bryan are not obvious political or intellectual twins. But the two men did share a core tenet: Christian faith sustains and even defines American life. In Bryan's political heyday, the glory years of populism, such a belief in the centrality of Christianity served no particular political creed. And on matters of political economy, Bryan's faith steered him, as the teachings of the carpenter of Nazareth might well, to the left; he believed that all Americans (white Americans, at any rate) deserved an equitable share of the country's material wealth. But when it came to the primacy of faith and how young people should be educated, the populist and the patrician were as one. From such an odd union comes interesting political fruit.

Buckley, in appearance, speech, and background, was anything but a populist. But he understood that many Americans' deep suspicion of the avant-garde and the unfamiliar, as well as their almost instinctual mistrust of the iconoclastic intellectual elite, was in tune with his own cultural conservatism and served it politically. Buckley well knew that Edmund Burke had made similar observations about the stolid English folk, arguing that they were natural allies of a conservative social order. Thus Buckley could, at times, sound like a man of the people: "[I would] sooner be governed by the first two thousand people in the Boston telephone directory than by the two thousand members of the faculty of Harvard University."[13] That such people in the Boston directory were likely to be fellow Irish Catholics and that it was Harvard, not his alma mater, that he was lampooning, certainly figured in Buckley's claim. But Buckley, at least partially, meant what he said: the tradition-abiding, religious majority of the American people have a greater sense for the necessity of the verities of life than do secular elites and thus could be trusted to make better political judgments.

Before Buckley became a public figure of consequence, sophisticated opponents of America's modernist, secular turn did most certainly exist. And some of these distinguished lights had success in the public square. J. Gresham Machen, a learned and nationally well-known conservative Presbyterian theologian, attacked the modernist turn in both American society and his own denomination in *Christianity and Liberalism* (1923). He argued that "[m]aterial betterment has gone hand in hand with spiritual decline. Such a condition of the world ought to cause the choice between modernism and traditionalism, liberalism and conservatism, to be approached without any of the prejudice which is too often displayed. . . . In the midst of all the material achievements of modern life, one may well ask the question whether in gaining the whole world we have not lost our own soul."[14] Machen was not alone in making a thoughtful, carefully argued case for a tradition-affirming religiosity in the face of the secular-scientific, modernist juggernaut, and his work has continued to be influential, even now.

But the most vocal champions of a Christian, God-fearing America, especially in the era right before William Buckley took center stage in the more refined venues of American public life, often preached in far more strident and less becoming tones. Eschewing subtleties, they looked for villains and found conspiracies. In particular, when they attacked secular modernism, they placed substantial blame for the nation's spiritual peril on the head of the Jew. During the first decades of the twentieth century, many of the best-known and aggressive adherents of religious conservatism in the United States tied their cause to anti-Semitism.

In the loosely connected movement of the Protestant Far Right, most popular in the Midwest and the South, evil Jews and demonic communists—quite often one and the same—played biblically cast, starring roles as Satan's legions, whose primary mission was to destroy the United States by spreading secularism and robbing God-fearing Americans of their fundamental—and fundamentalist—beliefs and values.[15] Reverend Gerald B. Winrod helped lead this campaign. In 1925, he founded the Defenders of the Christian Faith in Salina, Kansas, in order to fight the "forces of evolution" and "Modernism."[16] Jews, he informed his followers, working under "organized demon intelligences," were the leaders of these spirit-destroying forces.[17] In 1952, *Time* magazine reported that he was still at it, warning his diminishing number of followers that "the international Jewish banking fraternity" was moving fast to "sovietize" the United States: "Woodrow Wilson failed them. Franklin Roosevelt served them to the end of his days. Harry Truman remains their pawn. Dwight Eisenhower is their choice in this, the catastrophic year of 1952." Gerald L. K. Smith, whose heyday had been in the late New Deal years but who maintained a public role as head of the Nationalist Christian Crusade, was more direct in his 1952 attack on moderate Republican Eisenhower: "A dispatch out of London reveals that the leading Jewish paper [unnamed] of that city now admits that Eisenhower is a Jew."[18]

Such Jew-baiting had a long, if not particularly distinguished history in the United States and was, at least until the early 1940s, a usually unremarked upon aspect of life in America.[19] Nevertheless, in the 1930s, most political liberals, whose New Deal–solidified urban constituency included Americans of all religions, had almost completely weaned themselves from anti-Semitism and had reached out convincingly to American Jews. While many sophisticated, secularly oriented conservatives had done likewise—Senator Robert Taft, for example—conservative circles were far more likely to include men and women who abhorred Jews and enjoyed speaking publicly about their feelings.

Those conservatives who remained anti-Semitic did so for varied reasons. Followers of men like Gerald Smith and Gerald Winrod believed, at a practical level, that the influx of millions of Jews into the United States in the early twentieth century endangered America's traditional and essential status as a Christian nation. Jews, they believed with cause, would not convert to Christianity, and because America was by their definition a Christian nation, Jews could not become good Americans. Instead, Jews, for a variety of reasons and in a range of ways, would make America less Christian and therefore less good. Then, too, members of the Protestant Far Right believed, along with millions of other Americans, that Jews had villainously crucified Jesus and ever since refused to accept Christ as their savior. Damning evidence, to put the matter literally. And, in accord with Christians' accusations that spanned the centuries, these anti-Semites charged Jews with innumerable dastardly deeds, mostly involving money trickery against Gentiles. In the 1920s, Henry Ford with his millions of dollars and the Ku Klux Klan with its millions of followers had done their best to inculcate Americans with these beliefs. In the 1930s, powerful figures in the Catholic Church—including the famed Great Depression–era radio priest, Father Charles E. Coughlin, and Patrick Scanlon, editor of the *Brooklyn Tablet*, the influential newspaper of the Brooklyn archdiocese—had done likewise among their own coreligionists. To be a Christian-who-hated-Jews was to be part of a time-honored, constantly refreshed tradition in Western civilization; that is, anti-Semitism, an anti-Semite would argue, was a conservative virtue. Tolerance of Jews was a newfangled idea, something only liberals with their love of social experiment embraced, as they did the New Deal (a.k.a., the "Jew Deal").

At least some sophisticated and intellectually oriented conservatives shared some or all of these beliefs. William Buckley's own father believed that Jews were cultural interlopers who could not adapt to the spiritual truths that made the United States great and who thus endangered America's moral foundations.[20] But young Buckley rejected anti-Semitism as an atavistic impulse rather than a morally sound, grounded tradition. In breaking with the anti-Semitism of his father and of the disreputable sort of religiocultural conservatism that characterized elements of the Protestant Far Right and the Catholic Church, Buckley was doing his best to live by his own moral standards and to put a modern, religiously inclusive face on American conservatism.

Buckley's lively ecumenism occurred at a time when a new tolerance for religious diversity—restricted, as it was, to Catholic, Protestant, and Jew—was being celebrated, if not always observed, in America's political and cultural mainstream. Nazis, not Americans, were anti-Semites, and after news of the Holocaust became well known in the United States, few Americans found public or political diatribes against Jews acceptable (even as Jews remained the object of private prejudice and widespread exclusionary practice). Equally true, wartime unity and common sacrifice contributed to the diminishment, if not the end, of Protestant Americans' suspicion (or worse) of Catholics, another long-standing American tradition, and to the uneasy creation of a common religious front.

The rapprochement between Catholic and Protestant had been another project that had begun with religious liberals. In the face of the extraordinary rise in the 1920s of the Ku Klux Klan, which preached a fiery hatred of Jews, blacks, modern women, and especially Catholics, liberal Protestants had fought back. Working through the Federal Council of Churches and related ecumenical groups, liberal Protestants had reached out to Catholic Americans (and Jews, as well). By 1934, they had instigated a National Brotherhood Week, and during the war interfaith declarations against "godless fascism" became a standard call to spiritual arms throughout the United States. A 1942 Brotherhood Week statement, released by the National Conference of Christians and Jews, expressed the new American creed: "We the undersigned individuals of the Protestant, Catholic, and Jewish faiths, viewing the present catastrophic results of Godlessness in the world . . . realize the necessity for stressing those spiritual truths which we hold in common."[21] Such welcome sentiments had become, by the end of the war, conventional wisdom. President-elect Eisenhower, champion of such conventions, stated the relatively new view best in his famous 1952 aside to a *New York Times* reporter: "[O]ur government makes no sense unless it is founded in a deeply religious faith—and I don't care what it is."[22] After more than a century of Protestant attempts to denigrate Catholics in the United States, peace had been declared by leading Protestant worthies (though rearguard action would continue to be fought by a vocal minority of suspicious Protestants who feared "papalized politicians").

William Buckley, thus, was working in a cultural realm in which his Catholic beliefs and anti-anti-Semitism could be transmogrified into a seemly Christian stew of tolerant though insistent religiosity. For Buckley—and for most Americans—the enemy could be restricted to the godless foe. With the defeat of fascism accomplished and postwar America soaking in the warm water of religious brotherhood, the godly, instead of expending their energies fighting one another, could find common purpose in the fight against communism. Buckley had entered the crowded field of professional anticommunism with his first book, *God and Man at Yale*. He sought to cultivate his patch on this fertile ground with his second, *McCarthy and His Enemies*

(1954). Once again, he published with the conservative protomovement press, Henry Regnery Company. This time he was joined in coauthorship with his brother-in-law and erstwhile Yale debating partner, L. Brent Bozell.

Most everyone, by the early 1950s, had joined the anticommunist bandwagon. While a tiny number of liberals had supported the 1948 Progressive Party presidential campaign of Henry Wallace (Roosevelt's 1940 running mate), who promised to reach out to the monstrous Joseph Stalin, a vast majority of liberals had, soon after the end of World War II, embraced the anticommunist cause. Fair Dealer Harry Truman, after all, had launched the Cold War abroad in March 1947, proclaiming, "The free peoples of the world look to us for support in maintaining their freedoms. If we falter in our leadership, we may endanger the peace of the world—and we shall surely endanger the welfare of our own nation."[23] A few days later, Truman had followed up on that first salvo against Soviet-led international communism with a war against communism at home by implementing an anticommunist loyalty oath program for all members of the executive branch. In 1949, the quintessential liberal intellectual, Arthur Schlesinger Jr., published *The Vital Center*, which declared that fascism and communism were twinned totalitarian enemies of democracy and that only liberalism provided modern man (it was a very macho book) with a fighting faith in freedom and individual liberty capable of defeating them both. Tough-minded and full-throated anticommunism, then and for many years thereafter, was a project of both the liberal and conservative mainstream.

The question in the early 1950s, and for several decades after, was exactly how to fight the communist enemy. Liberals tended to focus on the international activities of the Soviet Union and placed their emphasis on containing the Red foe until its own internal contradictions caused it to implode. Richard Gid Powers, in his sympathetic history of American anticommunism, *Not without Honor*, observes that for liberals such as Arthur Schlesinger Jr., "there was no danger from domestic Communists that could not be handled by the constitutional methods of 'debate, identification and exposure.' To abridge civil liberties in an effort to fight communism was to betray the cause of freedom."[24] Liberals wanted to dismiss government employees disloyal to the United States and were all for rooting out communist spies, but they also believed that domestic repression aimed at ferreting out anyone who expressed sympathy with Marxist ideas or even the Soviet Union was too high a price to pay for the limited damage domestic communists and pinkish fellow-travelers could do to American society. Liberals trusted that individual Americans were intellectually capable of hearing communist propaganda or even reasoned Marxist disquisitions without falling prey to them. The democratic process and an open society, they argued, could handle domestic communists.

Conservatives, especially religiously based conservatives, disagreed. They lacked liberals' optimistic faith in Americans' ability to withstand the blandishments of communist propaganda—the Red snake was wily, and humans, they knew, were susceptible to temptation. They demanded a more vigorous offensive, especially on the cultural front, and young William Buckley was all for a full-bore attack on domestic communists. He, like most committed conservatives of his time, understood the war at home against the malevolent Left to be at least as important as the battle abroad against the Soviet octopus. For Buckley, then, like almost all on the Right, the Herculean efforts of Senator Joseph McCarthy were a godsend. While Buckley was well aware that the junior senator from Wisconsin was not without his sins, he believed that McCarthy deserved support, even enthusiastic support, especially as his enemies began to tear him down.

Buckley understood that Senator McCarthy was an easy man to dislike. The senator drank a great deal, often a quart of whiskey a day. Being drunk a good deal of the time made him sloppy in dress, manner, and speech. Either because of the drinking or his character or both, he lied a lot—about such things as his World War II record, the number of communists against whom he had evidence, and the nature of the domestic communist threat. He lied so often and so grandly that historian Richard Gid Powers argues, "In the mouth of McCarthy, the truths of anticommunism would turn into evil, malicious lies."[25] William Buckley disapproved of the excessive drinking and the occasional lying, but despite it all he both liked and admired Joseph McCarthy, as did his brother-in-law Brent Bozell, who had worked for McCarthy as a speech writer. And Buckley categorically rejected the notion that McCarthy's imprecisions damaged the anticommunist cause.

In this version, McCarthy grasped the big picture, and he believed that to inspire Americans sufficiently to support fierce actions against the communists and their domestic fellow-travelers, subtly was not in the cards. Thus Buckley, no shrinking violet himself, wrote in *McCarthy and His Enemies* that people must understand that "McCarthy is a publicist among publicists."[26] Just as liberal advocates Truman and Roosevelt had done, Senator McCarthy had to blow hard to move a largely inert public. That so many liberals had lined up against McCarthy and the entire project of ridding American public life of communists was further proof of the senator's need to exert himself even unto a certain degree of hyperbole. That McCarthy was a faithful Catholic, whose anticommunism partially stemmed, like Buckley's own, from the Church's long-standing leadership in the anticommunist cause contributed to the goodwill and ease between the two men of such otherwise different backgrounds.

Faithful Catholics had been hearing about the horrors of communism long before the Cold War with the Soviet Union began in the postwar years. Bishop Fulton Sheen, whose immensely popular prime-time television show in the early Cold War years featured anticommunist sermonizing, had been warning Catholic audiences for decades about the communist threat. In 1935, he blasted the Soviet Union as "the most anti-Christ nation on the face of the earth" and chillingly explained how the Soviets had symbolically replaced the miracle of Christ arisen with "a rotted corpse, the body of Lenin—a perfect symbol of that to which all communism must lead us all, unto dust, dissolution, unto death."[27] In 1938, in a packed Carnegie Hall rally condemning the leftist cause in the Spanish Civil War, the charismatic Sheen intoned, "We were silent before when 2,000,000 kulaks met death and 60,000 churches were closed by an atheistic government in Russia; we were silent before when 20,000 churches and chapels were desecrated, burned, and pillaged, and when 6,000 diocesan clergy were murdered in Spain." No more, he said, "the secret is out; those who cannot pull God down from heaven are driving his creatures from the face of the earth."[28] While many embraced the anti-communist cause in the 1950s, Catholic leaders, both in the Church and among lay people, had been at the forefront of the struggle long before most secular sorts had seen the light.[29]

Buckley stood with McCarthy. They were Catholic men who believed that the Soviet Union was more than a foreign policy problem; it was the embodiment of a stunningly evil force loosed in the world. Communists literally meant to wipe out the teachings of God. Why would anyone—liberals, that is—compromise with such a force or bind oneself in the struggle with rules made for ordinary political disputes?

The case of Owen Lattimore, detailed in Buckley and Bozell's *McCarthy and His Enemies*, demonstrated the divide between the conservative McCarthyite and the liberal anticommunist. Owen Lattimore was a leading American academic expert on China. He was also, as the saying went, "soft on communism." In the late 1930s, he had made public excuses for Stalin's murderous purges and show trials. During the 1940s, Lattimore demonstrated open support for the Mao-led communist forces battling for control of China. Despite that record and those sympathies, Lattimore maintained an advisory role as a China expert to American government officials. In the 1940s, he had counseled the Truman administration to accept the inevitability of a communist takeover of China. A communist China, he argued, would not be a problem for U.S. interests in the region. While the Truman government continued to support the corrupt and often incompetent anticommunist forces in China's civil war, it did so without enthusiasm or commitment. When Mao's communist forces won the war, the Truman administration blandly—and rightly—insisted that "[n]othing that this country did or could have done within the reasonable limits of its capabilities would have changed that result."[30] For Buckley and other ardent, conservative anticommunists this polite acceptance of the communist takeover of the world's most populous nation was appalling; they believed that American policy and not Chinese actions had caused the "fall" of China to the Reds.

Joseph McCarthy stated the matter bluntly: the fall of China could have been stopped by the American government. The Truman administration had not prevented the surrender of China because

American men loyal to communist doctrine had ensured it. The communists took China because the U.S. State Department gave it to them. Most specifically, the State Department let China go Red, McCarthy insisted, because the Ivy League–educated men of Foggy Bottom took counsel from one of their own kind, Owen Lattimore, who whispered that America's Chinese ally Chiang Kai-shek was finished and that a communist victory was inevitable. Lattimore had lied, McCarthy told the world, and he did so because he was the "top Russian espionage agent in the country."[31] This was the headline charge that turned McCarthy from a mere man to a timeless modus operandi: McCarthyism.

In fact, though Lattimore had expressed support for both the Soviet Union and the Red Chinese, he was not a Russian agent. He did not work for the Soviets; he was not paid by the Soviets; he did not take orders from the Soviets; nor was he, at any time, a member of any Communist Party. Few, if any, liberals at the time found any of McCarthy's evidence reasonable, nor did they accept his premise, that somehow the United States could have stopped Mao's armies from defeating the anticommunist forces of Chiang Kai-shek. They did find the senator's original, headline-making slander of Lattimore proof of the danger that McCarthy—and McCarthyism—presented to American democracy.

Buckley reversed the equation. He found liberals' anti-McCarthyism a danger to American society. And throughout *McCarthy and His Enemies* "Liberals" (always with a capital L) emerged for the first time as Buckley's primary antagonists. Buckley, while unwavering in his horror over communism, was beginning to articulate the position that would sustain him over the next several decades: the war at home was not between communists and anticommunists so much as it was between weak-willed, naive liberals and stout, principled conservatives.

Buckley supported McCarthy, even in his charges against Owen Lattimore, because he constructed the communist threat differently than did those liberal anticommunists who held to a narrow standard of evidence and a narrower sense of the threat facing the American people. Liberals argued that Lattimore was innocent because he was not a Soviet agent or even a member of the Communist Party. Buckley admitted that "McCarthy got off on the wrong foot" by accusing Lattimore of literally being a Soviet spy.[32] But the name given to Lattimore's crime, Buckley and Bozell explained in *McCarthy and His Enemies*, was less important than stopping the man from counseling government officials and the American people to support international communism.

Buckley applauded McCarthyism, in general, because its purpose was not merely to rid the federal government of out-and-out Russian spies. McCarthyism served a higher calling. Done right (and Senator McCarthy had not always done so), McCarthyism aimed to produce a necessary and salutary political orthodoxy: communism and communists, communist sympathizing and communist "fellow-traveling" should not have any place in American thought, American politics, or American institutions. A man such as Owen Lattimore might not be paid by the Soviets, but his sympathies for Chinese Red Communists made him a traitor to American values. Traitors to American values lost their right to advise the American government and to spread their traitorous thoughts to the American public. "Comsymps," in the lingo of the time, had to be "excluded from positions of public trust and public esteem."[33]

Buckley enjoyed being an enfant terrible. Celebrating McCarthyism at a time when Senator McCarthy's hold on the so-called mainstream American imagination was tremulous, at best, could be seen as an exercise in the kind of intellectual contrariness he greatly enjoyed. But raising the bloody flag of McCarthyism was more than that. Buckley, as his prior book on education at Yale also demonstrated, believed that a virtuous people needed to guard their culture zealously from the dangerously unorthodox—and communism, he claimed, was the most dangerously unorthodox idea of all. While liberals worshiped at the altar of civil liberties and exalted the good produced by the free exchange of ideas, Buckley offered a different perspective, a conservative one, on the meaning of freedom in a virtuous society.

In *McCarthy and His Enemies*, Buckley and Bozell spelled out this conservative position. "In short," they wrote, "it is characteristic of society that it uses sanctions in support of its folklore and mores, and that in doing so it urges conformity. What we call the 'institutions' of a society are nothing but the values that society has settled on over the years. . . . It is our institutions that make us what we are."[34] Americans, the authors argued, had the right and the necessity to protect themselves from those nonconformist ideas—un-American ideas—that threatened the nation's time-tested institutions: "McCarthy's function has been to harden the existing [anticommunist] conformity. . . . McCarthyism, then, is a weapon in the American arsenal. . . . [I]t is a movement around which men of good will and stern morality can close ranks."[35] Liberals, they scoffed, are "bewitched . . . with the value of innovation."[36] Thus, liberals are willing to chance any new expression and any new practice in the vainglorious hope that it might stimulate some exciting and somehow useful new feeling or thought. In such laxity Buckley saw depravity.

For Buckley, conservatism meant that one could be, and at times must be, soft on protecting civil liberties in order to be hard in the endless fight against deadly cultural corruption. Most cosmopolitan sophisticates celebrated the avant-garde and the quest for new stimulations. William Buckley, though quite urbane and cosmopolitan, in his own way, worshiped at the altar of those traditions that kept American society united and strong in religious faith, in free market principles, and in conformity to the overarching ideals expressed in the Constitution.

By time *McCarthy and His Enemies* was published, the senator was losing his hold on the American public and was already a despised figure in the hearts of America's dominant liberal intelligentsia. As partial result, Buckley's second book had a different impact than had his first. *God and Man at Yale* had sounded an alarm that shocked, titillated, and even inspired at least a portion of its intended audience of well-educated men and women worried about the liberal, secular drift of American life. Buckley's pro-McCarthyism volume merely weighed in—in dramatic fashion—on a debate that had long before become polarized. Still, Buckley's plunge into the fight increased his public profile and served to crystallize the conservative position on the anticommunist fight. Just as the Eisenhower administration, seeking to prove its moderate "modern Republican" way, was distancing itself from McCarthyism, Buckley was wrapping himself in its mantle.

Just after the book's publication, Buckley's invitation to speak before the Women's National Republican Club in New York was retracted by Republican moderates because of his too zealous McCarthyism. Revealing the deep divide within the Republican Party, a rival faction of conservative women responded by asking him to address their group, instead. Before an overflowing crowd, Buckley did what he did best: "Far from suffering from a reign of terror, it is my contention that we are living in an age when particularly the cowards speak up. Men who have never had the spirit to face up to their mothers-in-law are suddenly aware that they can now earn a badge of courage by denouncing Senator McCarthy."[37] Buckley, all who attended understood, was mocking as unmanly those moderate Republicans—whatever their office—who were running away from Senator McCarthy. Not yet thirty years old, Buckley was drawing a line in the sand between moderate Republicans and stalwart conservatives who, he believed, needed to stand up and take back the party. In the age of Eisenhower, Buckley was in a minority, but he was not, by any means, alone.

Buckley had never intended to be just a writer and speaker, brilliant as he was at both. Hoping to carry the fight to the enemy most directly, right out of college, he had decided to join the Central Intelligence Agency. After a pleasant hiatus, during which he married the beautiful, brilliant, and very conservative heiress, Pat Taylor, and wrote God and Man at Yale, Buckley had entered the then clubby world of espionage. But while he had been quite adept at the spy business, proving his mettle in Mexico by pushing an anticommunist agenda among Mexico City's student set, Buckley quickly came to miss the public role he had just begun carving out as a champion of the conservative cause. Covert life was not quite the same as life in the spotlight. Given his post-first-book-celebrityhood and the relative lack of intellectually charismatic and presentable figures on the Right, Buckley had several good opportunities back in the States. Thanks to family wealth, vulgarities such as a regular paycheck or job security were of little concern.

Buckley wanted to institutionalize and regularize his attack on liberal conventional wisdom by bringing to the public arena a reliable and respectable voice of accessible, intellectual conservatism. All the

major outlets of reasoned public opinion, he believed, were mouth-
pieces for liberalism. The high-end of the mass media was particularly egregious; the *New York Times* and the *Washington Post* both
scorned Senator McCarthy and conformed to the Rooseveltian line.
And a regular hornet's nest of little magazines all along the left-liberal
line drilled New Dealism and the thrills of secular modernism into
the hungry minds of college students, young professionals, and the
intellectually inclined. At best, a modest "We Like Ike" Republicanism was made available to readers via the major organs of the Luce
empire: *Time, Fortune*, and *Life*. And while a significant number of
newspapers, especially the *Chicago Tribune*, the *Los Angeles Times*,
the many papers of both the Hearst empire and the Scripps-Howard
chain, as well as syndicated newspaper columnists such as George
Sokolsky and Westbrook Pegler championed the free market and
were as anticommunist as Buckley, no intellectually credible, winning
magazine of opinion carried the flaming torch of true conservatism.
Buckley believed in the power of ideas and the sustaining value of
culture; ergo, he believed that conservatives needed a potent forum to
refine their principles, express their cultural preferences, and verbal-
ize, as Buckley would say, their policy choices.

When Buckley left the CIA in search of public influence, a few
periodicals of Buckley-like conservatism did exist, but all were
struggling for viability. A notable example was the *Freeman*—which
had published Buckley's first major article, a defense of Senator Joe
McCarthy. Albert Jay Nock, believer in the saving power of a cultured
remnant, had started the *Freeman* in the 1920s to warn against the
individual-crushing terror of the modern state and the idiocy of the
unlettered masses. It had been briefly resurrected by Frank Chodorov, a brilliant, no-holds-barred defender of anti-statist individual-
ism ("the State is our enemy. . . . [I]ts administrators and beneficiaries
are a 'professional criminal class'").[38] But Chodorov had proved to be
too aggressively contentious for his backers—an endemic problem
for intellectuals on both the Left and the Right—and had been forced
out. A new *Freeman* had been born in 1950, combining its efforts with
a small anticommunist journal, *Plain Talk*. An editorial in the first
issue declared that the *Freeman* embraced "traditional liberalism and

individual freedom"; the free market and limited government were its watchwords. Mostly, a coterie of conservative business owners footed the bill for the money-losing enterprise (an irony that seemed lost on the free market acolytes who ran it). But the magazine, in whatever iteration, remained moored in an isolated, conservative backwater. And it suffered from bitter editorial strife over the correct direction, meaning, and parameters of modern conservatism.

After Buckley's CIA adventure, the men who ran the *Freeman* had wanted to hire the ebullient Buckley as an editor, but he chose to work instead at the more tempestuous, higher-circulation, and newly conservative magazine, the *American Mercury*. The magazine had a storied past, having been founded in the 1920s, ironically enough, by the iconoclastic and atheistic H. L. Mencken. After Mencken departed, the publication had limped along for a number of years and then, in 1950, a conservative businessman had bought the ailing title, hoping to make it a flagship periodical of conservative opinion. William Bradford Huie, a prolific, popular writer whose wide-ranging works included *The Revolt of Mamie Stover*, a fictionalized account of a World War II Honolulu-based prostitute and madam, was made editor. Huie knew how to write and had entrepreneurial zeal, but he did not have conservative credentials or a particularly well-considered conservative worldview. Nonetheless, in 1952, Huie convinced Buckley to join the enterprise, promising to give the young publicist of the Right a free editorial hand.

Not surprisingly, given his temperament and capacities, Buckley found the experience of working under less-capable others at the financially and ideologically challenged magazine annoying, at best. He left the flagging affair just in time; under new ownership it was reinvented as a mouthpiece for anti-Semites and other fell forms of conservatism of which Buckley firmly disapproved. Buckley took leave from the world of employed labor, and while he pondered his future endeavors, he wrote the McCarthy book with his brother-in-law.

Despite his unpleasant experience working at the *American Mercury*, Buckley still believed that he could produce a substantial and successful magazine of the Right. He saw no competitor, and he saw substantial need. With characteristic certainty, he told a sympathetic lunch companion, the esteemed Dante scholar and Yale professor Thomas Bergin, "I can give the Right the kind of decent image it needs instead of the image that some people are giving it."[39] With financial help from his father and a small group of other wealthy businessmen, young Mr. Buckley launched America's great magazine of conservative opinion, the *National Review*.

In the conventional story of modern conservatism, the appearance of Buckley's *National Review* is often treated as a Lazarus-like story: through the words on its pages conservatism is brought back from the dead. John Judis, Buckley's biographer and trustworthy in so many ways, sets the stage for the 1955 appearance of the first issue of the *National Review* by writing, "At no time did the fortunes of the American right appear as dim as they did in 1954."[40] Buckley himself loved to portray the early years of his career as a crying in the wilderness: liberals ruled the citadels of culture and politics, and the masses had fallen prey to their machinations. Conservatives would have to fight hard, in well-organized ranks, to take back American civilization. Although this story has elements of truth, conservatism was hardly flat on its back.

While Buckley might have felt under siege, only a couple of years had passed since Senator Taft's death. And President Eisenhower, although not a Buckley conservative, was hardly a Rooseveltian liberal. Ike believed in limited government, a balanced budget, and the right of local people to determine their own community standards. In both the House of Representatives and the Senate, ardent, free market conservatives like the recently elected Congressman James Utt of Orange County, California, and stalwarts like Ohio Senator John Bricker and Indiana's William E. Jenner pursued communists and left-wingers with an unswerving passion. Then, too, books espousing an uncompromising free market capitalism, most especially Friedrich A. von Hayek's masterpiece, *The Road to Serfdom* and, not least, Buckley's own volumes, had been eagerly taken up by a large readership. In 1953, Russell Kirk, then a relatively unknown history professor at Michigan State, published with the indispensable Henry Regnery Company a massive tome titled *The Conservative Mind*. In it, Kirk laid out an American conservative intellectual genealogy and cheered on religious tradition, an ordered social hierarchy, and cultural prescription. Surprising both the author and the publisher, *The Conservative Mind* was widely reviewed and earned praise almost everywhere, including a glowing review in the *New York Times* and featured treatment in *Time* magazine.[41] On television, Bishop Fulton Sheen wowed audiences of his prime-time show, *Life Is Worth Living*, with paeans to religiosity and devastating attacks on communism. Upon winning the Academy Award in 1952 for Most Outstanding Television Personality, he said, "I wish to thank my four writers, Matthew, Mark, Luke, and John."[42] Conservatism, in both the political and cultural realm, was alive and well in America. Still, 1954 was a low point, to put it mildly, for Senator Joe McCarthy and his full-bore hunt for subversives, and Buckley, his ardent champion, had reason to feel besieged.

In that year, the Senate censured McCarthy. The senator had been losing support and gaining enemies steadily since he began his largely unsupported attacks on communists in high places in February 1950 at the Lincoln Day Dinner held by the Ohio County Women's Republican Club in Wheeling, West Virginia. Liberals had scorned McCarthy from the outset, and the senator had made an early, if generally silent enemy of Dwight Eisenhower by accusing Ike's friend, World War II Army Chief of Staff and then Secretary of State George C. Marshall, of being a communist. By 1953, liberals had been joined by legions of others as the senator's accusations became ever more wild.

Millions of television viewers in June 1954 had watched in disgust as McCarthy accused the United States Army of being soft on communism. The army's counsel, Joseph Welch, won general acclaim when he responded to McCarthy's attacks by stating, "Until this moment, Senator, I think I never really gauged your cruelty or your recklessness. . . . Have you no sense of decency, sir, at long last? Have you left no sense of decency?"[43] Public opinion polls taken in June showed that McCarthy, whose support had still stood at 50 percent in January 1954, had plummeted to 34 percent.

Right after the 1954 midterm elections, the cautious Senate voted 67 to 22 to censure McCarthy. Every Democrat present had voted against him, as had a majority of Republicans. Still, twenty-two Republicans had stood by McCarthy, and so did 34 percent of the public. As the 1952 Democratic presidential candidate Adlai Stevenson observed, the Republican Party was "half McCarthy and half Eisenhower."[44] McCarthy, politically speaking, had been mortally wounded, and he never recovered (he died from complications caused by alcoholism in May 1957), but McCarthyism, particularly in the Republican Party, remained popular. Hunting for communists, communist conspiracies, fellow-travelers, and Reds of various shades remained an enthusiastic pursuit in large parts of the United States. Conservatism of a McCarthyite kind was down but hardly out in 1954.

Still, liberals' successful efforts to destroy McCarthy put William Buckley and other ardent McCarthyites on the defensive and gave credence to the mainstream mass media claims that Americans sought a moderate, consensus-building, civil politics, as personified in the figure of President Eisenhower. A majority of American voters did surely feel this way. Thus, when Buckley began the *National Review* in 1955, he was, as he repeatedly stated, fighting conventional wisdom and powerful segments of the intelligentsia. But he was not alone as he began his efforts to create an intellectual beachhead for a resurgent conservative political movement.

Buckley raised money for his magazine from a disparate crew of wealthy men. Some, like the financier E. F. Hutton (who had helped fund the American Liberty League), had been fighting New Deal liberalism for many years. Then there was the South Carolina textile giant Roger Milliken, who although just a decade older than Buckley came from a family where fighting labor unions was a way of life. Relatively new to the conservative scene were a dedicated crew of Southern California businessmen who would continue to make their presence known in conservative circles for decades to come. Buckley's father had gotten the ball rolling with a gift of $100,000. While rich businessmen were not lining up around the block to support a sophisticated journal of conservative opinion, enough of them had opened up their checkbooks to Buckley.[45]

Buckley only needed a relatively small amount of capital, as he was not looking to produce and market a flashy, big-budget magazine to the masses. His goal, he wrote shortly before publishing the first issue, was to "influence the opinion makers" and not to grow a "grass-roots" constituency.[46] In a letter to the writer and lecturer Ruth Alexander, who had urged Buckley to reach out to the average voter, Buckley explained, "[W]e feel that before it is possible to bring the entire nation around politically, we have got to engage the attention of people who for a long time have felt that the conservative position is moribund." He continued "... once we have engaged in hand-to-hand combat with the best the Liberals can furnish, and bested them, then we can proceed to present a realistic political alternative around which we hope the American right, at present so terribly disintegrated, can close ranks."[47] Setting up the offices of the *National Review* in New York City, Buckley intended to take on the East Coast liberal intelligentsia that, he believed, controlled American political and cultural discourse. As would be typical of conservative intellectuals and publicists more generally, he ignored or simply did not take into consideration the power that conservative businessmen still exercised on Capitol Hill and in most state governments, nor did he ponder the influence conservative religious figures held in America's churches and on the airwaves. Buckley was focused on confronting those men—and few women— that had made liberalism a form of established conventional wisdom among the better-educated sort in the United States.

Buckley made his position clear in the first issue of the *National Review*, published November 19, 1955. Liberals, he warned, "[r]un just about *everything*. There never was an age of conformity quite like this one, or camaraderie quite like the Liberals.'" As a result, "Conservatives in this country—at least those who have not made their peace with the New Deal, and there is a serious question of whether there are others—are non-licensed nonconformists; and this is a dangerous business in a Liberal world, as every editor of this magazine can readily show by pointing to his scars." Despite risks of such damage to one's professional self, he promised, the men and women of the *National Review* would not bow to the liberal hegemony. Instead, Buckley rather dashingly proclaimed, the *National Review*, "stands athwart history yelling Stop." The new flagship of what Buckley hailed as "radical" conservatism rejected both the fear-mongering of the "irresponsible Right" (though he was coy in this first issue about the exact nature of that irresponsibility) and the compromising, temporizing spirit of the "well-fed Right" (read: Eisenhower Republicans). Buckley promised his virtuous readers to fight, with unflagging energy and scorn for all compromise, the liberal "relativism" that allowed college professors to teach the merits of socialism and left-wing intellectuals to confuse the American public as to the "superiority . . . of champagne to ditchwater." The *National Review*, Buckley gleefully ended, tongue in cheek, was "the hottest thing in town."[48]

Buckley was more than a witty writer who knew how to grab the public's attention. With youthful charm and prodigious intellectual energy, he convinced most of the leading lights of the intellectual Right to contribute to the *National Review*. The ardent and compelling foe of the Soviet empire, James Burnham, contributed a regular feature titled "The Third World War." Cultural traditionalists were powerfully represented by Russell Kirk, champion of an American conservative intellectual tradition, and Richard Weaver, who had gained fame (at least in conservative intellectual circles) by arguing that the West had gone desperately wrong in the fourteenth century when men began to pride themselves on recognizing an empirical, rather than a transcendent, reality. More topically, the best of the era's ex-communist, anticommunists came on board, eventually including Whittaker Chambers, famed for having worked in tandem with a young Richard Nixon to prove the Red ties of Alger Hiss, a star of the New Deal–liberal establishment. In 1957, somewhat overwhelmed by the complexity of running, editing, writing, and master-minding the magazine, Buckley brought on William Rusher as publisher. Rusher brought to the magazine a sharp business mind and also powerful connections to the conservative wing of the Republican Party and to conservative political activists outside of the Northeast. During its first few years, as intended, the *National Review* subscriber base remained small, but its fame—and that of its leading light—grew at a pace Buckley welcomed.

Buckley meant for the *National Review* to impress by force of its intellectual weight. And writers such as Russell Kirk and Frank S. Meyer delivered the goods, providing learned essays on heavy topics having to do with the nature of the republic or the political philosophy of Continental thinkers. Similarly, James Burnham refused to allow conservatives to bandy about simple solutions to the Soviet menace, challenging them instead to interrogate assumptions and ponder options. During its early years, the editors of *National Review* did demand orthodoxy on certain issues; for example, one must favor the exorcisement of Reds in high places, one must support traditional cultural standards, and one must condemn Eisenhower's me-too New Dealisms ("Budgetary Elephantiasis").[49] And an assertion that capitalism is good and communism (and all its pinkish relatives such as socialism and big government liberalism) is bad would suffice for almost all overarching questions of political economy. But the magazine did expect readers to accept an intellectual challenge. And especially in the areas of foreign policy, conservative intellectual genealogy, and practical political strategy, rigorous debate in the pursuit of conservative values, policies, and goals was part of the fun of the enterprise. The *National Review* did believe that conservatism could not be all work and no play.

Much of the Buckley wit poured forth in the parts of the magazine that were less forthrightly devoted to policy and politics. He personally enjoyed weighing in on the cultural news of the day. So, for example, in early 1957, when Steve Allen had the audacity to allow the movie star and admitted adulteress Ingrid Bergman to appear on his popular television show, the *National Review* blasted him and her: "The point is that once upon a time there was a thing called the public morality. Quite apart from Christian doctrine, certain prescriptions have grown out of a consensus of the people as to the requirements of social existence . . . not compounded out of superstition or prudery." To keep family life sound, *NR* proclaimed, one must maintain "social sanctions against the violator."[50] This high-flown, deliberately overblown rhetorical style in service to the moral high ground was part of *NR*'s charm. And writing about the piano-playing talk show host Steve Allen, and not always about Edmund Burke or José Ortega y Gasset, was meant to leaven the mix.

Especially during *NR*'s early years, Buckley crafted an ironic tone that made conservatives appear dashing and clever and calls for Christian virtue in the public square sound hip and rebellious—at least by the standards of the late 1950s. Thus, when a group of conservative college students met one wintry day in 1957 in New York City, Buckley himself explained to readers, "Fashionable colleges do not play host to students deranged enough to protest the prevailing orthodoxy . . . of the Liberal-Left." As a result, the intrepid youths were forced to gather in the shabby environs of a drab lower Manhattan meeting hall. But these "dissenters," Buckley wrote, refused to give in to the grimness of their surroundings; they met, they talked, they planned, and they gave hope that the "nonconformists" were on the march.[51] In Buckley's animated world, conservatives—especially young conservatives and most especially young, intellectual conservatives—were brave lions, and liberals were always, at best, simple sheep.

Not all was fun and games at the *National Review*. While Buckley meant to enlist a wide cast of characters in the conservative cause, not everyone was welcome. Policing the boundaries had to be a part of the enterprise, and that meant coming down hard on those who Buckley and the inner circle felt were giving conservatives or conservative principles a bad name. One who was deemed most unwelcome was Ayn Rand. Rand was a literary and pop philosophy phenomenon. A Russian émigré, she first captured national attention in 1943 with the publication of *The Fountainhead*. The novel features the superindividualist architect Howard Roark, whose creative genius is matched only by his scorn for all forms of collectivism; it was made into a major motion picture, starring the iconic Gary Cooper, in 1949 (another indication that celebrations of free market genius had legions of supporters in the immediate postwar years). Rand became a minor celebrity in postwar America, chastising those who refused to worship at the temple of the free enterprise system or to accept the right of the talented and able to do as they must to realize their individual destiny. Labeled by some a libertarian—though she never called herself such—she regarded the state as her enemy and the individual as the only measure of virtue. She first met Buckley in 1954 and earned his everlasting opprobrium by bluntly informing him, "You aarh too eentelligent to bihleef in Gott!"[52]

In 1957, Rand published *Atlas Shrugged*, a monumentally over-the-top novel that follows an immensely talented group of individuals as they fight to bring down an evil New Deal-ish society that takes from them the money they have earned and the freedom they deserve. So far so good, many a 1950s-era conservative might say—and many did. But for Buckley and his kind of traditionalist conservative, Rand mightily and dangerously missed the point. Two years before *Atlas Shrugged* pushed its way up the best-seller list, a Buckley fellow-traveler, Stephen Tonsor, argued that the free market was not the be all and end all of conservatism; it was simply a means to a much more virtuous end. Tonsor, a young history professor, wrote, "The leaders of the new conservatism are not now, nor will they ever be identified with the American business community. They are clearly identified with the natural law philosophy and revealed religion." "Economic determinism," Tonsor insisted, was the enemy, not the source, of conservatism.[53] While the businessmen backers of the *National Review* might not all have agreed—and while Senator Robert Taft would never have articulated the matter thusly—for Tonsor, for William Buckley, and for most of the writers operating nearest to the pulsing heart of the *National Review*, conservatism without the traditional religious faith that placed individual acts, even those of the finest of capitalists, in God's mighty hands, was an empty and even vile thing.

Whittaker Chambers, the ex-communist who had worked with Richard Nixon to take down Alger Hiss, wrote *National Review*'s blistering review of Rand's *Atlas Shrugged*. Buckley greatly admired Chambers's intelligence and integrity and gave him a free hand. Chambers was razor sharp: "Out of a lifetime of reading, I can recall no other book in which a tone of overriding arrogance was so implacably sustained. Its shrillness is without reprieve. Its dogmatism is without appeal. . . . From almost any page of *Atlas Shrugged*, a voice can be heard, from painful necessity, commanding: 'To the gas chambers—go!'" In the final analysis, Chambers argued, Rand saw life as nothing more than the merciless pursuit of individual pleasure: "For, if man's 'heroism' (some will prefer to say: 'human dignity') no longer derives from God . . . then Man becomes merely the most consuming of animals, with glut as the condition of his happiness."[54] By no means did all conservatives buy into the religiously transcendent, intellectually demanding ethos Buckley and his cohort brought to the conservative political project. But for those who wanted a morally potent, spiritually engaging, intellectually rigorous conservatism, without any hint of backwater Bible-thumping, the *National Review* provided the goods.

If Buckley wanted no truck with atheists, whatever their commitment to free market principles, he also wanted to guard his brand of intellectually respectable, morally certifiable conservatism from an embarrassment of zealotry that certain elements in the right-wing anticommunist forces brought to the fray. Most particularly, Buckley and the *National Review* team had to play a careful hand when dealing with the emergent might of Robert Welch's John Birch Society. Welch took the McCarthyism that Buckley celebrated in spoken and written form and ran far, far down the road with it. Welch, Buckley believed, was a kook, but he also observed that he was a popular kook with the most energetic and excitable of America's anticommunists.

Robert Welch was a genuine intellectual prodigy who had graduated college at sixteen and then become a highly successful candy manufacturer (Sugar Daddies, Sugar Babies, Junior Mints). He was one of many executives of a small- to medium-size business who abhorred the New Deal world spawned by Americans' response to the Great Depression. He had committed himself to the anti–New Deal labors of the National Association of Manufacturers, where he became a leading officer of the group and learned a great deal about the mechanics of spreading the good news of the free market system through pamphlets, advertisements, and most every form of the mass media. Welch, quite wealthy, became a financial supporter of Senator Taft, as well as of Senator McCarthy. Stymied in his bid to win elected office in Massachusetts— the candy magnate made Robert Taft look like a suave movie star— Welch threw himself into anticommunist pamphleteering. By 1958, he had published a couple of books with the Henry Regnery Company and begun a regular anticommunist newsletter (one of many circulating the country). At the end of that year, he launched an organization to teach Americans the truth about communist subversion in the United States and provide them with the tools to fight it.

Welch named his organization in honor of John Birch, a Baptist missionary and American intelligence operative in China who had been killed by Mao's communist legions in 1945. The John Birch Society preached the McCarthyite message with a vengeance: every communist victory abroad was produced by American communists at home, and those American communist subversives were everywhere. Welch taught that they controlled a panoply of supposedly liberal organizations such as the American Civil Liberties Union, the National Council of Churches, and the National Association for the Advancement of Colored People. But Welch went much further. Even into the highest reaches of the federal government, a communist conspiracy had taken hold of the United States. President Eisenhower, he calmly observed, with a flat certainty, was "a dedicated, conscious agent of the Communist conspiracy."[55]

When it came to fighting communism, Welch was to Senator McCarthy as McCarthy was to Harry Truman. By the very first years of the 1960s, the John Birch Society had spread like a wildfire, igniting excitement across the United States and gaining great popularity in Southern California, the Texas oil patch, the western suburbs of Chicago, and many other redoubts of conservatism. Welch and a committed group of western oilmen, midwestern manufacturers, and southern industrialists provided the society with plenty of funds with which to spread the JBS message.

The *National Review*, itself, had received funds from the successful candy man. But that did not mean that William Buckley, personally, found Welch to be a credible observer of political reality. Immediately after Welch founded the JBS in December 1958, Buckley wrote to him and bluntly rejected Welch's conspiratorial zeal: "I for one disavow your hypotheses. I do not even find them plausible."[56] But Welch, Buckley understood, had solid support among the most enthusiastic members of the anticommunist Right. So, Buckley felt forced to tiptoe around the question of how far to separate the *National Review* from the JBS.

The problem was a practical one. Energetic conservatives willing to go out and do the hard work of taking back American politics and society from the liberal establishment were not, seemingly, plentiful. The JBS foot soldiers, while not dependably rational in their analyses, were exuberantly committed to the conservative cause. They wrote letters to newspapers, petitioned politicians, held reading groups, proselytized among their neighbors, and, not insignificantly, subscribed to conservative publications. William Rusher, *NR* publisher and ever practical, underlined this reality for Buckley: "[T]he great bulk of our readership, of our support, and of the warm bodies available to us to lead in any desired direction lies in the more or less organized Right, and large segments of the Right are more simplistic than we are, or than we can perhaps in time bring them to be, and also far more closely tied to the John Birch Society than we are."[57] Buckley recognized the practical problem and had no wish to divide and thus weaken conservative forces. But Welch's fantasies so rankled him that in early 1962 he overrode, if only partially, his publisher's arguments. While careful not to attack the John Birch Society or its membership, in February, a *National Review* editorial blasted Robert Welch for "damaging the cause of anti-Communism" by "distorting reality and in refusing to make moral and political distinction." In the magazine's very first issue, Buckley had sworn to attack the "irresponsible" Right. Welch, the editorial concluded, had crossed a critical line: "There are bounds to the dictum, Anyone on the right is my ally."[58]

Buckley so wanted to spark a new, majoritarian conservative politics. Unfortunately, some of the most motivated shock troops for such a movement made him uncomfortable. Just as the John Birch Society made Buckley squirm, so too did a roaring mass of potential new recruits to the movement: white segregationists. At the cusp of the 1950s and 1960s, civil rights politics was replacing anticommunism as the nation's number one domestic concern. Southern African Americans, supported by white liberals and black northerners, had begun a massive organizing effort to tear down Jim Crow laws in the South. The Supreme Court had joined the effort foursquare with the *Brown v. Board of Education* decision, and the rest of the federal government, slowly, but in the eyes of segregationists inexorably, was joining the cause.

Buckley and the *National Review*, en masse, in the 1950s and early 1960s, opposed the civil rights movement and supported the segregationists. On rare occasions, a racist scent malodorously wafted from *NR* complaints about the civil rights revolution. Even Buckley, who knew better, exhibited a startlingly tone-deaf response, asserting early on, for example, that "the white community is so entitled [to "prevail" over black southerners, even when whites are in a minority] because, for the time being, it is the advanced race."[59] Here Buckley, in his enthusiasm for the white southerners' cause, seems to forget that the individual, not the "race," is the measure by which a conservative claims to guarantee liberty and freedom. And later (1965), echoing Mississippi Congressman John Rankin's infamous rant ("Slavery [was] the greatest blessing the Negro had ever known up to that time. It elevated him from the position of savage to that of servant"), Buckley managed to convince himself, at least temporarily—and to try to convince National Review readers—that whites' enslavement of blacks should best be seen as the process by "which American Negroes were rescued years ago" from the primitive conditions of Africa.[60]

Such racist or racially suspect sentiments were not the National Review's usual fare. Far more regularly, Buckley and the NR team dismissed arguments that used white supremacism to legitimate racial discrimination. Rather, they simply supported whites' right to segregate and discriminate on racial grounds for the same reason that Senator Robert Taft had: the federal government had no right to meddle in the affairs of individuals who wished to segregate and discriminate on racial grounds nor in the affairs of state governments who had the right to oversee local affairs such as education and municipal transportation or the social organization of drinking fountains and restrooms. Conservatives, after all, believed in limited national government and the right of local peoples to stay true to the traditions that sustained their communities. Buckley, like Taft before him, seemed to think little about the strong possibility that, say, black Mississippians might not actually voluntarily conform to the folkways of white supremacy. Nor did Buckley's religious principles seem to steer him toward an abhorrence of cruelly enforced and legally mandated racial inequality or induce, on his part, any sympathy for civil rights advocates' Christian-inflected calls for justice. As a result, the National Review gave much editorial space to the support of southern whites in their campaign to maintain their right to be racists, even as the National Review did not support racism, per se.

Supporting racists while not specifically endorsing racism did, however, complicate Buckley's line of argumentation. So many of the racists were unpleasant bedfellows. Thus, Buckley tried to urge southern whites to follow a moderate course, as opposed to using murderous violence, in their fight to maintain their right to racism. For example, after a particularly horrific bit of southern white barbarism visited upon the bodies of civil rights demonstrators in early 1957, Buckley offered this bit of wisdom: "However paradoxical it may sound, it is so that Northern ideologists are responsible for the outbreak of violence in the South, and that, nevertheless, no one is responsible for that violence save those who commit it." He continued, "Southerners guilty of shooting stray bullets into buses filled with Negroes . . . can rail against politicization of the Supreme Court, against the perversion of the Constitution, against the abstractions of radical anthropology, and every word of it may be true; but nothing they say can atone for, or in any way mitigate, their debasing brutality."[61] As with the Birchers, when it came to the whites' cause in the early days of the civil rights movement, Buckley tried to demonstrate some moral and intellectual reservations. But he saw in the white resistance a large army of conservative recruits, and he understood that as liberal politicians lined up in support of blacks' demands for racial justice, opportunity called.

Buckley had never intended to pursue a life of pure scholarly inquiry. The *National Review* was just one means to his true end: a resurgent, intellectually disciplined political conservative movement. So, besides editing his lively magazine, Buckley had been stirring the pot wherever and whenever he could. He had been president and continued to be an evangelist for the Intercollegiate Society of Individualists, a rather loosely organized group that delivered conservative publications to young people. He had become a regular on radio and television, and barnstormed the country delivering popular lectures on the perfidy of liberalism and the need for a conservative political movement. In 1959, he summarized much of his thinking in a major work, *Up from Liberalism*, the title a rather awkward play on Booker T. Washington's *Up from Slavery*. In the new book, he continued a theme that had become emblematic of his public discourse: liberals, because they held to no sustainable and revealed truths, obsessed too much about the purity of method—democracy, free speech, academic freedom—and too little about the need for virtuous results based on enduring truths: the precious necessity of economic freedom, civil order, the sanctity of the family, and the spiritual basis of life.[62]

In the early 1960s, Buckley became nearly a whirlwind on behalf of the conservative cause. In the fall of 1960, he was instrumental in helping a soon-to-be highly influential group of conservative students organize Young Americans for Freedom. YAF's founding document, "The Sharon Statement," named after Buckley's hometown in Connecticut, where the young people had gathered, was a paean to Buckley's instruction: "[I]t is the responsibility of the youth of America to affirm certain eternal truths. . . . [F]oremost among the transcendent values is the individual's use of his God-given free will."[63] Young, intellectually oriented conservatives found Buckley an irresistible presence and mammoth influence. They aped his seersucker style, his expansive vocabulary, and his acid pen.[64] In 1962, Buckley's intellectual aplomb and wit brought him a syndicated newspaper column that massively enlarged his audience (his public increased yet again in 1966 when he began hosting a syndicated television talk show, *Firing Line*). Perhaps even more important, by 1960, Buckley was becoming fully engaged in winning back the Republican Party to the truths of conservatism as he understood them. After several years of proselytizing, he had hopes that his words might be made political flesh in the form of Arizona Senator Barry Goldwater.

Between the early 1950s and the early 1960s, William Buckley had, more than any other individual, strengthened the conservative cause. In part, Buckley was himself the message: conservatives did not have to be gray men of sober mien; they could be funny and have fun. Wit as well as wisdom, charisma as well as character, were arrows in Buckley's quiver. In modern America celebrity matters, and Buckley, even with his Yale pedigree and his hard-to-pin down, upper-crust, mid-Atlantic accent, knew how to connect with people, or at least with his target audience, people of an intellectual disposition who enjoyed perspicacious display. Buckley combined his talents with a prodigious energy. All through the 1950s and 1960s (and for decades after!) "Chairman" Bill churned out prose, spoke far and wide, ran enterprises, guided organizations, and maintained an extraordinary network of friends and colleagues. He even ran for mayor of New York City in 1965. All this energy he produced in behalf of the conservative cause, even as he traveled the world, sailed frequently, dined well, and very obviously enjoyed life immensely.

But if the messenger greatly mattered, so did the message. At a time when "modern" Republicans took pride in accepting the outlines if not all the particulars of New Dealism, Buckley damned big government liberalism as a veiled variant of the communist evil. He maintained and deepened conservatives' long-standing faith in an unrestrained free market economics. More important, he took conservatives' narrow economic policy and contributed a culture to their cause. He rejected the relativistic empiricisms and pragmatisms of secular modernism and reminded conservatives that they stood for deeper values and revealed truths. "Active Christianity," Buckley proclaimed throughout the 1950s, was the bedrock on which human virtue and, therefore, American society, stood. Fighting godless communism was a calling, not just a political position. Without unbending faith in the revealed truths of God and country, Americans were mendicants before the shifting sands of popular fad and evil proselytizers. Buckley argued for a heroic conservatism, for a rebellious conservatism, for an unwavering faith in the traditions that had made the nation great (and where racism and other gross inequalities fit in that formula, he preferred not to dig too deep). Buckley built cultural platforms and constituencies that gave form and substance to the more forthrightly political movement that was, in the early 1960s, ready to charge forward in a bold attempt to seize the levers of national power.

THREE

BARRY GOLDWATER

Cowboy Conservatism, Race Politics, and the Other Sixties

BARRY GOLDWATER WAS NO BILL BUCKLEY. His sister believed that he had never read a book while he was growing up in Phoenix. He had gone to the University of Arizona, but he lasted only a year. Poised to run for the presidency in 1964, Goldwater was willing to wonder if he was smart enough to sit in the Oval Office. "Doggone it," he told conservative stalwarts at the *Chicago Tribune*, "I'm not even sure that I've got the brains to be President of the United States."[1] For Barry Goldwater, conservatism was not a matter of learning an intellectual genealogy or mastering a political philosophy. Conservatism was unvarnished common sense that came down to a basic truth: America faced dangers at home and abroad that could destroy the nation. So if you loved America as he did, communism had to be stopped. Liberty had to be preserved. And, in the face of those dangers, you do not comprise. You do not go soft on those principles. You stand firm. You stand united with other Americans who understand the danger. You point your finger at those who don't. That was Goldwater's message, and millions of people responded to it. Goldwater was a man of the people—or at least some of the people. He helped invent a modern, populist conservatism.

Barry Goldwater, though born to wealth and privilege in 1909, never saw himself as part of the national elite. He was a man of the West. He liked to hunt and hike. He did not go to Europe to look at paintings; he found his culture closer to home, taking photographs—good ones—of Arizona's canyons, mountains, and people. He took a measured role in his family's immensely successful Phoenix-based department store business and even had some national success with a merchandising gimmick ("antsy pants," boxer shorts imprinted with images of ants). Goldwater's Taftian faith in economic liberty and his disgust with labor unions and government interference came directly from his own experiences as a businessman. But running the family business never made his pulse race. Goldwater preferred to tinker with his beloved ham radio rig and electronic gadgets of all kinds. He loved to fly airplanes. After the Pearl Harbor attack he volunteered, at age thirty-two, for the air corps; he spent much of the last part of the war "flying the hump," carrying cargo over the Himalayas from India to China. His love of flying was lifelong. At war's end he came home.

By 1952, he was Arizona's U.S. senator, and eight years later his fellow conservatives were urging him to run for president; four years after that he won the Republican nomination. He was handsome and fit and he carried himself well. Blunt, straightforward, and sometimes even bellicose, Goldwater was going to put a rugged, masculine face to American conservatism.

Goldwater, of course, lost his 1964 bid to become president of the United States. Electorally, he was crushed. Conventional wisdom, post-election, was that America had rejected not just a man but a movement. American voters, as Goldwater's informal electioneering slogan stated, had been offered "a choice not an echo," and they had overwhelmingly chosen liberalism and rejected conservatism. True enough. But more-current conventional wisdom also is right— Goldwater was the John the Baptist figure who made conservative activists, many of them young, believe that the Republican Party could be won to their cause. And Goldwater, as he had intended, helped teach millions, including anticommunist militants, committed anti-secularists, pro–states' rightists, and dedicated segregationists, that they were, overarchingly, political conservatives—Republican Party conservatives. At a time when civil rights protesters marched down city streets and sat-in at drug stores and restaurants, willfully breaking the law in the name of higher truths, Goldwater introduced the national electorate to the rhetoric of law and order. Not least, Goldwater brought millions of southern whites to the conservative cause and unified and nationalized a grassroots right-wing movement.

Two issues dominated national politics at the advent of the 1960s: the threat of Soviet communism and the challenge African Americans were raising against racial injustice. No consensus existed within either major political party about how to respond to these issues. To a degree, a liberal-conservative divide could be ascertained. Congressional liberals almost always supported federal civil rights legislation and conservatives usually did not, but regional identity was a more decisive factor in determining how a member of Congress voted. When it came to international communism, liberals went after "Red" spies and fought to contain the Soviet Union. Conservatives did, too— but demanded far stronger measures against those they perceived as domestic subversives, while some talked vaguely about using military might to roll back and even defeat the communists. Despite these sometimes sharp rhetorical divisions, when it came to actual federal policy, not much had separated most conservative officeholders from most liberal ones on the civil rights and Cold War front before 1960. Economic policy, especially regarding labor unions, business regulation, and tax policy, was what most emphatically differentiated liberals from conservatives in Congress.

By 1960, political change was afoot. Liberals were becoming far more interested in pushing forward with the civil rights agenda that President Harry Truman had cautiously embraced in 1948 and that African American activists were demanding. And in the face of the communist takeover of Cuba, conservatives were banging the wardrum ever harder. Nonetheless, at the advent of the sixties, each political party had a conservative faction and a liberal faction and numerous people in the middle. That limited the range of political maneuverability on both sides of the partisan divide. During the 1960 presidential campaign, most well-informed voters would have been hard pressed to explain how the moderate liberal Democrat John Kennedy differed from the moderate conservative Republican Richard Nixon on the major issues.

Senator Barry Goldwater, unlike the two parties' nominees, did not care to seek out this moderate middle ground. By 1960, his rhetoric was sharp, and he seemed to promise altogether different policies. Senator Goldwater also understood that many voters saw the world differently than did the majority of national pundits and politicians who viewed American politics from midtown Manhattan or Capitol Hill. William Buckley had sought to modulate the volume and moderate the tone of some of these right-wing constituencies who feared what was happening to their nation. Barry Goldwater amplified them. He admired the right-wing activists who were fighting to reinvent politics in the United States. These grassroots conservatives reciprocated the feeling. By 1960, they had made Goldwater their champion.

In Phoenix and Amarillo, in Orange County and suburban Atlanta, all over America, but most numerously in the West, South, and Southwest, a lot of people—that is to say, white people, and more specifically, white Christian people—were angry. They were angry that communists and communist supporters, as they saw it, were bedeviling their children's schools by forcing religion out and anti-American textbooks in. That liberals and moderates mocked their efforts to restore God and tradition to the classroom as ignorant and irrational provincialism made them even angrier. They were angry, too, that Negroes, to use the polite term of the day, were demanding race-mixing and forced integration. Here again, that liberals and moderates chastised them as intolerant racists for voicing their reservations only fueled their fears and frustration. And as they watched liberals and moderates debate and bicker and nitpick over what to do about the international communist conspiracy even as the Soviet Union was on the march, they concluded that something evil was afoot in the corridors of power that ran through Washington and New York. The communists were winning, and the American government was standing on the sidelines.

These were people who had never turned on Senator Joe McCarthy. They cheered—and took notice—when Goldwater defended McCarthy in 1954 during the Senate censure debate as a man who had earned "honor and influence," and whose loss would be celebrated as "a strong victory for Moscow."[2] And while the *National Review* crowd distanced itself from John Birch Society leader Robert Welch's more dire warnings ("Dwight Eisenhower is a dedicated, conscious agent of the Communist conspiracy"), many of these dedicated anti-communist, Christian Americans listened to and learned from the JBS, which was rapidly picking up adherents and national attention (though much of it tended to be negative) in the immediate years after its formation in 1958. As a horrified *Time* magazine reported in early 1961, sell-out crowds numbering in the thousands paid to hear a "pink-faced and natty" Welch accuse the American government of being riddled with Reds and run by "comsymps."[3] Some of these same people and masses of others sought out publications from Fred Schwarz's Christian Anti-Communism Crusade or Reverend Billy James Hargis's Church of the Christian Crusade or Texas oil man H. L. Hunt's Life Line Foundation. While a few thousand read the intellectually rigorous *National Review*, many, many more studied the materials of the popular anticommunist pamphleteers, listened to them on the radio, and attended anticommunist study groups or lectures. By 1960, right-wing, anticommunist "suburban warriors" were on the march, forming a new rank-and-file, conservative, mass movement. Senator Barry Goldwater was their champion.[4]

William Buckley and his kind believed the communist threat to be civilizational in nature. The Soviet Union would, if it could, destroy freedom, liberty, and Christianity in the United States and in all other parts of the world. Many of the grassroots anticommunists, the sort who joined the John Birch Society or attended open-air anticommunist rallies in the late 1950s and early 1960s, shared this vision but joined to it an apocalyptic sensibility. They brought to the anticommunist cause a frisson of end-times, of an imminent final battle that would one way or the other determine man's destiny on earth if not in heaven.

Senator Joe McCarthy was the father of this imminent danger school of thought. In the 1950 Wheeling, West Virginia, speech that made his name, he quantified the risk of total destruction of the American way of life: "In less than six years the odds have changed from nine to one in our favor to eight to five against us. This indicates the tempo of Communism's victories and American defeats in the Cold War."[5] By the early 1960s, students of the school of imminent collapse warned that the "tempo" of the communists' victories had only increased. American life could well be soon destroyed. The Reverend Billy Hargis, attuned to the numerological sensibility of end-time preachers and their followers, offered a date certain. In a message broadcast on his anticommunist radio show heard on some 270 stations, he calculated that unless patriots reversed the tide, communists would completely rule the United States by 1974.[6] The most vehement of the Jeremiahs, Robert Welch, who was raised a fundamentalist Baptist in rural North Carolina, also offered numerical precision. Welch lamented in 1962 that the United States, as a whole, was already "50–70 percent under Communist control" and the "government of the United States is under operational control of the Communist Party."[7]

Senator Goldwater, like Bill Buckley before him, distanced himself from such specific arguments and from Robert Welch's more spectacular claims. Still, Goldwater, like Buckley, did not repudiate the Birchers themselves. And unlike Buckley, who privately felt that the members of the John Birch Society were kooky, the senator liked and respected the adherents he knew, telling reporters that Birchers "are the finest people in my community."[8] Goldwater did not separate

himself from the fiercest and most apocalyptic of the anticommunists; he sought out their support.

For many liberals, the John Birch Society, the Reverend Billy Hargis and his supporters, the students of Fred Schwarz's School of Anti-
Communism, and the members of For America, Texans for America,
the National Indignation Convention, and the multitude of other
grassroots groups that perceived a vast, domestic communist enemy
operating with impunity in the United States were horrifying but also
nearly inexplicable. What was wrong with these people? One simply could not, liberals complained, engage them in rational debate,
so ferocious was their dread of domestic subversion, so broad was
their definition of the threat, and so certain was their belief that Red
conspiracies were already in control of much of American life. Most
liberals had felt the same way about the rabid followers of Senator
McCarthy in the early 1950s. The whole phenomenon seemed to
them to be a manifestation of something almost wholly outside normal American politics.

A group of top-shelf, mainly liberal American intellectuals did
their best to explain the right-wingers to liberal audiences in a
widely reviewed and distributed book, first titled *The New American
Right* and then revised and reissued as *The Radical Right*. The first
edition came out in 1955 and was devoted to interpreting the rise
of McCarthyism, and the second came out in 1963; it included the
earlier essays but added chapters devoted to the Birchers and their
militant anticommunist compatriots.[9] Richard Hofstadter, arguably
mid-twentieth-century America's finest historian, spoke for most of
the essayists when he condemned the militant anticommunists as
psychologically damaged, pseudoconservatives.

First, Hofstadter asserted that right-wing Americans suffered from
a virulent form of status anxiety, not unlike the psychological malady,
he said, that had afflicted rural populists of the late nineteenth century. Contemporary right-wingers—whether they were small-town
businessmen, midsize manufacturers, or working-class tradesmen—
felt themselves to be losing a cultural place of pride in a new, secular, mass media–driven, corporate, capitalist world. As a result, these
men (and Hofstadter, like so many of his intellectual contemporaries,

almost exclusively spoke about men, ignoring the legions of right-wing women) had turned to scapegoatery and conspiratorial thinking to resolve their status anxiety predicament. He further deduced that these anxious folks had "little in common with the temperate and compromising spirit of true conservatism in the classical sense of the word. . . . Their political reactions express rather a profound if largely unconscious hatred of our society and its ways—a hatred which one would hesitate to impute to them if one did not have suggestive clinical evidence." The anticommunist militants, in other words, were psychological basket cases, alienated from true American culture because they suffered from (and here Hofstadter relied on the German émigré scholar Theodor Adorno) an "authoritarian personality."[10] Adorno had coined the phrase to explain how and why Germans had become Nazis.

In 1962, Hofstadter added a short postscript to his scathing attack. He admitted that in his first take on the anticommunist zealots he had missed part of the story. "Cultural politics," he allowed, not just a form of lunacy, might explain the motives of some of the right-wingers. For Hofstadter, as for many other liberal political commentators in postwar America, the idea that cultural or religious beliefs—and not economic self-interest—could, let alone should, determine an individual's political orientation was a deeply unsettling hypothesis. Operating in the midst of relatively widespread national prosperity, he offered up one of his many elegant formulations: "Hard times mobilize economic group antagonisms; prosperity liberates the public for the expression of its more luxurious hostilities."[11] Hofstadter, like many a liberal commentator before and after, feared the fury such "cultural politics" could unleash. Writing so soon after World War II, the historian did not need archival evidence to recall how well Adolf Hitler's murderous rage against the Jews played with Germany's unhappy citizenry.

At the advent of the 1960s, many liberals, including John Kennedy, hoped that domestic politics could stay tightly focused on the mechanics of economic policy. They looked to Roosevelt's New Deal as their paradigm. And they sought to avoid the political wars inspired by religiocultural crusades that had resulted in such public policy debacles as Prohibition. They continued to hope that an ever more educated and pluralistic national citizenry would soon outgrow its "irrational" attachments—its "luxurious hostilities," as Hofstadter had ironically labeled them—and find a reasonable comity amid shared economic security.

William Buckley and his merry band of conservative intellectuals despised this materialist, even Marxist, formulation in which man was reduced to economic creature and government to a necessary Big Brother tasked narrowly with expert management of the nation's economy. They believed in the politics of moral crusade and religious affirmation; a virtuous citizenry should demand public policies that affirmed Americans' core beliefs and defended against apostasy of all kinds. Goldwater, at a gut level, felt much the same and caught the *National Review* crowd's attention with his blunt defense of spirituality and morality in politics.

From his first days on the national scene, Goldwater had linked his uncompromising, Taftian championing of economic liberty with spirited calls on the need for self-discipline and religious faith. The nation must, he warned, reject the blandishments of big government and soft-on-communism liberals and instead "return to faith in the flag, Bible, family, and self." Faith in the verities, he suggested, and not in government, offered Americans their best bulwark against life's many financial and personal uncertainties. Repudiating Franklin Roosevelt's claim that a benevolent government would best protect Americans from the "hazards and vicissitudes" of modern life, Goldwater told a crowd of Southern California Republicans who had gathered for an annual Lincoln Day dinner, "We still have many Donner Passes and deserts to cross. No government can smooth out the hills and valleys of the world."[12]

Goldwater offered Americans the strict and enthralling discipline of the wagon train. Put your faith in the Lord, work with your neighbors for the good of your local community, but above all, be self-reliant—because the Donner Pass, which here seems to be a metaphor for the challenges of both the free market and the vast uncertainties of mortal life, will certainly put you to the test. Donner Pass is named after the California-bound Donner party of 1846, some of whom resorted to cannibalism after being snowbound for months on the east side of the Sierra Nevada mountain pass.

Goldwater added to his conservative reputation with his ferocious attacks on organized labor's most articulate and politically aggressive champion, United Auto Workers leader Walter Reuther. Fighting labor unions was, in the late 1950s, still at the heart of the conservative cause, and Goldwater, who had begun his political career as an ardent advocate in Arizona of the Taft-Hartley Act's antiunion, "right-to-work" clause, was among the Senate's most dedicated antiunionists, arguing that industrywide bargaining was "an evil to be eliminated."[13] Goldwater used his seat on the Senate Select Committee on Improper Activities in the Labor or Management Field to excoriate Reuther and the UAW's efforts to use its impressive war chest to support pro-union Democratic politicians. Even as the Democratic senators on the committee, whose chief counsel was the very young Robert Kennedy, went after corrupt union figures such as the Teamsters's Jimmy Hoffa, Goldwater relentlessly pursued Reuther: "I would rather have Hoffa steal my money than Reuther stealing my freedom."[14] In a heated moment, Goldwater avowed that Reuther was a "more dangerous menace than the sputnik or anything Soviet Russia might do to America."[15] Goldwater had managed to link well-to-do economic conservatives' disdain for organized labor with grassroots conservatives' fear of internal subversion. From such artful rhetoric is a political coalition born.

Goldwater's boundless energy and buoyant speechmaking on behalf of conservative principles in the late 1950s produced excitement in the tight circle of conservative political activists and power brokers who were actively seeking a champion. They wanted someone who could take on both liberalism and the "modern" Republicanism (what they called New Deal "Me too-ism") of the Eisenhower administration. The man at the center of this particular conservative network was the intellectually gifted and politically savvy former dean of Notre Dame's law school, Clarence "Pat" Manion.[16] Since Taft's inglorious defeat at the hands of Eisenhower and the moneyed East Coast internationalist interests that supported the general, Manion had been on the lookout for a new conservative political leader. Using his influential weekly radio show, *The Manion Forum of Opinion*, and his connections in the as yet only loosely affiliated world of conservative politicians, *National Review* intellectuals, John Birch Society activists, and well-to-do industrialists, Manion began to promote Barry Goldwater as the conservative candidate for the 1960 Republican Party presidential nomination.

Goldwater was not, however, Dean Manion's only choice for presidential candidate in those early days. Manion, like several other conservative political operators, understood a hard truth about the national electoral map. He knew that to win the White House, conservatives needed somehow to bring to their cause the voters of two very different regions—and two different partisan political identities. Heartland Republican conservatives, the kind of voters who had supported Ohio Senator Robert Taft, had to be given one kind of champion. At the same time, Manion proposed, antiliberal, segregationist southern whites, who increasingly resented the national Democratic Party's turn away from its longtime obeisance to southern traditions of white supremacy, had to be given another sort of candidate. Southern whites, Manion believed, had not yet, in large numbers, learned to call themselves conservatives, and most assuredly, they did not see themselves as partisan Republicans.

A great majority of white southerners hated the GOP for historic reasons that had been, in essence, bred into the bone. The Republican Party had been founded in 1854 as the champion of free labor and as the uncompromising abolitionist opponent of the South's "peculiar institution." From the time of the War against Northern Aggression (known in the North as the Civil War) and through several "Lost Cause"–worshiping generations thereafter, southern whites, in massive numbers, pledged themselves to the Democratic Party. Franklin Roosevelt and his New Deal had further cemented white southerners' ties to the Democrats. First, Roosevelt personally linked himself to the South, making much of his heartfelt connections to Warm Springs, Georgia, where he had gone to recuperate from polio and then built his "little White House." More important, the New Deal had been particularly well-received by Depression-era, economically challenged whites in the historically poor South, who also appreciated Roosevelt's accommodation in most policy matters to their codes of racial hierarchy.

Because Manion believed that white southerners would not vote for a Republican, he wanted the conservative cause to promote two candidates: a third-party candidate in the South, akin to the 1948 States Rights Party candidacy of South Carolina's then governor, Strom Thurmond, and a regular Republican candidate, Goldwater, who could capture votes in the Midwest and, it was hoped, assorted other northern states. If all went as planned, the two conservative candidates would overwhelm the one nonconservative Democratic candidate. This three-way race would prevent any one candidate from achieving a majority in the Electoral College tally, which would move the presidential decision into the House of Representatives where, in a grand compromise, Goldwater would win. It was a complicated scenario but not impossibly so.

Just one day after Manion spoke with an ambivalent Goldwater about running for the 1960 Republican presidential nomination, Goldwater proved that Manion's elaborate two-candidate conservative scenario was unnecessary. On May 16, 1959, Goldwater spoke in Greenville, South Carolina, before a small group gathered together at the humble Republican South Carolina annual state convention. He had been invited there by Roger Milliken, the young, Yale-educated, antiunion textile magnate (and *National Review* financial angel), who was the mainstay of the small state's GOP. Mostly, Goldwater gave his usual speech, condemning labor unions, damning communists, and blasting big government. But for the occasion, a rare visit for the peripatetic speechmaker to the GOP-unfriendly Deep South, he also let loose on the Supreme Court. The Court's decision in *Brown v. Board of Education* that schools must be racially desegregated was, Goldwater thundered, "not based on law." Moreover, President Eisenhower's recent decision to federalize troops to enforce that decision was plain wrong. Desegregation orders, unlawful in their essence, he stated in his typically blunt fashion, must "not be enforced by arms."[17] Prominent South Carolina Republican W. W. "Duck" Wannamaker later wrote to Goldwater, "You are not only a great American, sir . . . but you could pass for a great Southerner any time, any place."[18] Barry Goldwater, the Arizona cowboy, was whistling "Dixie," and his white southern audience went wild. Word of

Goldwater's southern success quickly reached Dean Manion. Manion was excited: Goldwater played in the South. Goldwater, the man from the West, could show people in both the North and the South that, in their own different but overlapping ways, they were all conservatives together.

In 1959, Goldwater was not a man well known to most Americans, nor was he even a figure of renown among conservatives. His Senate career had been a humble one, and Arizona, still an underpopulated state far from the centers of the mass media, was not an easy launching pad for a national candidate. To give Goldwater a national presence, Manion came up with an unlikely plan. Goldwater should produce an extended manifesto spelling out his conservative political beliefs. The notion was odd for two reasons. First, Goldwater was, to be kind, not much of a writer or, for that matter, a careful thinker. Second, books of political theory and policy exposition "authored" by second-tier politicians had not proved to be the stuff of which best sellers were made. Even Senator Taft, at the height of his career and widely known as an intellectually gifted man, had failed only a few years earlier to find an audience for his own policy-oriented book. Nonetheless, Manion pushed on, and Goldwater, while stating that he could not and would not author such a book himself, agreed to the project if Manion could find an actual writer.

So, where to go for an author? Well, in 1960 it seemed all roads to a bona fide intellectual conservatism led to the House of Buckley. In this case, Manion's request for a ghostwriter went not to Bill Buckley but instead to Buckley's brilliant if erratic brother-in-law, Brent Bozell. Bozell had already done some speechwriting for Goldwater and had a good feel for Goldwater's views and what views Goldwater was willing to send into the public arena under his name. Bozell knocked out *The Conscience of a Conservative* in a few weeks time. The prose, and the thinking behind the prose, sounded a good deal more like the erudite, Yale-educated, Catholic intellectual Bozell than it did "antsy-pants" Barry Goldwater. Senator Goldwater did not care. He glanced at the typescript, had his regular speechwriter check the manuscript pages more carefully, and told Manion to go ahead with it. Surprising everyone, the book became a massive best seller. The conservative media, not surprisingly, loved it. The arch-conservative *Chicago Tribune* informed readers that there was more "hard sense in this slight book than will emerge from all of the chatter of this year's session of Congress [and] this year's campaign for the presidency." The widely syndicated columnist Westbrook Pegler, best known for his vitriolic attacks on the labor union movement, announced, "Senator Barry Goldwater of Arizona certainly is now the successor to Senator Taft of Ohio as defender of the Constitution and freedom."[19]

Much to the bemusement of Manion and Goldwater, the mainstream press took up the book, as well. *Time* magazine, like many other mass circulation periodicals, gave *The Conscience of a Conservative* and Goldwater major coverage, though it was of the man-bites-dog variety: "He thoroughly belies the U.S. liberals' caricature-belief that an Old Guardist is a deep-dyed isolationist endowed with nothing but penny-pinching inhumanity and slavish devotion to Big Business."[20] *The Conscience of a Conservative* had hit a political nerve, and the book made Goldwater a major public figure in the United States.

A good deal of what made *The Conscience of a Conservative* both a best seller and a kind of bible to the growing cadres of conservative rank and file was its winning combination of hard-nosed policy language (Goldwater) and high-minded justification (Bozell) for such toughness. So, on the one hand, the book blasts welfare payments to the poor and needy and, more generally, the entire notion of a government-mandated social safety net as dependency-creating claptrap that robs Americans of the individual discipline and strength of will the country is built on. But, on the other, this harsh policy prescription is couched in a language of moral rectitude:

> Liberals tend to look only at the material side of man's nature. The Conservative believes that man is, in part, an economic, an animal creature; but that he is also a spiritual creature with spiritual needs and spiritual desires. What is more, these needs and desires reflect the *superior* side of man's nature, and thus take precedence over his economic wants. Conservatism therefore looks upon the enhancement of man's spiritual nature as the primary concern of

political philosophy. Liberals, on the other hand—in the name of a concern for "human beings"—regard the satisfaction of economic wants as the dominant mission of society.[21]

The editors at *Barron's*, the venerable business weekly, cheered on this conservative formula: "Its success springs in part from the author's ability to give humanitarian reasons for following policies which usually have been associated with lust for gain."[22] Just a few years earlier, Senator Bob Taft had defended his anti–New Deal policies by calling on the rights of property holders. Liberals called Taft a hard-hearted bastard only interested in protecting the rich. Goldwater, with more than a little help from Bozell, turned the tables. Liberals, he said, are the hard-hearted materialists. They care little, if at all, for the dignity and spiritual life of the less well-off. It is conservatives who safeguard the moral character and long-term happiness of their fellow citizens.

Goldwater sang from the same hymnal when it came to the explosive issue of racial justice in the United States. Conservatives, he asserted, are not racists. He personally believed in integration: "It so happens that I am in agreement with the objectives of the Supreme Court as stated in the *Brown* decision. I believe that it is both wise and just for negro children to attend the same schools as whites, and that to deny them this opportunity carries with it strong implications of inferiority." Tough words, undoubtedly, for any Ku Klux Klansman turning the pages. But then Goldwater made it equally plain that his thoughts on the problem were just that, a personal observation not intended to indicate a support of government-mandated integration. Neither as senator or, if the stars should so line up, as president, would Goldwater support any effort to inflict his sentiments on the people of the South (black southerners quickly drop up out of his assessment of who counts as a southerner). He writes: "I am not prepared, however, to impose that judgment of mine on the people of Mississippi or South Carolina.... That is their business, not mine. I believe that the problem of race relations, like all social and cultural problems, is best handled by the people directly concerned ... [and] should not be effected by engines of national power."[23] In the political context of the early 1960s, Goldwater was politely giving white segregationists the green light to do what they thought they must to fight the federal government and black southerners' efforts to end white supremacy.

Goldwater was staying the course with the 1896 Supreme Court decision that *Brown* overturned. In *Plessey v. Ferguson* the Court had ruled that state-mandated segregation of blacks and whites was constitutional insomuch as such issues were simply a matter of a given state's "liberty to act with reference to the established usages, customs, and traditions of the people, and with a view to the promotion of their comfort and the preservation of the public peace and good order."[24] For Goldwater and for most conservatives, a call for liberty (remember the 1930s-era Liberty League) always trumped the demand for equality. And when liberty was joined to concerns about "traditions" and "the preservation of the public peace and good order," the debate for many conservatives was over.

The Conscience of a Conservative, dreamed up by Dean Manion, written by Brent Bozell, and author(iz)ed by Barry Goldwater, neatly summed up the state of conservative virtue, as they saw it, in 1960: champion economic liberty (fight communism, labor unions, and federally mandated business regulation); respect tradition (even—or especially—if it means supporting segregationist white southerners); and demand public order (criticize the disruptive protests of the civil rights movement). The question before Goldwater and his backers was would such a formula sell to the American voter? The issue turned out to be moot in 1960. Vice President Richard Nixon, having long courted the power brokers at the county, state, and national level within the Republican Party, had the nomination sewed up. And Nixon did not run as a conservative. He hewed to the moderate Republicanism of President Eisenhower.

On the civil rights issue, Nixon went even further than Eisenhower. In a convention battle over the GOP's plank on civil rights that pitted conservatives such as Goldwater and the Texas senatorial candidate John Tower against GOP liberals led by New York Governor Nelson Rockefeller, Nixon sided with the liberals (Nixon was agnostic, even indifferent, about the whole issue but thought he needed Rockefeller's support in the Northeast). The Nixon-endorsed GOP position on civil rights was even stronger than that of the Democrats. The Republican Party officially supported federally mandated school desegregation, voting rights for black southerners, and a long list of other civil rights movement causes. The Republican Party civil rights plank concluded: "In summary, we pledge the full use of the power, resources and leadership of the federal government to eliminate discrimination based on race, color, religion or national origin."[25] Nixon was no liberal, but he seemed determined to show Americans that he was not a conservative, either.

Goldwater was disgusted by Nixon's compromise with Rockefeller, but he was far from heartbroken about how things had turned out. He had hardly expected to be the GOP nominee—over and over he had said he was not running, despite the efforts of many around him to round up delegates. In his speech before the 1960 convention, where he formally released those few delegate votes that had been pledged to him (in those days a majority of delegates were chosen by the state party, not through open primaries or caucuses), he promised to support Nixon with every ounce of his strength. Goldwater was a conservative, but he was also a party man. He wanted his fellow conservatives to be party men, also. He told his followers to stop threatening to walk away from the Republican Party. It was time for conservatives, his people, to cowboy up: "Now, let's put our shoulders to the wheel for Dick Nixon and push him across the line." And then he launched his bid—conservatives' bid—to take over the Republican Party: "Let's grow up conservatives. If we want to take this Party back, and I think we can someday, let's get to work."[26]

Between 1960 and 1964, following Nixon's defeat by John Kennedy, conservatives organized in an unprecedented way to make the Republican Party their party and to gain the presidential nomination for their man, Barry Goldwater. Senator Taft and his supporters had never been able to generate a national, grassroots base of support, let alone an activist movement to support his bid for the Republican nomination. They had not even tried. Goldwater's supporters meant to challenge conventional political wisdom, which placed the power to nominate in the hands of a few party kingmakers operating in "smoke-filled backrooms." Conservatives in the early 1960s were at the forefront of creating a more democratic process of nominating major party presidential candidates.

Goldwater watched this movement unfold from the sidelines. He was ambivalent almost to the end about the fight to win the nomination. The great political journalist Theodore White, accustomed to the savvy, hands-on style of political masterminds like Franklin Roosevelt and Richard Nixon, wryly observed, "Goldwater's favorite style in politics is exhortation, he is a moralist, not an organizer. . . . He arouses emotion—he does not harness it."[27] Goldwater's lack of interest in the mechanics of securing the Republican nomination did not matter to the men and women working to win him the presidency. Especially in the earliest years, those leading the crusade were fighting for a cause, not just for a man. And in the early 1960s, the conservative political cause was being waged at both the state and the national level and both from within and from without the Republican Party. Those working directly to win the nomination and then presidency for Goldwater were joined by separate conservative political movements around the country, some of them in unexpected places, including the state of Texas.

In 1961, political lightning struck in Texas, electrifying both the conservative cause and the Republican Party. A short, hard-drinking, onetime associate professor of political science at Midwestern University in Wichita Falls, Texas, shocked the political establishment by winning a special election to become the first Republican senator from Texas since Reconstruction. John Tower had run as a proud conservative, and Barry Goldwater had come to Texas and campaigned hard in his behalf.[28]

While Texas in the early 1960s was a complex place politically—being half western, half southern and all Texan—Tower's victory there signaled the changing partisan nature of politics in the old Confederacy and thus, potentially, the United States. Texas was, overall, not a liberal state, though most voters in the early 1960s still did not label themselves as conservative.[29] Tower had run full out as a conservative, championing states' rights, and he had bluntly stated that unlike his Democratic opponent (who also ran as a conservative), he would never be used by northern Democratic liberals to run roughshod over the principles Texans (he meant white Texans) held dear. Just a year earlier, Tower had run against the incumbent Lyndon Johnson for the same Senate seat and waged an unprecedentedly strong campaign for a Texas Republican. Tower had been beaten, but a lot of Texans had grown disgusted with Johnson's liberal turn on the issue of race relations, and a good many longtime "yellow dog" Democrats had begun to lose their partisan allegiance to the Democratic Party.

Johnson had become a civil rights advocate for a lot of reasons; whatever else he was, Johnson was a complicated man. But among those reasons was his desire to become a nationally reputable figure in the Democratic Party and not a regional southern politician. Johnson wanted to be the Democrats' 1960 presidential candidate, and he understood that no segregationist could win the party's nomination. So by the late 1950s, Johnson had begun to change his racial politics, as well as his image, playing up his western roots, rather than his southern ones. His increasing commitment to serious civil rights legislation frustrated his southern allies in Congress and infuriated many of his Texas supporters. The *Richmond News Leader* editorialist and fierce defender of white supremacy, James Jackson Kilpatrick, was appalled: "Before a cock could crow thrice, this son of Confederate Texas was denying every identification with his Dixie brothers. A southerner? Not he . . . he was a Westerner, podner."[30] In Texas, many whites regarded Johnson as a race traitor. "Lyndon Johnson may be a Texan to the rest of the U.S.," wrote one angry Texas woman, "but to us in Texas he just lost his citizenship.[31] In 1960, even as the westerner Barry Goldwater increasingly linked his political fortunes to the South, the onetime southern politician Lyndon Johnson was becoming a westerner. For both men, race politics was the reason.

In 1961, conservative Republican John Tower made the case that at least in Texas the Republican Party had replaced the Democratic Party as the anti–civil rights party. Tower's victory proved that the South was ever less a one-party region. That change, dreamed of by Dean Manion and a host of other politically savvy conservatives, meant that Barry Goldwater had a chance to make his own lightning strike, smash the old partisan electoral map, and thereby win the presidency.

On October 8, 1961, a small group of men, most of them serious political operatives, met in Chicago to plan Goldwater's path to
the Republican Party presidential nomination. The group was diverse
in a 1950s Republican sort of way: white men from both the South
and the North attended; the head of the American Medical Association Political Action Committee was joined by the publisher of the
National Review; and several of the men were young. Given the evolution of the conservative movement, it is worth noting that none of
them was directly linked to religious or culturally conservative organizations. F. Clifton White, a New York state Republican Party county
chairman and leader of the national Young Republican Clubs, had
organized the meeting; he was to be the nuts-and-bolts guy. White
had one of the best political minds in the country, and for conservatives to win elections and not just debates, they would need men like
him to map out the political terrain.

In the era before presidential primaries played a fundamental role
in the process (the Democrats first opened up the nominating process after their 1968 convention debacle), winning over each state's
delegation was a delicate and deliberate operation. In 1964, of the
1,309 voting delegates at the Republican convention, only 540 were
selected through open primaries. The rest were chosen through
arcane and complex rules that varied state by state. White and his
allies began mapping out a strategy to work those rules, as well as
target a few primary states, and so win the nomination for Goldwater
and the Republican Party's conservatives. They needed to build support in the Taftian Midwest, the segregationist South, and as much
of the West—California, a primary state, being key—as they could.
The South alone had some three hundred delegates. In 1961 no one
know for certain how the contest would play out for the Republican
nomination, but most predicted that the liberal New York Governor
Nelson Rockefeller would be the party favorite.

Nelson Rockefeller's front-running bid for the nomination illus-
trates how many liberals and moderates, especially of the Northeast
variety, still inhabited the GOP in 1964. Grandson of Standard Oil
founder John D. Rockefeller, Governor Rockefeller was, not surprisingly, a staunch anticommunist—but no more so than that other son

of wealth, John Kennedy, who had won the presidency in 1960 running as a Democrat. However, like most members in good standing of the East Coast superwealthy elite, he was an ardent economic internationalist, dedicated to world-stabilizing and global market enhancing organizations like the United Nations. For much the same reason, Rockefeller supported the national economic-stabilizing policies of the New Deal such as the Social Security system and was a strong advocate of civil rights legislation. He was even an early and ardent environmentalist. Conservatives hated him.

Rockefeller was a force of nature. A man of immense self-confidence and energy, Rockefeller loved politics and policymaking. He was so self-assured that he did not seem to think anyone would mind when he decided to divorce his wife of some thirty years in 1962 and marry a much younger women the following year—and only one month after her own divorce. In the early 1960s, such behavior was deemed scandalous by many, including fellow northeastern moderate Republican Senator Prescott Bush (father of one president and grandfather of another). Rockefeller, the Connecticut senator announced, was a "destroyer of American homes."[32] Many Americans, most especially Republicans, felt much the same way. When Governor Rockefeller strode into the ballroom where the National Federation of Republican Women were meeting, his new wife Happy on his arm, a number of Republican women made a scene by rising from their chairs and disdainfully marching out the doors.[33] Such feelings intensified when the new marriage again made headlines in spring 1964 when Happy gave birth to Nelson Jr. While sexual and gender politics had yet to become the stuff of stump speeches or campaign pledges (in part because feminism, the sexual revolution, and so many other aspects of cultural change had yet to be powerfully manifested), many Americans felt them at a visceral level. Rockefeller's personal liabilities made the Goldwater team's efforts to win the nomination for their man, despite the best efforts of the party's northeastern power brokers, all the more likely.

The conservative political operatives dedicated to winning the Republican nomination for Goldwater, even with Rockefeller's implosion, still had to beat back the efforts of the party's northeastern wing to select a—any—middle-of-the-road candidate. To do so, the

Goldwater team had to unify and politicize a grassroots activist base. A whole host of men and women would be brought to the battle. In the South, the leaders of the Goldwater effort were generally younger men of the "New South." Unlike many of the men who led the Democratic Party in the South, they were not vulgar racists, though none were friends of the civil rights movement exploding all around them. Theodore White, referring to the old-style southern Democrats as "red-neck, demoniac leaders," offers a sympathetic portrait of this new breed, writing that they were "men between thirty and forty years old, city people, well-bred, moderate segregationists, efficient, more at ease in suburban cocktail parties than when whiskey-belting in courthouse chambers."[34] John Grenier was their leader. Grenier was born in New Orleans in 1930, a banker's son. He earned his undergraduate and law degrees at Tulane University. He was a fighter pilot in Korea with the Marine Corps and then went north to New York University, adding a master's degree in taxation law to his credentials. Shortly thereafter, he returned to the South, to Birmingham, Alabama, a booming industrial city. Grenier spoke foreign languages; he played tennis; by all accounts, he was brilliant. Almost immediately he was a major figure in the city's elite circles. He decided to become active in Alabama politics—Republican Party politics.[35]

Alabama politics were complicated. In the early 1950s, the progressive Democratic Governor "Big Jim" Folsom (he stood 6 foot 8 inches) had somehow managed to beat back the racist tide by making a populist appeal to working people—black and white. He told whites to beware when politicians start race baiting. When they scream, "Whip the Nigger!" he warned, "then you know damn well they are trying to cover up dirty tracks."[36] But by the late 1950s, in the face of a dynamic civil rights movement and the Supreme Court's intervention in behalf of black southerners, a great majority of whites in Alabama were not listening. Alabama's two Democratic senators played to the racism that was so ingrained in white southern culture. At the same time, both men were also economic liberals who supported efforts to bring federal money and support to their relatively poor state. Mostly, Alabama statewide office holders were hard-hearted white supremacists but also modest economic liberals, often of a populist persuasion.

George Wallace led the pack. Wallace had first run for governor in 1958 but lost to fellow Democrat state Attorney General Jim Patterson. Patterson had made his name by successfully banning the NAACP from operating in Alabama and had been enthusiastically embraced by the Ku Klux Klan. Wallace thought an endorsement by the Klan was too much even for Alabama's white segregationists, so he chastised Patterson: "[H]e is rolling with the new wave of the Klan with its terrible tradition of lawlessness."[37] But Wallace had misjudged the white electorate. They were in no mood for moderation in the face of black southerners' challenges to white supremacy. A successful Alabama businessman explained why in 1958 he supported Patterson over Wallace: "I'd rather have Attorney General Patterson attacking the Communists in the NAACP than running down an organization [the KKK] devoted to maintaining our way of life."[38] For a great many white southerners, communist subversion—again, an expansive term for many Cold War Americans—had much less to do with Soviet spying and much more to do with African Americans' quest for equality. Wallace learned from his defeat. He told his campaign team, "Well, boys . . . no other son-of-a-bitch will ever out-nigger me again."[39] In 1962, he ran for governor again, made sure that he "out-niggered" everybody, and he won. Not only did he become governor, he became nationally famous for his defense of the white southern way of life.

That was the world in which southern Republicans in the early 1960s lived. John Grenier, their Alabama leader, never intended to out-nasty, if you will, George Wallace or others of his ilk. Racial politics was not what drew John Grenier, or Barry Goldwater, to politics or to the conservative cause. Grenier wanted to rid southern politics of the often corrupt, often buffoonish men who preached and sometimes even practiced—like "Big Jim" Folsom—economic populism. He wanted his state, his region, and his nation to embrace low-tax, private property–protecting, probusiness policies produced by intelligent, forward-thinking men like himself. But if the white southern uproar over civil rights agitators and liberal national politicians could help Alabama Republicans and the conservative Republican Party in the South more generally, then so be it.

National Review publisher William Rusher, a leading Goldwater man, put the matter bluntly in a hard-nosed analysis of the Republican's chances of beating Kennedy in the 1964 election. In the aftermath of the 1962 congressional elections, in which southern Republicans had nearly doubled their share of the vote since 1958, he wrote in the *National Review* that the "Republican Party, like it or not, has a rendezvous with a brand new idea." The South, he told his readers, was ready to vote Republican if the party would offer whites an anti–civil rights candidate. Liberal Republicans, he underlined, were not willing to do that; they wanted to remind everyone that the Republican Party had been created to end slavery; and they even insisted that "any Republican concession to Southern sentiment is a venture in sheer racism." In honor of their party's heritage and their personal belief in equality, Republican liberals, moderates, and even a few conservatives, Rusher acknowledged, felt duty-bound to support national civil rights legislation. Rusher insisted that the conservative cause reject such soft-heartedness.

He reminded conservatives that southern Democrats had long championed racism and sought out, he said, the support of "the primitive wool-hats" (an old-time political epithet similar to "rednecks"). The new Republicans of the South, stalwarts such as John Grenier, were the racial moderates. The GOP need not go after the Klan vote. They just needed to win over white moderates who made up much of the southern middle class and who populated the South's booming suburbs. These were the people who made up the fast-growing New South, born out of postwar prosperity and industrialization. And if those people also opposed federal efforts to end white supremacy, and if, Rusher wrote, they made "no apology for opposing the Warren Court's breezy ventures in social pioneering . . . it may well be that here they have something to teach conservatives of the North."[40] Rusher left unsaid what that lesson might be, but he, like Grenier and like Goldwater, did make it clear that he was no ally of the civil rights movement.

Somewhat surprisingly, Rusher did not point out that some thirty years earlier the great liberal Democrat Franklin Roosevelt had almost as brutally sacrificed African Americans to his larger political agenda. He, too, had sided with the white South to keep those voters and their representatives loyal to him. Most white politicians had been selling out African Americans for one reason or another since the end of Reconstruction.

In the early sixties, though, that sort of cruelty was no longer practiced by white politicians with impunity. Since World War II, Americans had been undergoing an intense racial education. Nazism had given racism a bad name. The onset of the Cold War had made sophisticated Americans, interested in winning the peoples of Africa, Asia, and Latin America to the American side, increasingly uncomfortable with the ugly picture Jim Crow segregation painted of American life. Most important, the civil rights movement had upended American politics. African American activists had put their bodies on the line to prove that they did not choose lives of racial subjugation. By the early 1960s, whites could not just ignore racism. Civil rights activists forced white Americans to look squarely at the barbaric face of white supremacy and choose sides in the epic battle for racial justice. Goldwater, of course, chose to side with the racists. He had his ideological reasons, but he also knew the politics of racism. Even before he was serious about gaining the Republican nomination, shortly after Nixon's defeat, he remarked to a group of white Republicans in Atlanta that, given Kennedy's increasing support of the civil rights movement, the GOP was "not going to get the Negro vote . . . so we ought to go hunting where the ducks are."[41]

On November 22, 1963, at 1:40 p.m., CBS cut away from its broadcast of *As the World Turns*. The newsman Walter Cronkite announced that the president had been shot. Then, in a live feed from Dallas, viewers saw the banquet room where the president was to have spoken; the camera closed in on a black waiter. He was crying. A reporter said, "The president is dead."[42]

Kennedy, only a few months earlier, had made civil rights his issue. He had waited a long time. He knew that to embrace racial justice was to give away much of the white southern vote that had enabled him to win by so narrow a margin the presidency in 1960. He told Martin Luther King Jr., "I may lose the next election because of this." But he also said, "I don't care."[43] Kennedy took no pleasure in moving his party from the firm ground of economic liberalism to the politically treacherous terrain of racial liberalism. He knew that he was turning loose the kind of "cultural hostilities" Richard Hofstadter had earlier remarked upon. But by 1963 he saw no alternative: the moral stakes seemed a simple matter of black and white.

Just days after Kennedy's death, newly inaugurated President Lyndon Johnson told the American people that together they could best honor John Kennedy by passing national civil rights legislation. "We have talked long enough in this country about equal rights," he said. "It is time now to write the next chapter, and to write it in the book of laws."[44] Over the next several months, with Johnson using every means at his disposal to move passage of the Civil Rights Act, Congress battled over the course of that legislation.

Southern Democrats led the fight to stop it. Although northern Democrats pushed hardest to move a strong bill forward, overwhelmingly Republicans endorsed the measure. While many Republicans were wary of the large powers the act gave the federal government—and some worked for months, unsuccessfully, to limit the applicability of the act and aspects of its enforcement provisions—the party supported the legislation. The Republican National Committee in Washington had sent notices around to all Republican members of Congress reminding them to lambast the Democrats for their long and sordid history of race baiting and to remind civil rights activists and their supporters that the GOP was the traditional party of civil rights.[45]

Senate Minority Leader Everett Dirksen, who had first been elected as Illinois senator in 1950 and who considered himself a conservative in the Taftian mode, was hesitant at first about expanding the power of government to countervail racial discrimination, but when the time came to vote, he showed no equivocation. The first important ballot came when the Senate moved to end southerners' Senate filibuster. Dirksen rose to observe that they were that day meeting on the one hundredth anniversary of Abraham Lincoln's nomination by the Republican Party to a second term as president of the United States. Then he took a page from the French writer Victor Hugo: "Stronger than all the armies is an idea whose time has come." "The time has come," he growled, "for equality of opportunity in sharing in government, in education, and in employment. It will not be stayed or denied. It is here!"[46]

Goldwater had to disagree. He took no pleasure in standing against the Civil Rights Act alongside the more virulent racists in American public life, but stand with them he did. When he rose on the Senate floor to mark his break with his party's leadership, he spoke, historian Rick Perlstein tell us, "rapidly, tonelessly, head down, as if reading into the record." He could not, he said, allow "the loss of our God-given liberties." The Civil Rights Act, he continued, would make the federal government into a "police state" and would lead to "the destruction of a free society."[47]

Goldwater did not come away from the occasion unscathed. Senator Dirksen charged him on the Senate floor with fighting for a base cause against an act that history demanded: "Utter all the extreme opinions that you will, it will carry forward. You can go ahead and talk about conscience! It is *man's* conscience that speaks in every generation!"[48] Dirksen was right. The 1964 Civil Rights Act passed the House overwhelmingly with 138 Republicans and 152 Democrats voting for it. In the Senate, twenty-seven Republicans joined forty-six Democrats to pass the act; only six Republicans, joined by twenty of twenty-one Southern Democrats, opposed it. Goldwater had done what he thought he must. President Johnson had done what he thought was right. He also understood the politics. In a remark that echoed what John Kennedy had told Martin Luther King Jr., Johnson told his staff on the day he signed the bill into law, "I think we just gave the South to the Republicans for your lifetime and mine."[49] He was, in essence, right.

The 1964 Republican Presidential Nomination Convention opened July 13, less than two weeks after President Johnson signed the Civil Rights Act into law. Goldwater's people had done what few had thought possible back in 1961. They had the nomination in the bag. Conservatives won the nomination for Goldwater by out-organizing the Republican Party's moderate and liberal factions, the same factions that had controlled the nominating process for the prior three decades. In the southern states, John Grenier and other relatively young Republicans such as Roger Milliken breathed new life into the Republican Party. Unlike prior Republican leaders, who were typically more interested in patronage jobs and personal perquisites than trying to win elections, the new leadership focused on bringing in new supporters and winning political power by throwing themselves into the greater conservative cause. They had an easy time lining up delegates for Goldwater—his major opponents were northeastern civil rights liberals: New York Governor Nelson Rockefeller, Massachusetts patrician Henry Cabot Lodge, and, late in the game, Pennsylvania Governor Bill Scranton. Elsewhere, the struggle was harder and, more often than not, won on the ground through the extraordinary efforts of grassroots volunteers motivated by high principle and organized by savvy political operatives who understood how the Republican Party and its presidential nominating process worked.

Among the groups active in the nomination fight were the Young Americans for Freedom, the organization that William Buckley had helped foster in 1960. At a strategic political level, in the early 1960s the YAF differed fundamentally from its rivals on the other side of the political spectrum. New Left groups such as Students for a Democratic Society and the Student Non-Violent Coordinating Committee were experimenting with an array of more participatory and even libratory forms of democratic practice; they had little use for mainstream party politics and much scorn for the pragmatic, even cautious, liberal wing of the Democratic Party. The traditionalist YAFers were far more practical about gaining political power in the United States. They always saw their role as being at the vanguard of the conservative faction within the Republican Party.

In January 1963, the YAF newsletter *The New Guard* endorsed Goldwater for the Republican presidential nomination, making the YAF one of the very first organizations on the Right to fully embrace Goldwater's still unannounced and reluctant candidacy. Leading YAF members then formed Youth for Goldwater and threw themselves into the fray. Working closely with Dean Manion, Clif White, and other stalwarts on the Right, the YAF legions captured the Young Republican National Federation, an important organizing forum with deep roots in every state. Using the YRNF, they concentrated on winning party caucuses by planting their people, state by state, into the local Republican Party. Working with the Goldwater campaign, they also targeted unaffiliated or disaffected young people floundering in the murky tides of apathetic youth culture. The campaign even formed an ersatz folk-singing group, The Goldwaters, who sang catchy lyrics such as: "Barry's gonna win in '64/The New Frontier will be no more" and "Hang down your head, left-wingers/Hang down your head and cry/Well, take one last look at the White House/Before you say goodbye." Goldwater was both touched and excited by the passions his YAF adherents brought to the cause.[50]

Robert Welch's John Birch Society, as the *National Review* publisher William Rusher had predicted, also played a key role in fighting for delegates and rounding up support for Goldwater at the local level. Their presence was much attended to by the national mass media, which pictured the JBS as a scary bunch of nuts. Even the conservative publisher of the *Los Angeles Times*, Otis Chandler, well aware that the JBS was popular in California (the state had some three hundred chapters), issued a stern editorial warning his readers that the Birchers "sow distrust, and aggravate disputes, and they will weaken the very strong case for conservatism. . . . What is happening to us when all loyal Americans are accused [by the JBS] of being Communist dupes unless they subscribe to radical and dictatorial direction of one self-chosen man? . . . Subversion, whether of the left or the right, is still subversion."[51] Some of the most visible figures of the conservative cause—but never Barry Goldwater—made it clear that the JBS was not invited to their party, and the mainstream mass media targeted the JBS for ridicule throughout the campaign season. Regardless, members of the JBS soldiered on for Goldwater.

Birchers might have appeared as dangerous extremists to many Americans, even fellow conservatives, but by any standard they were impressively dedicated political activists. Birchers belied the mythical image of late 1950s, early 1960s quiescent, domesticated, apolitical "Leave It to Beaver" suburbanites. They held regular meetings in small groups all over the country in which they discussed right-wing books and articles, listened to tapes made by Robert Welch, and carefully planned local political actions. By 1964, local JBS chapters had successfully worked to take over PTAs, run members for school board membership, confront ministers, labor leaders, and politicians they believed to be communists, open dozens of defiantly right-wing bookstores, launch massive congressional letter-writing campaigns (impeaching antisegregationist Supreme Court Chief Justice Earl

Warren was one of their pet causes), and spend many a weekend going door to door giving away pamphlets, talking local politics, and looking for new members.

In 1964, the men and women of the JBS, numbering upwards of forty thousand (with some estimates of the group membership—the organization kept the number secret—running as high as one hundred thousand), were well trained and attuned to the practicalities of their local political battlefields. For Goldwater they led petition drives, attended precinct caucuses, and in every useful way attended to the business of winning delegates. In caucus states, where delegates often were selected through local meetings of Republican Party members, disciplined cadres who could be counted on to show up and to vote by bloc were indispensable. Goldwater understood that the Birchers were politically flammable, but he admired their unbending commitment to him and their cause and, in the nomination fight, he understood their utility.[52]

California was at the epicenter of the grassroots Goldwater campaign to win the Republican nomination. In this winner-take-all primary state, the candidate with the most votes received eighty-six delegates. Those delegates were important to Goldwater. But winning the vote in California would also show Republican Party regulars that the Goldwater campaign had electoral reach; it was not just a cabal of zealous operatives, it was also a popular movement. In the California primary grassroots conservatives proved themselves. They won the state delegation for Goldwater and became a force that would endure well past the 1964 presidential campaign. The YAF and the John Birch Society were a part of the California conservative movement, but so were many others. In California, as in many other states, the Goldwater campaign brought together small, often locally oriented groups, members of national conservative groups, as well as many unaffiliated but politically concerned people into a vital, unified movement.

Anticommunism, broadly understood, unified most of the Goldwater volunteers in California. Dr. Fred Schwarz, who had started the Christian Anti-Communism Crusade (CACC) in Iowa in 1953, helped galvanize the movement. He had moved his operation to Long Beach, California, in 1960 and in early 1961. Taking time from his peripatetic travels in behalf of his national crusade, he helped organize the Orange County School of Anti-Communism, which was quickly followed by the Southern California School of Anti-Communism.

Dr. Schwarz warned that communism meant to destroy the American family and Christianity. Communists hated the "diseased bourgeois class" and considered the families that sustained it to be "animals." Schwarz first made sure that Americans understood that in the Soviet Union families just like theirs had been torn apart, with children taken from parents, husbands sent away to deadly work camps, and millions left to starve to death. Here, just a very few years after Stalinism, he did not have to exaggerate the horrors, only report them. Schwarz then warned that if—and given current conditions, he claimed, it was not so much if as when—the communists took over America, middle-class families would be similarly targeted for devastation and death. Second, he informed his audiences that "Communism is the enemy of God and of Christ and his Gospel."[53] If, or when, communists seized control of the United States they would replace Christianity with soul-murdering atheism. For Schwarz and others who taught at the schools of anticommunism, the threat of communism was not something that was happening "over there." The communists—and here is where hyperbole and hysteria came to the fore—were already here, and they were winning. As one lecturer, a staff member of the House Un-American Activities Committee, reported in a Southern California School of Anti-Communism meeting in 1960, "Communists have infiltrated our radar defense and communications networks, newspapers and other printed media, education, art and labor unions and have gained by court decisions ruling that their activities are merely political."[54] Schwarz warned, "At present rates of progress, Communism will have conquered the world within a generation."[55] There was no time to waste.

More than fifteen thousand people participated in the Anti-Communism Schools in Southern California in 1961, and numerous celebrities, including John Wayne, Pat Boone, Roy Rogers, and Ronald Reagan, rallied the students. The organization raised more than a $1 million.[56] Like the JBS, the schools asked for more than a polite hearing; they promoted activism. Ardent anticommunists found each other at the CACC events and then worked together to politicize their neighbors and communities.

These activists saw multiple threats to their beliefs. Many, especially women activists, battled the "collectivist menace" they believed threatened their children's schools. They alerted other parents to school officials they perceived to be communists or communist sympathizers for prescribing "progressive education" and for making evolutionary biology and sex education a part of the curriculum. A host of religious leaders linked Christianity to the anticommunist, pro–free enterprise cause. Megachurch pioneer Robert Schuller assured his flock, "[Y]ou have a God-ordained right to be wealthy. . . . Having riches is no sin, wealth is no crime. Christ did not praise poverty." And the archconservative Catholic Cardinal of Orange County, Francis McIntyre, warned of the dangers of communist-linked secular humanism and encouraged his priests and parishioners to listen to Robert Welch and read John Birch Society publications.[57]

Doctors and dentists played a large and visible role in the burgeoning movement. They fiercely opposed liberals' plans to create massive government programs that would, in their eyes, sovietize medicine and ruin their livelihoods. They were joined by real estate developers, bankers, construction company owners, industrialists, and entrepreneurs of all kinds who fought to keep government economic regulation and taxes to a minimum. As historian Lisa McGirr writes, these were men whose own life stories in the booming postwar economy of California confirmed "their strong belief that hard work, individual entrepreneurship, and intelligence paved the road to success."[58] In addition, the flourishing defense industries of Southern California, led by Lockheed, Northrop, McDonnell Douglas, and Hughes, were full of supporters for the ardently promilitary policies of Senator Goldwater. These were the people who formed the activist base of the Goldwater campaign in California, joining together in volunteer political organizations, including the United Republicans of California.

Few of these people saw themselves engaged in temperate political debates with other well-meaning Americans about the state of science education or the appropriate level of social services for poor people in a rich nation or the place that government oversight should play in the private sector. In 1964, many believed that they were locked in a final battle with agents of international communism who controlled legions of liberal dupes, fellow-travelers, and out-and-out minions of the Soviet Union.

In early 1964, two ardent conservative authors offered detailed accounts of the treachery the conservative movement faced in winning its battle to elect Goldwater. John Stormer, chairman of the Missouri Federation of Young Republicans, self-published *None Dare Call It Treason*, which explained how communists and their allies ("the collectivists") had infiltrated American education, churches, press, radio, television, mental health organizations, labor unions, charities, and the American government. In a typical passage, Stormer explained, "The weapons of hate and fear by which the collectivists have moved a generation of Americans to sell their freedom and integrity for security would never have worked had American roots in basic Judaic-Christian traditions not first been severed."[59] Conservatives in California alone distributed some five hundred thousand copies of Stormer's polemic. An equal number of Phyllis Schlafly's *A Choice Not an Echo* (a phrase Goldwater had used in announcing his presidential candidacy) were also distributed just in California before the state Republican primary.[60] Schlafly, an ardent anticommunist and Republican Party activist, warned that for decades "secret kingmakers," dedicated to their own international economic interests, had chosen the Republican presidential candidate. They placed their internationalist agenda ahead of American interests. They practiced "an America Last foreign policy." They had conspired to defeat Robert Taft. Now, they meant to stop Goldwater and place Nelson Rockefeller atop the 1964 Republican ticket. Schlafly offered rank-and-file conservatives a winning populist message that put them on the side of the people against a secret cabal of the superwealthy.[61] In 1964, liberal and moderate Republicans had no polemical weapons like those offered by Schlafly and Stormer.

Goldwater campaigned heavily in California right before the primary vote. At a Memorial Day speech in Riverside, he gave his own expansive version of the communist threat. Mimicking the voice of a liberal, big government bureaucrat, he squeaked, "Don't worry about Mom and Pop, don't lay aside any money, enjoy yourself, the Federal

Government will take care of Mom and Pop." Steely-eyed, he warned, "*this* is the ultimate destruction of the American family. When this happens, Communism will have won."[62]

Thousands of volunteers went door to door on primary day, turning out the vote for Goldwater. The head of the Republican Party in Los Angeles believed those volunteers were vital to the outcome: ". . . those bumbling, disoriented, inept amateurs who are out stomping around from door to door asking for votes for Goldwater. They make people feel that someone is interested in *them*."[63] In California's white communities, as well as in white communities around the nation, the passion, the heated rhetoric, and the grassroots mobilization were almost all on the side of the conservatives.

In June 1964, Republican primary voters gave California's convention delegation to Goldwater. The vote was close, as liberal and moderate Republicans still dominated Northern California, but in Southern California, especially in fast-growing Los Angeles and Orange County, conservatives ruled. With California, the nomination was Goldwater's, and just a few weeks later, in mid-July, the Goldwater legions gathered at the Cow Palace in San Francisco to nominate their champion.

The 1964 Republican Convention was a high watermark for political conservatism. Not until 1980 would it be eclipsed. Presidential campaign pundit Theodore White concluded, ". . . this was a new thing in American conventions—not a meeting, not a clash, but a coup d'état."[64] White was indulging in a bit of hyperbole; still, the party of the "modern" Republicans had been beaten. The Massachusetts moderate, Henry Cabot Lodge, after a miserable appearance before the Goldwater-dominated platform committee, retired to his hotel room and scanned the delegate list: "What in God's name has happened to the Republican Party! I hardly know any of these people!"[65] The party that had made a separate peace with the New Deal, refused the leadership of Senator Taft, and joined with liberal Democrats to pass big government civil rights legislation had been out-organized and out-mobilized by a new conservative movement.

Goldwater paid homage to that movement in his acceptance speech. His virtues were their virtues: "The good Lord raised this mighty Republic to be a home for the brave and to flourish as the land of the free—not to stagnate in the swampland of collectivism, not to cringe before the bullying of communism." He echoed their traditionalist credo, urging Americans to "return to proven ways— not because they are old, but because they are true." And he lambasted big government liberals: "Those who seek to live your lives for you, to take your liberties in return for relieving you of yours, those who elevate the state and downgrade the citizen must see ultimately a world in which earthly power can be substituted for Divine Will, and this Nation was founded upon the rejection of that notion and upon the acceptance of God as the author of freedom."

Goldwater delegates roared in approval when he blasted the Johnson administration for failing to keep Americans safe from the disorderly protesters, lawless agitators, and urban criminals that, he said, liberal policies had fostered and even encouraged: "Security from domestic violence, no less than from foreign aggression, is the most elementary and fundamental purpose of any government, and a government that cannot fulfill that purpose is one that cannot long command the loyalty of its citizens. History shows us—demonstrates that nothing—nothing prepares the way for tyranny more than the failure of public officials to keep the streets from bullies and marauders." Goldwater had invented the politics of law and order.

Senator Goldwater reserved some of his harshest words for the liberals and moderates within his own party: "Those who do not care for our cause, we don't expect to enter our ranks in any case. And— And let our Republicanism, so focused and so dedicated, not be made fuzzy and futile by unthinking and stupid labels." Then, after dismissing the left-wing of his party, he gave a full-throated welcome to the right-wing activists, John Birch Society members most specially, who had been vital to his victory: "I would remind you that extremism in the defense of liberty is no vice. And let me remind you also that moderation in the pursuit of justice is no virtue."[66]

Liberals watching the convention were shocked, especially by the ode to "extremism." Nelson Rockefeller called Goldwater's statement "dangerous, irresponsible and frightening." The *New York Times* concluded that the Goldwater takeover of the Republicans had lowered "a once great party to the status of an ugly, frustrated faction."[67] And the pollster and pundit Elmo Roper concluded, "Total control of the Republican Party passed into the hands of its most conservative elements."[68] A bemused reporter turned to Theodore White right after the "extremism" riff and said Goldwater was actually "going to run as Barry Goldwater."[69]

Lyndon Johnson, who was going to run as an avowed liberal, was pleased by the outcome. Earlier in the year, when the political insiders began to reckon that Goldwater just might take the Republican nomination, Johnson had handicapped his chances against Goldwater and liked his odds. He told his speechwriter Richard Goodwin, "What the man on the street wants is not a big debate on fundamental issues. He wants a little medical care, a rug on the floor, a picture on the wall, a little music in the house, and a place to take Molly and the grandchildren when he retired." Economic liberalism—New Deal liberalism, in other words—was still the ticket, and Johnson meant to hammer home the risks Goldwater and his principled conservatism would bring to the Social Security system (Goldwater would make it "voluntary") and to the widespread prosperity and stability that government safeguards had brought to the American people. LBJ, in his campaign, was going to offer them more of the same—big programs that would help Americans pay their medical bills and clean up their communities and improve their children's schools. But President Johnson also had decided that he would risk all that goodwill by not deviating from the path he had laid for himself. There would be, he swore, ". . .no compromises on civil rights. . . . Those civil righters are going to have to wear sneakers to keep up with me."[70] He had decided by early 1964 to bet his presidential legacy and the political future of liberalism on the cause of racial justice.

Johnson and his campaign team would not run away from the president's economic and racial liberalism, but they would also do their best to place Goldwater's conservatism in the worst possible light. Much energy would go into suggesting to voters that Barry Goldwater wanted to go to war with the Soviet Union and "Red" China and that if he became president, he would jump at the chance to drop atomic bombs on miscellaneous people. Goldwater gave the Johnson campaign plenty with which to work: he had made numerous public statements tailor-made for negative ads aimed at scaring the bejesus out of numerous Americans. In his last preprimary campaign rally in California, Goldwater had thundered, "I charge that today this nation is following in the most disastrous foreign policy in its entire history. . . . We are at war and we should admit it!"[71] He had, at one point, vowed to cut off diplomatic relations with the Soviet Union. He wanted to militarize space. He blasted "Communist-induced hysteria on the subject of radio-active fallout" and demanded an end to the 1963 Nuclear Test Ban Treaty. He pledged to help instigate "a full fledged Resistance" in communist-controlled countries and, if need be, to "move a highly mobile task force equipped with appropriate nuclear weapons to the scene of the revolt . . . to compel a Soviet withdrawal."[72] And just a few weeks before he won the Republican nomination, Goldwater had made a series of ambiguous statements regarding the use of atomic bombs in Vietnam and China. He was asked on ABC's *Issues and Answers* what he would do to cut off communist supply lines to South Vietnam (the United States was then still in the "training" and "nation building" stage in Vietnam). He responded that one option was "defoliation of the forests by low-yield atomic weapons" and then responded to a follow-up question about the role of the communist Chinese in the region by suggesting that they, too could be targeted: "You might have to . . . If we decide to go into this war in a full-scale way, we certainly would have to make the decision on strategic supplies for the enemy at the same time." Later, to journalists, he repeated, "If I had my choice, I would go into South China. It would be fairly easy."[73] Such casual war-mongering and possible atomic bombing set the stage for Johnson's negative attack ads on Goldwater.

The Johnson campaign ran a number of commercials attacking Goldwater's bellicosity. One of them, though aired only once as a paid ad and then pulled amid controversy, became legendary. The one-minute spot showed a little girl pulling petals off a daisy, counting as she did so. As she approached ten, she looked up, frozen-faced; a man's voice boomed a countdown, and then as the camera closed in on the girl's face, an atomic bomb exploded. As the mushroom cloud formed, President Johnson, voice-over, intoned, "These are the stakes, to make a world in which all of God's children can live or to go into the dark. We must either love each other or we must die."[74] Decades later, the ad is still potent.

Goldwater, the reluctant presidential candidate, lost big. Johnson received 61.1 percent of the vote, a higher total even than that of his hero, Franklin D. Roosevelt. In defeat, Goldwater received almost 7 million fewer votes than Richard Nixon had in 1960. In Republican strongholds in New England and the mid-Atlantic states, many of the party's liberals and moderates had refused to support Goldwater. Many other Republicans, skittish about Goldwater's attacks on Social Security, farm supports, or other cherished government programs, turned away from the principled conservative. Black voters, who had given about 70 percent of their vote to John Kennedy, went nearly unanimously for Johnson, as the number of their votes, thanks to the civil rights movement and the centrality of racial justice issues to the election, had increased by nearly a million. White backlash in the North against Johnson appeared to be minimal, even in communities, such as Philadelphia and New York, that had experienced violent racial conflict. While some northern whites' discontent with the changing racial justice policies of the Democrats was visible and increasingly vocal, it lacked enough salience to push them Goldwater's way. (Electoral signs of change were, however, registered: in California, even as Johnson won easily, an anti–open housing measure passed by a ratio of approximately 2 to 1.) Roosevelt's New Deal coalition had nearly held together. Still loyal to the Democrats were most Catholic and ethnic, working-class whites, Jewish Americans, African Americans, as well as East and West Coast secular and internationally oriented middle- and upper-middle-class voters.[75] Only one group had deserted the Democratic Party: southern whites.

Right after Goldwater had won the Republican nomination, he received a surprise visitor: Alabama Governor George Wallace. Wallace had been running, somewhat quixotically, for the Democratic presidential nomination and had been garnering a great deal of press attention. Wallace asked Goldwater if he might like the Alabamian to join him on the ticket as his vice presidential running mate. Goldwater, explaining that he must run with a Republican, graciously begged off, but Wallace decided that he would, though still a Democrat, support Senator Goldwater's candidacy. He appeared on the CBS program *Face the Nation* and praised Goldwater's civil rights policy and his strong support for law and order in the face of rising crime rates. Soon thereafter, Wallace followed up with some "rare philosophical observations" about his recent conversion to conservatism. In the pages of *Playboy* magazine, the governor explained, "Originally, a liberal was a believer in freedom. But the name has been taken over by those who believe in economic and social planning by the federal government to interfere in everybody's business. The liberalism of today shows a loss of faith in the individual. Conservatives still believe in the individual, in private enterprise." Governor Wallace sounded just like the late Senator Robert Taft! He then echoed Senator Goldwater: ". . . just because I believe Alabama should do good things for her people . . . does not mean I believe the government has the right to tell a businessman whom he can hire and whom he cannot hire, a café or restaurant or motel owner whom he can serve and whom he cannot, a homeowner whom he must and must not sell his house to. A Conservative tries to preserve freedom for business and labor."[76] George Wallace, educated in the southern populist tradition and *still faithful to it*, had become a self-proclaimed convert to conservatism. Prior to that conversion, he had justified his opposition to equal rights for African Americans by using racist language that demeaned black Americans and by insisting that white southerners had the legal authority, based on the principle of states' rights, to maintain their traditions and customs—which just so happened to include racial segregation and discrimination. After his conversion to the conservative cause, Wallace instead justified his opposition to civil rights legislation and equal opportunity for African Americans by using phrases like "property rights," "faith in the individual," and "preserve freedom." Over time, many whites in the North as well as the South, for many reasons (and, for certain, often not racist ones), would resist government-mandated equal rights for African Americans and other minority groups by embracing this new paradigm.

Wallace's conversion was emblematic, too, of the changing national voting patterns and national party identification of a great many white southerners. South Carolina Senator Strom Thurmond slammed home this new political reality when he announced shortly before the November election that he was renouncing his membership in the Democratic Party and would ever after be a Republican: "The Democratic Party has abandoned the people. . . . It is leading the evolution of our nation to a socialistic dictatorship."[77] For a number of years, most other white southern politicians did not switch political parties. They maintained their allegiance to the Democratic Party for reasons of legislative seniority and local political loyalties. Most of them, however, made it clear that they rejected the racial justice politics of the national party and the label of liberalism, which post-1964 had become so tightly identified with those racial politics. Sam Nunn, who ran successfully for the Senate as a Democrat in Georgia in 1972, for example, eagerly trumpeted George Wallace's support of his candidacy and denounced his Republican opponent for "trying to make me out as some sort of liberal, but nothing could be farther from the truth. . . . I am a common-sense conservative from one of the most conservative, common-sense counties in our great state."[78]

Goldwater won only six states in 1964. One was his own state of Arizona (which he won by just half a percentage point), but the rest were in the Deep South: Alabama, Mississippi, Georgia, Louisiana, and South Carolina. In Mississippi, where the black citizenry was still almost completely disenfranchised, Goldwater received 87 percent of the vote. White southerners were fast learning that they were conservatives and that when it came to presidential politics, they were Republicans.

Most Americans had not learned the same lesson. Goldwater's belief that he could teach a majority of voters that "in their hearts" they, too, were conservatives had not been borne out. In 1964, amid general peace and prosperity, with memories of the Great Depression still fresh and the martyrdom of John Kennedy still raw, a majority of voters stayed loyal to the New Deal liberal precepts of the Democratic Party. The struggle for racial justice was roiling the nation, but most whites in the North and West saw the civil rights movement and the federal government's embrace of it as a fight against the ugliest forms of legalized southern segregation—it was not about their communities. Liberals still dominated the culture and the polity.

William Buckley understood these factors. He had not been deeply involved in Goldwater's campaign, though he had hoped to be (Goldwater's staff seemed to be jealous of Buckley and distrustful of his East Coast intellectual ways). Cheerleading from the outside, he had been a realist all along about Goldwater's chances. In September 1964, at the national convention of the Young Americans for Freedom, the group he had been so instrumental in creating and whose members had thrown themselves so passionately into the Goldwater campaign, Buckley explained that their time, conservatism's time, had not yet come. Presciently, he told them, ". . . any election of Barry Goldwater would presuppose a sea change in American public opinion, presuppose that the fiery little body of dissenters, of which you are a shining meteor, suddenly spun off nothing less than a majority of the American people." Americans, he said, were not ready for "the true meaning of freedom." They had been, he argued, tricked and fooled and mystified by a liberal mass media and hordes of liberal intellectuals and scholars. Their conservative insurgency, he argued, needed to aim not at election day but at "future Novembers; to infuse the conservative spirit in enough people to entitle us to look about us, on November fourth, not at the ashes of defeat, but at the well-planted seeds of hope, which will flower on a great November day in the future."[79] Buckley, as usual, had put the matter elegantly, but even he did not realize how many years it would be before his movement captured the White House.

Goldwater lost big, but in his name a forceful grassroots conservative movement aimed at national power had taken shape. An extraordinary number of men and women had been mobilized by the Goldwater campaign. More than one million of them had been stirred to contribute money to the campaign; in 1960, only forty-four thousand had donated to Richard Nixon.[80] In the aftermath of the election some conservative activists would step back, and within the Republican Party moderates would do their best to push the conservatives back. But Goldwater had helped to reduce the power of liberal Republicans and to ensure that moderate Republicans, in the years ahead, would lean toward the conservative movement activists. And every Republican presidential candidate after Barry Goldwater would reach out and seek to expand the new, white conservative base in the South that he had helped to create. Barry Goldwater had been a flawed candidate. His ill-considered talk of atomic bombs and Asian land wars had given liberals the language with which to mock him, transforming his campaign slogan from "In your heart, you know he's right" to "In your guts, you know he's nuts." But Goldwater had inspired a generation of conservative activists, blooded them in a presidential campaign, and shown them the grit and political power of "old bare-knuckles frontier conservatism."[81] As Bill Buckley said, the times were not yet right for Goldwater's message, nor was the conservative coalition yet broad enough or strong enough to take national power, but the conservatives' day was coming.

FOUR

Phyllis Schlafly

Domestic Conservatism and Social Order

After Barry Goldwater's defeat in 1964, his key supporters in
the Republican Party came under attack by the moderates and the
liberals they had so gleefully displaced. Phyllis Schlafly faced that fire
head-on. Schlafly had been a central figure in Goldwater's run for
the presidency, first as the author of *A Choice Not an Echo* and then
as the tireless, ardently conservative Vice President of the National

Federation of Republican Women (NFRW). With the financial help of a group of wealthy California conservative women, she had also recorded a twenty-minute speech—framed by images of her loving children and husband—in which she asked Americans to vote for Goldwater and reject what she called the dangerously weak national security, communist-appeasing policies of Lyndon Johnson and his secretary of defense Robert McNamara: "Do you want to risk your family and children on the Johnson-McNamara policies?"[1] The sponsored address was broadcast all over the country. Schlafly represented all aspects of conservatism in the early 1960s: inspired by her unwavering Catholic faith and by her belief in the character-building, economically sound principles of the free enterprise system, she was an ardent anticommunist who believed that American liberty built on a strong spiritual foundation was God's gift to the world, which it was humankind's duty to preserve.

Like many other stalwart conservatives, Schlafly had tied her fortunes to Barry Goldwater's presidential run. With his failure, his enemies in the Republican Party were also hers. In the post-1964 fallout, the moderate pragmatists in the GOP, the "modern" Republicans who had backed Eisenhower and then Nixon, targeted Schlafly for removal from the party machinery. These GOP moderates succeeded, in the short-term, in purging her from a leadership role. Ironically, her fall from power placed her on the road to her greatest political and personal triumph. From her new position outside the cautious Republican Party apparatus, Schlafly helped engineer the triumph of the "New Right" in American politics.

Well before feminism was revitalized in 1960s America, Phyllis Schlafly proved that a woman—or at least (large caveat) a brilliant and fiercely self-disciplined woman—could do most anything she wanted: run for public office, write important books, find meaningful work. But just because women could triumph in such arenas without the coercive intervention of a paternalistic government does not mean they should, said the self-same Phyllis Schlafly. In a well-ordered, benevolent Christian society—in American society—women should always put their familial duties first, as she believed that she did.

In the 1970s, when American feminists and their supporters attempted to mandate women's right to full equality under the Constitution, Schlafly stood in their way. She said that a moral order based on family values, not on feminists' demands for full equality, is what America needed to keep women and their children safe, secure, and spiritually strong. In a dangerous world, in which subversive, immoral, and atheistic forces sought to destroy the American way of life, women guarded those family values and through that guardianship they best proved their virtue and earned their own value. Liberal feminists, Schlafly said, put individuals and not families first. Absolute, legally mandated equality would hurt, not help, women, their families, or American society. Liberal feminists, Schlafly said, want women to be just like men. The women's libbers even wanted women to fight in wars and die in combat.

Feminists, Schlafly said, failed to understand that God made women and men different from each other because men and women had different roles to play in life. She taught conservatives that family values were at the heart of their multifaceted cause. She showed that family-values politics could create a tidal wave of new conservative women activists. As the threat of domestic communism lost its hold on the American public's imagination and its centrality in the conservative movement, Schlafly helped conservative Americans see that subversion had a new name. In so doing, she swelled the ranks of conservative activists and voters, building a grassroots movement and a dedicated political base. In the 1970s, when even well-educated, middle-class young women wore blue jeans and learned to speak out loud about their sexual desires, Phyllis Schlafly wore pearls and pumps. She was a lady in a land awash in gutter talk. Her hair was perfect. To her followers, she was an exemplar of disciplined respectability in a time of slovenly permissiveness.

Schlafly had not set out to be the nation's conservative voice on matters of family life and gender roles. She had built her political reputation on the right as a militant anticommunist. But she perceived in the women's liberation movement and the general ethos of sixties culture a political opportunity she could not resist. She knew that her people felt themselves drowning in the liberal tide that had washed over the banks of university campuses and big cities and into the homes of America's broad middle class. The feminists insisted that "the personal is political." Schlafly and her allies would show feminists and their supporters how right they were by making the battle over women's equal rights a war about the enduring value of womanhood, motherhood, and wifely duties in America. This was a war conservatives could fight and thought they could win. Once again, conservatives would argue that equality—the liberals' shibboleth—was not Americans' primary value; first came the need to maintain a moral order on which society depended. Schlafly, her followers, and her allies believed that moral order depended on sustaining a traditional religious family life in which women's special and different roles as wives and mothers were not destroyed by the Left's love of radical, untested change.

Phyllis Schlafly, born in St. Louis in 1924 to a devout Catholic family, could well have been, given her family's economic travails during the Great Depression, a New Deal Democrat. Her father, John Stewart, lost his job in 1930 and never regained secure full-time employment in the private sector. Her mother, Dadie, became the family's primary breadwinner, working in the poorly paid women's sector of the economy, first as a department store clerk, then public school teacher, and finally as a librarian. If narrowly defined economic self-interest alone determined political consciousness, the Stewarts, daughter Phyllis included, should have been Roosevelt Democrats. But Phyllis's mother and father scorned New Deal work relief programs and social provision policies. They rejected what they considered to be Roosevelt's undermining of the free enterprise system. Though facing adversity, the Stewarts continued to believe that hard work, self-discipline, and adherence to religious faith were the means by which a virtuous life was earned and a moral order was established and maintained. Phyllis inherited those beliefs and never found reason to doubt them.[2]

Schlafly (still Phyllis Stewart) began her political work in the immediate postwar years in the anti–New Deal, Taftian, economic conservative cause. She had not set out to find employment defending the free enterprise system. After a stellar academic career that had ended triumphantly with an M.A. degree in political science at Radcliffe College, earned before she had even turned twenty-one (Schlafly had won a scholarship to attend Radcliffe but her coursework was largely done at all-male Harvard, which had only in 1943 begun to allow Radcliffe women to attend Harvard classes), Schlafly went to Washington, D.C., in 1945, planning to work for the federal government. Facing a tightening job market and stiff competition from returning veterans who received preferential treatment in government hiring, she became instead a researcher at the American Enterprise Association (later the American Enterprise Institute).

A better job for Schlafly's political education would be hard to imagine. The AEA had been formed in 1943 by a group of powerful New York City–based businessmen who had been mulling over how to respond to the primacy of New Deal economics in national policymaking. They were far from the only businessmen infuriated by New Dealers' success in disciplining the free enterprise system and raising taxes on the wealthy. The men who led the National Association of Manufacturers, the Chamber of Commerce, and many other probusiness organizations and trade associations fought actively in the political trenches, producing tracts aimed at shifting public opinion, testifying at hearings, and lobbying members of the government. A few of American's richest men, some of whom had been active in the anti-Roosevelt American Liberty League, such as General Motors's Alfred Sloan, took another tack, starting foundations to battle the leftist turn. The Sloan Foundation poured money into educational efforts aimed at teaching young people that the free enterprise system, not big government, produced economic security and guaranteed individual liberty. The AEA, however, was the only group that brought together conservative academicians with leading businessmen to produce rigorous analysis of economic legislation and broad economic policy.

Rather than embrace a narrow politics of economic self-interest as did the Chamber of Commerce or aim at changing mass public opinion as did the Sloan Foundation, the AEA vowed to prove to key government decision makers and influential (and intellectually oriented) members of the public how and why specific promarket policies benefited American society and why most business regulation and taxes hurt the American people. The AEA, in other words, was an innovative probusiness, conservative think tank. Schlafly only worked for one year at the AEA, but as her biographer Donald Critchlow observes, it was there—not at Harvard—that she was educated as a political conservative: "Her religious faith, now combined with a well-formed conservative ideology, created a formidable political outlook."[3] Schlafly also learned how to take complex ideas about politics and policy and communicate them in striking and simple phrases that nonexperts, whether they were congressional representatives or voters, could grasp and appreciate.

Schlafly decided to return to St. Louis, where she immediately continued her rapidly developing interest in conservative politics She worked as campaign manager for a Republican congressional challenger to an incumbent liberal Democrat and also as a researcher for a politically minded banker. Her congressional candidate lost, but Schlafly's commitment to Republican Party political activism had begun, just as her work at the bank helped her to develop her writing and research skills in the conservative cause. By 1949, Schlafly had become a force in local, probusiness, conservative politics. She was a whirlwind, and she was only twenty-four years old.

Schlafly never intended to pursue a career single-mindedly. In October 1949, she married Fred Schlafly, a prosperous, highly accomplished, and politically conservative much older man. While she, herself, was a good deal older than the average bride of her era (about half of all women married in 1949 were twenty or younger), she was not exactly an old maid. Once married, she immediately quit her paid position and became Mrs. Schlafly, happily creating a home across the Mississippi from St. Louis in Alton, Illinois. The Catholic couple began having children, six in all. Schlafly was, to be anachronistic, a stay-at-home wife and mother but of a highly unusual kind.

Schlafly's husband was a well-connected and intellectually sophisticated Senator Taft–supporting Republican. The Schlaflys' marriage was built, in part, on their companionate political passions. He respected her beliefs and admired her talents; from the beginning he urged her to continue her political work. With his encouragement and permission, she did continue that work, even as she raised her six children. In 1952, defying the gender conventions of the times, Mrs. Schlafly ran for Congress. The local county Republican Party leadership had wanted her well-to-do lawyer husband to run, not her. But after Fred turned them down, they looked to Phyllis, who at twenty-seven had already become a highly visible and effective political figure in the community, serving as a volunteer for the Illinois Federation of Republican Women and the Daughters of the American Revolution. With her husband's blessing, Schlafly said yes.

Schlafly ran as a housewife candidate with her toddler in tow. She made her status as a woman, a wife, and a mother central to her campaign. While she commanded an extraordinary body of facts and figures to support her political stands, she positioned herself publicly not as a onetime Washington, D.C., policy expert or young but experienced political veteran, but as a married lady whose mission was simply to bring to Congress the commonsense virtue that her sex and wifely status taught her. So, she would say, "as a housewife, I am greatly concerned about the fact that we have the highest prices and highest taxes in our country's history." In a similar vein, "I feel very disturbed about the corrupt situation in politics. I think that women should get into politics and do something about it." And most pointedly, "In former years . . . a woman's place was in the home. Today, American women must stand together if we are to protect our home."[4]

There was nothing cynical about the traditional feminine persona Schlafly offered voters, one that she would, in essence, maintain over the course of her political life. It was not, in other words, a persona crafted for political manipulation. Her feminist critics in the 1970s could never understand this about Schlafly. They thought that, at a minimum, she was a hypocrite. How could a woman, they said, be so dedicated to public life, so outspoken in her opinions, so energetic in her political organizing, book writing, and speech giving and yet reject the feminist cause that stood above all for making sure every woman had the opportunity to participate fully, fairly, and equally in all aspects of American life? What these feminist critics did not understand was that Schlafly never thought of herself as an exemplar of women's absolute right to seek self-fulfillment and equality in American society. She saw herself as a follower of a very different kind of American tradition. In Schlafly's 1952 congressional race—and thereafter—she drew on the venerable and respected American tradition of "republican motherhood."

Dating back to the nation's founding, a variety of women (and men, too) have argued that women are by nature and social position more capable of protecting the nation's virtue than are men. Politically driven men, the argument goes, are motivated by personal ambition for high office and the need of economic advancement in a competitive marketplace to be fierce partisans; their goal, too often, is naked or cloaked self-interest. The Constitution, with its relentless attention to governmental checks and balances, was in part structured by the Founders in accord with this premise. Because, the argument continues, women are different by nature (less ambitious and selfish, more nurturing and altruistic), and because women have for religious and cultural reasons been long excluded from so many individualistic endeavors, instead earning their socially respected and religiously inspired place in life through the caring for others (children, husband, and elderly parents), they have traditionally been shielded from the corrupting hunt for personal power and gain. One of nineteenth-century America's best-known female public figures, Catherine Beecher, was so fixed on the vital role women needed to play in bringing virtue to the American citizenry that she fought the effort to allow women to vote in the United States. In a famous and widely reprinted 1871 speech, "Address to the Christian Women of America," she warned that allowing women to participate in the hurly-burly world of partisan politics would only harm the nation. Once women could vote and participate fully in the pitched battles of party politics, she feared, they would lose their special role as selfless nurturers; their ability to speak disinterestedly in behalf of the nation's virtue would be lost in the swamp of special-interest pleading and self-interest.[5] Whatever the merits of this claim, women deployed it in the service of various political purposes, ranging from Beecher's antisuffrage stance to Jane Addams's Progressive Era argument that women's selfless virtue made them natural urban reformers.

Schlafly was an heir to this flexible, gendered political tradition, which until at least the 1960s was not seen by most Americans as particularly liberal or conservative. Even after the advent of the women's movement, a small number of women on the Left argued that women had a different, more nurturing, less belligerent nature than men and that it was this special nature—not their individual ability and character—that made women valuable political activists. Like most everything Schlafly did, she used this gendered tradition extraordinarily well. Even so, claiming that her special role as nurturing woman gave her a vital understanding of the nation's political problems carried with it risks. Especially on the Right, many men, and some women, too, were dismissive of the claims that women had a legitimate role to play in national public life, even the somewhat self-abnegating role of "republican mother." During the long years of the Roosevelt era, for example, a number of the more vituperative members of the "Old Right" had tremendous fun viciously mocking First Lady Eleanor Roosevelt for her energetic efforts to look after the less fortunate among the American people. The anticommunist, anti–New Dealer Gerald Smith was among the wittiest of her many hecklers. His parody of Edgar Allan Poe's "The Raven," attacked Mrs. Roosevelt for "Never sitting, never quitting, [n]ever knitting." Along the same lines, an exacerbated Smith accused President Roosevelt of being less than a man for his inability to make his wife "stay home at least one-half of the time."[6] Schlafly faced some of this sexist vitriol, as well, and by no means just from fellow conservatives.

Both her Republican primary challenger and her eventual Democratic opponent tried to use her sex against her. Schlafly shrugged off the attacks from her Republican primary adversary, winning her party's nomination but losing in the general election to her Democratic rival. She, at least, believed that her sex had nothing to do with the outcome, arguing that she may have lost some votes as a woman but that she probably picked up a few, as well; she lost, she said reasonably enough, because her district leaned heavily Democratic. Still, gender issues always surrounded Schlafly, and she knew it. She was not blind to or always accepting of the restrictions gendered conventions and men's actions placed on her. But rather than struggle for a society in which women were freed from binding restraints, she took her new political experiences and ever-improving communication skills and

threw herself into a fight for the values she believed were most important to the nation: a morally sound and religiously strong society. In
the 1950s and 1960s, she believed that anticommunism was the cause
that spoke most directly to that fight.

In the fight against communism, Schlafly was politically active
throughout the 1950s and 1960s both in women-only organizations,
especially the National Federation of Republican Women and the
Daughters of the American Revolution, and in work that seemingly
took her well outside of traditional female activities. She walked a
thin line between a protofeminist engagement with the public world
on egalitarian terms and a traditionalist understanding of women's
roles. Schlafly's many anticommunist activities gave her good opportunity to manage this balancing act.

Not unlike the morally charged abolitionist struggle of the nineteenth century and the prohibition cause of the early twentieth, the
right-wing anticommunist movement provided ample room for
women to participate in accord with traditional gender roles. Historian Michelle Nickerson argues that while men dominated the leadership ranks of the cause, women filled the grassroots, activist base.
These women worried about Soviet foreign policy, but they acted
much more directly to stop what they perceived to be domestic communist subversion. Lucille Cardin Crain, for example, published the
Educational Reviewer, a quarterly bulletin that warned concerned
readers about a multitude of school textbooks that she believed to
be communistic. PTA meetings in conservative bastions such as
Southern California were filled with "citizen-housewives" who came
together to hear speakers (usually men) warn about such dangers as
"How the Communist Menace Influences the Minds and Thinking of
Our Youth." These wives and mothers dedicated themselves to ridding
their children's schools of teachers they perceived to be communists
and of the kind of textbooks about which Crain had warned them.[7]

Phyllis Schlafly shared in these concerns about the Red infiltration of schools, libraries, and anywhere else vulnerable minds were at
risk. She, like many other women active in the school textbook fights,
ardently believed (as did William Buckley) that neither education nor
civil society, in general, were places where Americans, especially the

young, should work out their own views through an exposure to wide-open debate. Schools, in particular, should be places where young people were educated to be patriotic citizens. In a speech to the DAR, she stated her position in characteristically blunt fashion: "It is part of the Communist strategy . . . to destroy the feeling of pride we have when we see the Stars and Stripes unfurled. . . . In order to save our religion, our freedom, and our Constitution, we need the alertness of vigilantes, the fidelity of 100 percent Americans, the spirit of the flag-waver, the fervor of the nationalists, and the courage of our super-patriots."[8] Throughout the 1950s, Schlafly worked hard locally to warn people about the threat of communist subversion, collaborating with numerous Catholic and civic groups to spread information about the threat and to sponsor anticommunist speakers. Her concerns, however, were always about both the threat of domestic subversion and the danger—imminent, apocalyptic danger, she believed—of Soviet attack.

In 1958, Schlafly partnered with her husband and her husband's sister to join her religious faith to the anticommunist cause. They formed a national Catholic organization, the Mindszenty Foundation, dedicated to fighting communism. Named after a Catholic cardinal who had been imprisoned in brutal conditions in Hungary, the foundation had two, interconnected goals: to inform Catholics of the persecution of their coreligionists in communist-governed nations and to alert them to the threat communism posed to them within the United States. Members of the advisory board, as well as a cofounder of the group, Father C. Stephen Dunker, were all Catholic clerics who had personally suffered at the hands of Chinese, Soviet, or east European communist dictatorships before making their way to safety in the United States.

Many of these clerics took a strong line not only against the ongoing religious persecution in communist nations but at any hint of perceived communist subversion within the United States. Given their own experiences at the hands of the communists, these were not men given to couching their anticommunism in a carefully discriminating fashion. They were perfect allies for Schlafly's crusade. For example, advisory board member Most Reverend Cuthbert M. O'Gara made his anticommunist reputation in the late 1950s by accusing the American Catholic Church of allowing communists to subvert Catholic schools. After this charge was politely dismissed in a private letter to O'Gara by the leadership of the National Catholic Educational Association, O'Gara blasted back, "I am amazed that your letter is such a complete admission of your ignorance of what is actually going on in educational circles." He then attacked the anticommunist credentials of the NCEA official and insisted that every single Catholic college should be investigated for Red infiltration; every professor and every relevant assigned book should be examined, and parents of every student should be offered the opportunity to challenge the dedication of every school's anticommunist efforts. Men such as O'Gara made the foundation controversial within the American Catholic Church (so much so that cofounder Father Dunker was forced to leave the foundation by his Church superiors). Nonetheless, the foundation had chapters all over the United States and regularly sponsored anticommunist events that drew thousands of spectators, making it a major force on the Catholic anticommunist Right and a contributor to the larger anticommunist conservative movement.

Schlafly played a major role in the foundation's efforts. She oversaw its very successful education programs and continuously warned followers through its publications to beware of communist influences in television, the movies, and public institutions. The Cardinal Mindszenty Foundation, at both the national and chapter level, proudly followed the broad-brush style of anticommunist attack made famous by Senator Joe McCarthy and vigorously defended by William Buckley.[9]

During the late 1950s and early 1960s, anticommunist work, often through the foundation, took up much of Schlafly's nonfamily time, even as she remained a vital actor in local civic and Republican Party affairs. She wrote, researched, worked the phones, and gave speeches locally, honing her organizational and communication skills, while she also baked her own bread, cooked meals, shopped, breastfed each of her babies, and kept a careful eye on her children's education and social life. Friends and family were in awe: "You'd call Phyllis and while she was on the telephone talking to you, she'd be typing and there would be a gurgling, cooing sound from one baby on her

lap, and the noises of two of three others close by playing games."
Another noted: "She's able to shut out everything else. . . . Very few
women are. If the kids are running around and spilling the jam and
cocoa, you feel that you have to go and see what is going. She is totally
able to let them go on with the jam and the cocoa and not get up."
Then, too, at the Schlafly household the children were expected to do
their part, which included not spilling the jam and cocoa while their
mother was busy. A onetime summer helper with the children was a
bit more ambivalent about the situation. Recalling the emphasis on
punctuality, proper dress, carefully maintained and kept schedules,
and the general importance of discipline and order, she characterized the household as "old-fashioned, sort of like I imagine it was in
Victorian England." Schlafly would probably have been pleased with
that description.[10]

Not surprisingly, both Phyllis and Fred Schlafly were early supporters of Senator Barry Goldwater. Fred Schlafly was good friends
with fellow Catholic lawyer Clarence Manion, who had led the Goldwater boomlet in 1960; at Manion's urging, both had joined the Draft
Goldwater Committee.[11] Phyllis Schlafly was a powerful advocate for
Goldwater in the Illinois Federation of Republican Women, which
she headed in 1960. At the 1960 Republican convention, she invited
Goldwater to speak at the Illinois Federation luncheon, where she
introduced him as a "living lesson in the virtue of standing firm on
principle, even if you are a minority of one."[12]

Between the 1960 and 1964 presidential elections, Schlafly kept to
her busy schedule fighting communism and raising her family. She
was particularly successful in her leadership of the IFRW, where she
brought in thousands of new members, in part, by warning them that
subversive forces planned to destroy the moral and spiritual fabric of
American society. The federation, she wrote in late 1962, stood at the
ramparts defending America's four most vital freedoms: "Freedom
to Keep our Religious Heritage, Freedom from Obscenity, Freedom
from Criminal Attack, and Freedom from Communist Conspiracy."[13]
Schlafly, like many of her less articulate conservative women allies,
was incensed that the Supreme Court, led by the modern Republican
Chief Justice Earl Warren, had recently issued rulings banning prayer

in public schools and limiting the government's right to censor sexually explicit materials such as books and movies.

During the early 1960s, the civil rights movement captured the moral imagination and political heart of many Americans who believed that the struggle against racial disenfranchisement, legally mandated segregation, and endemic discrimination was the central battle for freedom and equality of their time. Schlafly was indifferent or opposed to all aspects of that cause, which she perceived to be divisive, disorderly, and socialistic if not completely communistic. She believed far greater issues were at stake in the United States: left-wingers meant to destroy Americans' moral fiber and leave them defenseless against a growing communist peril. Throughout Illinois, white women responded to her call to defend their America against the darkening tide of secularism, communism, criminality, and moral relativism.

As the 1964 election drew closer, Schlafly began focusing more on Goldwater's nomination. In June 1963, she made her first major appearance in the national mass media, blasting the liberal New York governor and presidential hopeful, Nelson Rockefeller, on moral grounds in *Time* magazine: "I've been taking a private poll of Republican women I meet all over [Illinois], and their reaction is nearly unanimous—they're disgusted with Rockefeller. . . . The party is not so hard up that it can't find somebody who stuck by his own family."[14] Schlafly announced her support for Goldwater immediately after he wrote to her and other activist supporters declaring his candidacy; she put herself forward as a GOP convention delegate. In early 1964, while pregnant, she decided she could best help Goldwater by writing a book attacking the Rockefeller wing of the Republican Party, which she and fellow conservatives feared would find a way to steal the nomination from Goldwater. She memorably titled the book *A Choice Not an Echo*.

Schlafly banged out the short book in a few weeks' time. Her theme was unrelentingly pounded home in chapter after chapter: East Coast internationalist moneyed elites, since 1936, had stolen the Republican presidential nomination from the conservative rank and file who made up the Republican Party. Robert Taft, in 1952, had been the most egregious victim of this carefully engineered theft. "The kingmakers," as Schlafly deftly labeled the conspirators, were far more dedicated to furthering their own international economic interests than they were in protecting the American people from Soviet communism. She named names, including Morgan banker Thomas Lamont; Governor Nelson Rockefeller's banker brother, David Rockefeller; and GM president Alfred Sloan (an odd choice, given that he strongly supported Robert Taft in 1952!). "A small group of secret kingmakers," she revealed, "using hidden persuaders and psychological warfare techniques manipulated the Republican National Convention to nominate candidates who would sidestep and suppress the key issues."[15] The kingmakers' tricks included use of Gallup polls, which rely on numbers "so few that the exact number is a dark secret which Gallup will not reveal."[16] Her tone throughout was not meant to calm the soul.

In an over-the-top touch consistent with the conspiracy theory–mongering of the John Birch Society and allied organizations, Schlafly devoted a chapter to a kind of parallel and/or overlapping set of kingmakers, the "Bilderberg group." These well-connected, rich and powerful men from North America and Europe, she suggested, conspired (successfully?) to control the world's political economy, as well as America's destiny. If that there were not enough, Schlafly also revealed, in a pitch-perfect, antielitist note, that they swilled "wines imported directly from France."[17]

The Bilderbergers did exist. Starting in 1954 and continuing for many years thereafter, a high-powered and well-connected group of North American and European academics, diplomats, journalists, and businessmen met annually—and privately—to discuss world affairs and improve relations between their allied nations. But as Schlafly knew, they were hardly secret puppet masters controlling the fate of the free world. Schlafly, somewhat cynically, threw in the Bilderberg connection to give her readers some red meat to chew on. She admitted as much to a friend: "This is the sort of thing that our people lap up and love."[18] Regardless of the conspiracy theory fillip, factual errors, and inflated language, enough truth resided in her larger point—at least since the mid 1930s, East Coast wealthy internationalists played a major role in selecting GOP presidential candidates—to keep the book in the land of the politically rational (or as

Schlafly titled one chapter, "Who's Looney Now?"). And she certainly was right that Governor Nelson Rockefeller and a host of other East Coast–based Republican liberals and moderates were desperate to stop the nomination of cowboy conservative Barry Goldwater.

Schlafly, in accord with the grassroots style of the conservative anticommunist movement, self-published the book and marketed it herself to fellow activists. Like Goldwater's *Conscience of a Conservative*, it was eagerly embraced by conservatives all over the country. The kingmaker theme, as was her main purpose, helped fire-up grassroots conservatives against East Coast super-moneybags Nelson Rockefeller. Schlafly also inspired Goldwater supporters with a populist defense of his intellectual gifts. Rather than fight liberals' claim that Goldwater was too simple-minded to become president of the United States, Schlafly embraced the critique and turned it against Goldwater's enemies, calling them a bunch of elitist "eggheads" too smart for their own good—or for the country's. Sure, she said, Goldwater saw things in a simple, straightforward, commonsense way. That was a good thing. "Egghead reasoning," she wrote, claims that the president "must have sophisticated—not simple solutions. Contrary to this argument, civilization progresses, freedom is won and problems are solved because we have wonderful people who think up simple solutions!"[19] Often marketed in bulk numbers to activist groups around the country, particularly in hotly contested California, *A Choice Not an Echo* sold an astonishing 3.5 million copies in 1964. According to one survey, 93 percent of convention delegates said they had read Schlafly's book, and 26 percent said that it had led them to support Goldwater.[20]

The book, with its front cover photo of the attractive author in her characteristic pearl necklace, made Schlafly a celebrity among conservatives. She was in great demand as a speaker and was feted at the convention. She starred, as noted, in a televised testimonial for Goldwater; "These are the six reasons I am voting for Barry Goldwater," she began after viewers had seen her children playing with their father. Schlafly was a television natural. Between the convention and the election, Schlafly pushed hard on the anticommunist front by coauthoring a book with retired navy Admiral Chester Ward, called *The Gravediggers*. She self-published the book and used the same cover design that had worked so well for *A Choice Not an Echo*—a simple title above the now well-known photo of a smiling, pearl-necklaced Mrs. Schlafly. *The Gravediggers* argued that liberal President Lyndon Johnson and his kind were laying the groundwork for a Soviet military defeat of the United States. "American gravediggers," she reported, "are not communists. They are card-carrying liberals. They will not commit the crime. They will merely dig the grave."[21] The Soviets, she explained, supplied these liberals with "made-in-Moscow slogans" aimed at sapping Americans' ability to maintain the massive "fire-power" needed to stop a Soviet attack on the United States. "Slogans are Communists' best gimmick," she explained; they "are injected into our communication system by Soviet agents and their dupes to poison our pipelines of information."[22] President Johnson, though no communist, played a key role in this pipeline poisoning, while Barry Goldwater, "the irreplaceable man," was all that stood between the Soviets and "the lives of your children."[23] Schlafly sold some two million copies of the book.[24]

Schlafly seemed on her way to national prominence as a Republican Party star and conservative spokeswoman on the communist threat. She had been elected first vice president of the National Federation of Republican Women, with its half million members, shortly before the presidential election, and she expected to be elevated automatically—as had been the rule for several years—to the presidency of the organization when the sitting president left office in 1966. But Goldwater's crushing defeat put all party conservatives on the defensive, and Republican moderates and liberals did their best to take back the GOP from the Goldwater crowd. Their success was limited, but they did take down Phyllis Schlafly.

Schlafly faced opposition within the Republican Party not from the "kingmakers" she described so vividly in *A Choice Not an Echo* but from pragmatists who believed that the GOP risked becoming a permanent minority party if it did not move away from the Right and back to the Eisenhower-like middle-of-the road. These pragmatic party stalwarts were joined by the diminishing number of GOP liberals who felt vindicated by the margin of Goldwater's defeat. A group of these Republican liberals, who had banded together in 1962 to form the Ripon Society, even hoped that Goldwater's defeat would mean their revival. They argued that the GOP, as represented by Abraham Lincoln and Theodore Roosevelt, was and should continue to be America's progressive party; its future lay not with southern reactionaries but with "the new middle classes of the suburbs of the North and West . . . the young college graduates and professional men and women of our great university centers—more concerned with 'opportunity' than 'security.'"[25] (This provocative idea, an updated Taftian economic conservatism joined to social progressivism went nowhere at the time but would be reinvented by a later generation of Republican activists—conservatives—in the early 1990s.) In 1965, the pragmatists, with the liberals' support, deposed Goldwater's Republican National Committee chairman and replaced him with one of their own. But the general party mood was not fratricidal. Most Republicans (with the exception of a good many of the liberal faction) simply felt that the party had gotten a bit too wild and that it was time to swallow a few aspirins and get back to the business of winning elections. Unity, not more ideological battling, they believed, was the best anodyne. The tried-and-true scrapper Richard Nixon would be the immediate beneficiary of this party-building campaign.

Mrs. Schlafly failed to fit in with this unity campaign. She was perceived by many of the modern Republicans and all of the liberals as an uncompromising champion of the divisive conservative diehards or as one of Schlafly's key opponents in the NFRW put it, "the nut fringe."[26] During the Republican convention back in July 1964, Schlafly had publicly accused "anti-Goldwater" Republicans of working "to break up the party and support Lyndon Johnson in the fall election." In a published interview, she told the Young Republicans of California that these apostates were "small in number and will not be any great loss."[27] While Barry Goldwater himself had expressed similar sentiments, in the postelection hangover era Schlafly's outspoken comments made her a target of the party unifiers. Instead of ascending automatically into the presidency of the NFRW, Schlafly found herself in a political war.

She lost that war, which dragged on through 1966 and into the spring of 1967. The battle was covered by the national mass media, which treated the contest as a major marker in the Republicans' post-Goldwater direction. The *New York Times* titled its first of several articles "GOP Women Face Right-Wing Test: Meet This Week to Elect a New Head in Bitter Fight." *Time* magazine, in the sort of sexism that was typical of the era, recognized the ideological stakes but treated the contest as a cat fight: "There was none of that man-to-man, shake-hands-and-come-out-fighting spirit that marks male contests for power. But then, the two contenders for the presidency of the National Federation of Republican Women were, naturally, women, and in politics the dame game is not the same as the masculine variety. Nor is it very ladylike." According to the *Times*, Schlafly blamed "New York liberals" for the fight; one of her followers, quoted in *Time* magazine, was less polite, pointing her finger at "the liberal rats." Schlafly's opponent, a Californian businesswoman and pioneering aviatrix, simply accused Schlafly of being too divisive a figure to lead the NFRW. Demonstrating the tangled gender politics of the time, the *anti*-Schlafly faction cited in the magazine story also argued that "any responsible mother with all those children ought to be home with her family."[28] Schlafly countered, "It is high time that the Federation has a president who is a wife and mother."[29] The vote in spring 1967 was close—much closer than the GOP middle-of-the roaders had expected—but Schlafly was deposed. The mass media, Republican stalwarts, and political observers of all stripes saw Schlafly's loss as more evidence that the conservative movement had been dealt a death blow by the Goldwater defeat.

Schlafly interpreted events differently. She did accuse liberals of having stolen the election from her, and like everyone else she recognized that Goldwater's supporters in the Republican Party were under siege. But to Schlafly, that was not the worst part of it. She had been purged, she wrote soon after the election, because she was a conservative woman who lived a traditional life based on family values. All women, she wrote in her usual blunt style and referring to herself in the third person, were treated with contempt by the party's male leaders: "Many men in the Party frankly want to keep women doing the menial work, while the selection of candidates and the policy decisions are taken care of by the men in the smoke-filled rooms. . . . In Phyllis, they recognized one who could not be neutralized or silenced." But Schlafly was not making an impassioned call for some sort of gender-free equality in politics. Her concern was less about equality in the abstract and more about ideology in particular. The party, she argued, was making a bad mistake in continuing to reward professional women without traditional family ties and responsibilities, such as her victorious opponent, with leadership of the National Federation of Republican Women. The party was telling "mothers of young children" that "they could be peons in the precincts but were barred from the highest office in the Federation." Schlafly was doing more than standing up for all women in politics, she was speaking directly to her belief that "the values of ordinary American women" were being ignored or worse, by the male politicians who ruled both political parties.[30] In making this claim, Schlafly began to stake out a new political territory and to organize like-minded traditional, religious, conservative women.

By the end of 1967, when Schlafly published her accusations about how and why the Republican Party purged her from its leadership, American society was in the midst of a rights revolution that was fast changing the legal, political, and cultural status of women. The kind of professional, working women that Schlafly had enjoined the Republican Party from rewarding had successfully allied with proponents of equal rights for African Americans and other racial minorities to ensure that the 1964 Civil Rights Act—the act that Barry Goldwater had opposed—also made employment discrimination against women illegal. Then, to push the reluctant federal government to enforce this provision, liberal feminists had formed the National Organization of Women in 1966. By the late 1960s, inspired by the civil rights movement in particular, but also by the massive movement for social change that was drawing millions of Americans to protest against the Vietnam War and for a more equitable and democratic nation, young and not-so-young women had formed a boisterous, multifaceted women's liberation movement. Though Phyllis Schlafly paid little attention to this development at first, by the early 1970s, fighting it became central to her life and her conservative politics.

Feminism was hardly a new cause, though few Americans in the late 1960s or later knew it. In the United States women's right activists had fought for political and legal equality since the early nineteenth century. Several generations of women had struggled for the right to vote, to hold public office, to serve on juries, and to control their own property. Success was recent; women's federal voting rights were scarcely half a century old. Only in 1920, with suffragists having worked both sides of the political aisle, was a women's right to vote guaranteed by passage of the Nineteenth Amendment to the Constitution (not coincidentally, feminists also succeeded in pushing through similar measures in the same time period in several other nations, including Australia, England, New Zealand, Germany, Holland and the brand new, one-party Soviet Union). These were not politically partisan battles, although Republicans were generally more sympathetic to women's rights. Almost immediately after passage of the Nineteenth Amendment, some American feminists began working to pass a women's equal rights amendment, aimed primarily at employment discrimination.

Women activists, however, divided over the proposed Constitutional amendment. Many progressive women, dedicated to preserving hard-won protective legislation aimed at safeguarding women (but not men) from dangerous and onerous workplace conditions, opposed the ERA. They feared that working-class women would lose more than they would gain from it. A great many professional women disagreed. They argued that protective legislation only contributed to men's claims that women were not capable of working like men; it allowed such men to argue that the widespread and legal exclusion of women from the vast majority of well-paid, high-status jobs—or even decently paid, middling-status jobs—was justified and natural. Given this sort of class politics, it was not surprising that the Republican Party in 1940, generally opposed to paternalistically safeguarding any worker's right to special protections, formally supported the ERA in its party platform and that Senator Taft was among the GOP supporters. In the 1950s, President Eisenhower reiterated GOP support for the ERA. While the Democratic Party had also come to support the ERA, despite opposition from its labor union bloc, the debate within the ranks of women activists over the issue of special rights versus equal rights for women had not been completely resolved in the early 1960s. However, by the mid-1960s modern feminists, with little stake in the old debate about the special needs of women industrial workers, had overwhelmingly decided that the loss of some protective legislation that favored women was worth the price if it meant that women would gain a legal guarantee of full equality in all aspects of American life.

While a general notion of gender equality unified most feminists, by the early 1970s much divided and factionalized the women's liberation movement. Feminists had no party line on the roles that capitalism, religion, sexuality, and family life played in oppressing or liberating women. By 1970, a time when the nation was divided by the Vietnam War, racial justice issues, and the counterculture, groups of liberal feminists clashed with factions of radical feminists who were challenged by divergent feminists of color who debated a mixed bag of feminist separatists. What gender equality could and should mean in the United States, what it was to be a "liberated" women in America and the modern world, was not something that feminists, as a whole, could agree on. Still, most feminists concurred on a few general principles.

Betty Friedan laid out some of those principles in her 1963 bestselling book, *The Feminine Mystique*, which would sell more than three million copies. Friedan argued that women needed more than a pleasant home with husband and children to find satisfaction in their lives and to contribute to their society. In white-hot prose she damned American society for instilling in women the belief that only "neurotic, unfeminine, unhappy women . . . wanted to be poets or physicists or presidents" and that "truly feminine women do not want careers, higher education, political rights." She continued, "The feminine mystique has succeeded in burying millions of American women alive. There is no way for these women to break out of their comfortable concentration camps except by finally putting forth an effort—that human effort which reaches beyond biology, beyond the narrow walls of home, to help shape the future." Women, wrote Freidan, should be valued and should value themselves for more than their ability to have and nurture children and to attract and keep a man; "to break out of the housewife trap and truly find fulfillment as wives and mothers," she insisted, American women had to fulfill "their own unique possibilities as separate human beings."[31] While some more radical feminists would find Friedan too accommodating to the traditional female roles of wife and mother, and though *The Feminine Mystique* was clearly oblivious to the different travails women of color and poor women faced in the United States, Friedan's book and subsequent speeches, writings, and political organizing did much to launch, legitimate, and provide intellectual foundations for the women's movement that grew in numbers and influence throughout the 1960s and 1970s.

As Friedan's polemic indicates, women's demands for change could not be satisfied by policy changes alone. Feminists wanted women and men alike to recognize the cultural, as well as the social and economic, oppression of women. Protesters attempted to "raise" people's consciousness by demonstrating how often a woman's value in America was reduced to her physical attractiveness and her marital status. At the 1968 Miss America pageant, women's liberation protesters set up a "freedom trash can" into which they threw instruments of oppression: false eyelashes, girdles, wigs, and cosmetics. Others protested at bridal fairs, mocking the enormous expense of weddings and the marketers who promoted the wedding day as a woman's greatest accomplishment. Their signs read, "Always a Bride, Never a Person." These women, in accord with the simultaneous radicalization of the racial justice movement, New Left, and antiwar cause, were often deliberately vulgar and mean-spirited in an attempt to shock people into new ways of thinking. Some mocked brides, singing, "Here Comes the Slave, Off to her Grave." And some showed contempt for the domestic activities of millions of women (though few understood their claims that way) by waving placards that read, "Fuck Housework." These efforts did provoke thought, though not all of it was favorable to the cause.[32]

Feminists also produced an avalanche of books and articles, and in 1971 a leading group of women's liberation advocates that included Gloria Steinem launched a mass market magazine, *Ms.* These publications asked women to ponder how and why women had been made to subordinate their hopes, their desires (including their sexual ones), their careers, their education, their health, and their happiness to men.

And they asked why society did so little, if anything, to prevent men from harassing them, mocking them, beating them, and raping them. In the early 1970s, these feminists confronted a legal system that rarely prosecuted rapes or wife beating; a business world that almost never punished men who demanded that their female subordinates provide them with sexual favors; a religious establishment that asked for women's faith but forbade them from being rabbis, priests, or ministers; and, in general, a society that denigrated ambitious, independent, and intelligent women. To explain this world, feminists invented a new word: *sexism*. Like contemporary racial justice activists, many advocates of the women's liberation movement were angry, serious, and uncompromising in their demands for fundamental change.

In the early 1970s, the Equal Rights Amendment for women was seen as thin gruel by the more radical members of the women's liberation movement, but nearly all feminists supported it. So, too, did an overwhelming majority of Congress. After a decade of monumental civil rights legislation aimed primarily at guaranteeing equality for African Americans, almost all congressmen saw a vote for the ERA as a no-brainer. The key passage of the ERA simply stated: "Equality of rights under the law shall not be denied or abridged by the United States or by any State on account of sex."[33] In June 1970, after almost no deliberation, the House voted 350 to 15 in favor of the ERA. In the Senate, events unfolded more slowly, and some vocal opposition was raised; still, the ERA passed on a vote of 84 to 8. Literally within minutes, the Hawaii state legislature passed the amendment, as well, and an avalanche of other state legislatures rushed to join the ratification process.

Enter Mrs. Schlafly. Between House and Senate passage of the ERA, Schlafly denounced the proposed Constitutional amendment. Her megaphone was the monthly newsletter she had begun as a way to communicate with the three thousand women who had stood with her in her run for the presidency of the National Federation of Republican Women in 1967. "What's Wrong with 'Equal Rights' for Women?" she asked in her February 1972 newsletter. Up until that time, Schlafly had largely ignored the booming women's movement. She had been politically active, even running again (and losing) for

Congress in 1970, but her focus had not shifted from that of her Goldwater days. Communism, especially the threat of Soviet attack, had remained her fundamental cause, and she feared that President Nixon (whom she had supported) was turning out to be no better than his liberal Democratic predecessors when it came to standing up to the enemy. Still, amid the social chaos of the late sixties and early seventies, generated, to her mind, by the combined forces of a countercultural Left, Schlafly recognized that the religious, culturally sound America in which she believed was under an extraordinary attack. She chose to enter the fray, picking a target that suited her longtime commitment to American family life as she envisioned it. She never intended to make the ERA and the women's movement her primary focus.

In making her attack on the ERA and feminism, Schlafly turned the logic of the women's movement completely on its head. Betty Friedan, the National Organization of Women, and more radical feminists argued that women faced economic discrimination, legal inequities, restrictive gender roles, and a culture that subordinated women to men. They contended that American women faced lives of diminished opportunities and systemic disempowerment. A society based on ideals of liberty, freedom, and equality for all must end not only racism but sexism. Schlafly mocked the very idea, insisting instead that "of all the classes of people who ever lived, the American woman is the most privileged."

Feminists, Schlafly claimed, missed the whole point of what it was to be a woman. "Women have babies and men don't," she pointed out, and as a result society is organized to protect women so that they may properly raise those children. Some societies may not be so organized, but that is surely not to their credit. "We have the immense good fortune to live in a civilization which respects the family as the basic unit of society," she observed. "Our Judeo-Christian civilization has developed the law and custom that, since women must bear the physical consequences of the sex act, men must be required to bear the other consequences and pay in other ways. . . . [A] man must carry his share by physical protection and financial support of his children and of the woman who bears his children." This complementary relationship between men and women guaranteed social stability and provided a moral framework for family life.

Schlafly continued in this vein for several paragraphs. She insisted that while men might find achievement through their work, often taking "30 to 40 years for accomplishment," women were far luckier: "A woman can enjoy real achievement when she is young—by having a baby." She dismissed feminists' constant complaints about violence against women by looking instead at the socially embedded cultural traditions that led men not to beat women but to protect them: women "are the beneficiaries of a tradition of special respect . . . which dates from the Christian Age of Chivalry. The honor and respect paid to Mary, the Mother of Christ, resulted in all women, in effect, being put on a pedestal." "The traditions of chivalry" she noted, meant that men not only defended women but were willing to work long hours to buy their brides diamond rings and then their wives "a fur piece or other finery." In a Taftian move, Schlafly further argued that women in America are the "most privileged" because of the genius of free enterprise, which has produced numerous labor-saving devices that have turned the drudgery of housework into a breeze: "The great heroes of women's liberation are not the straggly-haired women on television talk shows and picket lines but Thomas Edison who brought the miracle of electricity to our homes . . . or Elias Howe who gave us the sewing machine." Schlafly and her feminist foes were not seeing the same world. Schlafly did not mince words: "The claim that American women are downtrodden and unfairly treated is the fraud of the century. The truth is that American women never had it so good. Why should we lower ourselves to 'equal rights' when we already have the status of special privilege?"

Schlafly was not blind to the discrimination women faced in the workplace and elsewhere in society. Just as Robert Taft and Barry Goldwater had noted that African Americans faced racial discrimination, Schlafly knew quite well that women and men were not given the same educational and employment opportunities. She even seemed to go further than Taft and Goldwater when she wrote that she supported "necessary legislation" to stop such discrimination (although she did not in her essay or later writings explain what kind of legislation she meant and she never supported antidiscrimination legislation of any description). But as Schlafly saw it, discrimination was really beside the point. Feminists who demanded the ERA, Schlafly told her readers, were not really interested in fighting discrimination, either: "[T]his is only the sweet syrup which covers the deadly poison masquerading as 'women's lib.' The women libbers are radicals who are waging a total assault on the family, on marriage, and on children. . . . Women's lib is a total assault on the role of the American woman as wife and mother, and on the family as the basic unit of society." The ERA, Schlafly concluded, was the means by which feminists intended to destroy America.

Supporters of the ERA, Schlafly asserted, wanted to outlaw traditional American women who took pride in being feminine and who devoted themselves to their families. She offered three examples. First, she argued, the ERA would make women equally subject to be drafted into the military (she was writing at a time when the draft was still in effect and the war in Vietnam was still raging). Second, the ERA would end women's right to financial support from their husbands, making it possible for a husband to demand that his wife go to work. Third, it would end women's near-automatic right to custody of their children in the event of a divorce. The ERA, in other words, would cost women far more than they would gain. "The women-libbers," Schlafly wrote, "don't understand that most women want to be wife, mother and homemaker—and are happy in that role. . . . We do not want to trade our birthright of the special privileges of American women—for the mess of pottage called the Equal Rights Amendment." She finished with a call to arms: "Tell your Senators NOW that you want them to vote NO on the Equal Rights Amendment. Tell your television and radio stations that you want equal time to present the case FOR marriage and motherhood."[34]

Schlafly sent out the newsletter with no particular expectations. A month later, one of her supporters phoned her with extraordinary news: her article had been circulated among Oklahoma state legislators as they prepared to vote on the ERA. Bolstered by Schlafly's argument, the legislators had voted against ratification.[35] Schlafly wasted no time. She began to organize, first contacting her supporters from the NFRW. Quickly, however, many more women who had never before been involved in politics flocked to the cause. Overwhelmingly, they were religious women, mostly evangelical Christians, but Catholics and Mormons as well. Schlafly had tapped a new constituency for the conservative cause.

In October 1972, she launched a new organization: STOP ERA (Stop Taking Our Privileges). By early 1973, the organization was national. Phyllis Schlafly and the conservative women who believed in her had found their new political battleground. They would be joined in their fight by men and women, most of them deeply religious, who feared that the ERA would destroy traditional gender roles. They linked the fight against the ERA to related issues, most important the battle over abortion rights and the status of homosexuals. A new kind of conservative coalition was lining up against the supporters of gay and women's liberation. Americans were dividing themselves into two camps over issues of sexuality and gender, and conservative politicians liked their chances in this new political war.

Schlafly had important allies in her fight, men and women who would help redefine conservatism in the 1970s. Among the most prominent and useful was North Carolina Senator Sam Ervin who led the fight against the ERA in Congress. Ervin was a Democrat, part of that last generation of southerners who had come to political maturity at a time when the Republican Party in his home state stood for Abraham Lincoln and not Barry Goldwater. For some twenty years, Ervin had been best known for his fulminations against any and every form of civil rights legislation. In his first term as senator he had proudly coauthored the "Southern Manifesto" that had castigated the Supreme Court for ending mandatory segregation of the races in public schools. The nonviolent campaigns against racial discrimination in the early 1960s only inflamed his disgust for what he called the "snivel rights" movement. He blasted the 1964 Civil Rights Act, insisting that "[n]o men of any race can law or legislate their way either to economic or social equality in a free society," and he called the 1965 Voting Rights Act "an insulting and insupportable indictment of a whole [white] people." "Equality," he insisted, could not be bought at the cost of "the freedom of the individual." Senator Ervin, like Barry Goldwater, genuinely believed that individual liberties, and not a zealous pursuit of equality, were the wellspring of American justice. He would, in fact, win praise in the 1970s from the American Civil Liberties Union and Common Cause—organizations usually associated with the Left and not the Right—for his unbending commitment to protecting individuals' rights from coercive government power. His principled stance became evident to the nation when he helped lead the effort to hold President Richard Nixon accountable for his "Watergate" misdeeds. But Ervin was dedicated to more than a simple weighing of individual liberties and equal rights. He was a proud traditionalist who believed in the racial hierarchies in which he had been raised and that had been passed along generationally among whites in his community.

Given that disposition toward racial hierarchy, Ervin, not surprisingly, was flabbergasted by feminists' demands that women should be given the same rights, responsibilities, and opportunities as men. Men and women, he orated, are fundamentally different, and those differences should be and must be reflected in the laws of the land, just as they are expressed in custom and tradition. Men, he believed, had their superior qualities, such as greater strength, which made them natural protectors of women. But women too had special faculties. Like Schlafly, and like so many women reformers of the nineteenth century, Ervin insisted that women, because of their sex, their role as mothers, and their natural inclination to be helpmates to their husbands, had the ability to bring moral order to the fierce and competitive world that men made. Women, unlike men, he stated, could readily distinguish between "wisdom and folly, good and evil." Ervin acted on this belief; he was one of the few members of Congress to hire women to work on his professional staff. The senator was not an easy man to pigeonhole. Still, as Donald Mathews and Jane Sherron De Hart, historians of the North Carolina ERA ratification battle, write, "Ervin believed he was defending timeless values against ephemeral fad, superficial posturing, and political pressure, all of which he identified with feminists. Their refusal to concede the rationality of legal distinctions based on physiological and functional differences imperiled society."[36] Ervin, who had failed in the mid-1960s to convince his

Senate colleagues that civil rights legislation was wrong, failed in the early 1970s to turn the Senate against the ERA, but his courtly arguments did win the attention of Mrs. Schlafly.

Schlafly had been following the Senate debate over the ERA and had written to Senator Ervin to commend him for his leadership, as well as to send him a copy of her "What's Wrong with 'Equal Rights' for Women?" newsletter. Within a few months, Schlafly had convinced Ervin to use his congressional free mailing privileges to send out massive numbers of anti-ERA packets. By early 1973, she had coordinated with Ervin to send anti-ERA materials to STOP ERA activists in twenty-four states and to legislators considering ratification in twenty-five states.[37] In 1972, North Carolina elected its first post–Reconstruction era Republican Senator, Jesse Helms, who also threw himself into the anti-ERA cause. Helms, who would become a nationally important conservative champion by the end of the decade, built a close alliance with Schlafly.

Schlafly worked with members of Congress, but the real battle over the ERA, she knew, was at the state level, where the ratification fight was being waged one state at a time. In that conflict, Schlafly proved herself to be a grassroots organizing genius. She held workshops, set up chapters, traveled from battleground state to battleground state, and taught her people how to win. Throughout the 1970s, as the ERA war raged, Phyllis Schlafly became the most recognized figure on either side of the battlefield. For many Americans, the ratification fight over the ERA defined a new conservative-liberal divide. On the one side were the feminists, demanding equality for women and an end to sexism. On the other side were "traditional" women who insisted that America must support "family values," respect and protect the role of wife and mother, and recognize that men and women had different roles to play in a virtuous and stable society.

Those "traditional" women believed in Phyllis Schlafly's leadership, and those who joined the cause adored her. Carol Felsenthal, a liberal feminist who wrote a biography of Schlafly in the immediate aftermath of the ERA battle, was floored by anti-ERA activists' personal commitment to Schlafly: "Her supporters became positively misty-eyed when talking about their Phyllis." Schlafly showed her people how to make grassroots politics work; she inspired them to commit to community leadership. She provided the arguments and the evidence they needed to fight the ERA, but even more, she taught STOP ERA organizers how to raise money, how to get publicity, how to make politicians pay attention, and how to connect with other women who had never done anything political before in their lives. Schlafly even told her women what dress colors and makeup looked best on television. She videotaped them to help them become better debaters and modeled for them the calm, well-informed, disciplined, and cheerful feminine demeanor to which most politicians, who were overwhelmingly male, responded positively. What she taught them, Schlafly instructed, they were responsible for passing to the women in their chapters. For the housewives and mothers who joined the movement, STOP ERA was inspirational and life-changing. As feminists might have said, it was empowering. It was exactly the kind of participatory democracy left-wingers had thought they had cornered the market on in the 1960s and early 1970s.[38]

Schlafly was fighting the ERA, but she was also creating a powerful, well-trained activist base for the larger conservative movement. She used her newsletters, as well as her workshops and meetings with the STOP ERA activists, to teach her volunteers, most of them new to politics, how their struggle against the ERA fit into the larger conservative movement. Schlafly was creating a critical component of a revitalized, highly motivated, and savvy conservative Republican political base. Here were conservative legions who would raise money for, vote for, and convince their neighbors to vote for conservative candidates and issues.

Once Schlafly organized masses of women against the ERA, the seemingly uncontroversial amendment that most had seen as a sure thing began to lose support in state legislatures. A majority of state legislators, having been beseeched by STOP ERA activists to protect them from unwanted changes in their lives, began to vote against it. For many a state legislator during the early rush to ratify, a vote for the ERA had been a fairly easy way to show the ladies back in the district that he had their concerns in mind. Schlafly and her legions argued that legislators, in fact, were choosing a side in the battle between those who believed in time-tested, traditional gender roles that had governed America for generations and those who would upend family life, promote sexual promiscuity, mandate state-funded abortions, endanger women's economic security, endorse homosexuality, and even force women to go to war, where they would face death and sexual violation. Given that framing of the issues, the ERA began to flounder, especially among the many male state legislators who were dubious about really having women take their place as men's equals in politics, business, and at the dinner table.

Phyllis Schlafly, having done her best to craft the ratification vote in that way, then instructed her women in how to keep the heat on. First, they had to do the basics: organize legislative letter-writing campaigns, hold petition drives, and personally lobby their representatives both in their home districts and at the state capitol. Demonstrating once again her extraordinary ability to pack a powerful political punch in shorthand, Schlafly came up with compelling political tactics. Among the most pointed of those strategies was the fresh-bread offensive. When STOP ERA activists lobbied state legislators, they gave each of them (or at least all the men) freshly baked loaves of bread with an attached sticker: "from the breadmakers to the breadwinners."[39] STOP ERA wanted male legislators to understand that their women saw the roles of men and women as complementary. They did not want the world that came with legal equality, most especially financial independence. Traditional women wanted what they believed a mother and wife deserved—economic support from her husband.

Phyllis Schlafly used secular arguments, with an occasional heartfelt injection of religious language, to fight the ERA. Many of the people who joined her were more straightforwardly inspired by their religious beliefs. Among the most motivated was the leadership of the Church of Jesus Christ of Latter-day Saints. Under church leadership, Mormon women became powerful opponents of the ERA and feminism more generally. Given their church's beliefs about the roles of men and women, Mormons were natural allies of the cause. The Mormon Church newspaper, *Deseret News*, announced its opposition in February 1975, the day before the Utah state legislature was to vote on the ERA. The paper reminded readers of "the fact that men and women are different, made so by a Divine Creator."[40] Mormons believed that difference to be not just a biological fact but a sacred one. Mormon women were regularly and emphatically instructed by Church leaders to reject the women's liberation movement and to "Maintain Your Place as a Woman," which meant accepting their submission to men in all spheres of life, including the religious, secular, and domestic.[41] Such submission was a prerequisite for a "man and wife" to achieve exaltation in the "celestial kingdom" of heaven. The stakes, for believers, could not be higher.

Still, for Mormons, as for other religious groups, change in religious doctrine was always possible. Right up until the 1970s, Church leaders stated that according to their sacred doctrine no "Negro," owing to inherent unworthiness, could ever become a priest (a status almost all male Mormons—but no females—gain at the age of twelve). Nor could any "Negro" enter the "celestial kingdom" except as a servant to a white family. And in the late 1960s, a prominent leader and later president of the Mormon Church, Ezra Taft Benson, could not have made clearer his opposition to African Americans' struggle for equal rights in the United States: "Not one in a thousand Americans—black or white—really understands the full implications of today's civil rights agitation. The planning, direction, and leadership come from the Communists, and most of those are white men who fully intend to destroy America by spilling Negro blood, rather than their own."[42] But in 1978, at a time when the Church was under intense social, economic, and governmental pressure on race issues, its leaders announced that they had received a divine message giving African-American and African black men status equal to that of white men in the Church.

So, even as the Mormon Church was coming under great pressure in the 1970s over its race practices, the leadership decided to make the issue of women's subordination to men not just an enduring religious belief but a political priority. Historian Neil J. Young contends that the insertion of the Mormon Church into this secular, political battlefield was a deliberate decision by its leadership to become a far more powerful force in American politics, more generally. At a time when rapid social and cultural changes were testing Mormons' traditional practices, the Church, under the guidance of its new leader Spencer W. Kimball, a committed conservative who took office at the end of 1973, meant to become a firm shepherd for its own flock and for the national community as well. The Church leadership girded itself for this struggle by emphasizing that the head of the Church was not just its president but a "Prophet" who worked as "God's mouthpiece on earth." To reject the Church leadership's teachings on the ERA or on feminism, in other words, was to go against God.[43]

The result of the Mormon leadership's decision to fight the ERA was impressive. Before 1975, a majority of Mormon legislators in the Congress as well as in a variety of states had voted to ratify the ERA. And in 1974, a survey by the Church's own newspaper had shown that 63.1 percent of Mormons in Utah supported the ERA. After Prophet Spencer Kimball explained the Church's opposition to the amendment, support for it evaporated among the faithful, and Utah's state legislature voted resoundingly against it.

Mormon women, in particular, became a major force in actively fighting the ERA. In Utah, in 1977, some fourteen thousand of them turned out to rally against the amendment and the entire feminist agenda. They worked actively with Phyllis Schlafly's STOP ERA throughout the United States and were a decisive factor in convincing legislators in Idaho, Nevada, and Virginia to vote against or to rescind previous support of the ERA. Mormon women also organized against the ERA using their own national Church-linked network, the women-only Relief Society. For Mormon women, who were expected to submit to men's leadership in religious as well as secular matters, fighting the ERA became a way to prove their loyalty and importance to the larger mission of the Church. A great many embraced that cause resolutely.[44]

The Mormons were far from alone among deeply religious Americans to join the fight against the ERA and feminists' attacks on restrictive gender roles. The Virginia-based Baptist minister Jerry Falwell, whose syndicated radio and television show, the *Old Time Gospel Hour*, had made him a national figure, helped convince the Virginia state legislature to reject the amendment. He spoke for many evangelical Christians when he stated, "A definite violation of holy Scripture, ERA defies the mandate that 'the husband is the head of the wife, even as Christ is the head of the church' (Ep. 5:23). In 1 Peter 3:7 we read that husbands are to give their wives honor as unto the weaker vessel, that they are both heirs together of the grace of life." He was quick to add that "because a woman is weaker does not mean that she is less important."[45] Similar understandings fueled other Protestant ministers, dedicated to a literal reading of the Bible, to oppose the ERA and the larger feminist cause.

In the early 1970s, political pundits thought Phyllis Schlafly's battle to stop the ERA to be both hopeless and more proof of the political marginality of "Goldwater" conservatives. By the late 1970s, Schlafly had proved them wrong on both counts. She and her supporters had stopped the forward progress of the ERA and had successfully lobbied several state legislatures to rescind previous passage of the amendment. When liberals in Congress, facing the failure of the ERA to be ratified by the states, managed to extend the ratification deadline to 1982, Schlafly led the effort to battle the extension in Idaho through the federal courts. She was assisted by the Mormon Church and, most critically, by the Mountain States Legal Foundation, an organization that had been originally funded by the conservative businessmen Adolph Coors to fight government economic regulation, tax policy, and management of public lands. Schlafly's war had brought together economic conservatives and working-class evangelical Christians, Mormons, and Catholics. Not since the heyday of the anticommunist movement had such divergent groups cooperated so well nor mobilized en masse so energetically on political issues. Against all odds, this conservative coalition led by Phyllis Schlafly killed the ERA.

Schlafly also worked tirelessly to join her legions' battle against the ERA to other fierce cultural battles that began to rage in the 1970s. Almost from the beginning of her anti-ERA campaign she linked the feminist cause to the burgeoning gay liberation struggle. In her September 1974 *Phyllis Schlafly Report*, she told her readers that the ERA would mandate the legalization of lesbian and gay marriage. She warned that the women's liberation movement had actively embraced lesbianism. (Betty Friedan, speaking for many liberal feminists, had

feared that the "lavender herring" would damage the women's movement in the eyes of many Americans, but, after a long, internal, divisive fight over the issue, she and most liberal feminists had eventually
decided to put principle over short-term pragmatic politics and allied
with openly lesbian feminists and advocates for gay civil rights.)[46] The
ERA, Schlafly continued, was just the first step in liberals' crusade to
extend legally mandated equality not just to women but to homosexuals. And while legal scholars mostly rejected Schlafly's claim that
the ERA would automatically legalize gay marriage, her larger argument that the women's movement and liberals, more generally, were
supportive of equal rights for lesbians and gay men was true.

Religious and cultural conservatives had long been concerned
about issues of sex and sexuality, including but not restricted to
homosexuality or gay rights. They had protested liberals' advocacy
of sex education in the schools, acceptance of sexually explicit books
and movies, and tolerance for sex outside of the boundaries of traditional marriage. They believed socially mandated sexual control and
individual sexual discipline were fundamental to the health of the traditional family and a necessary prerequisite to a moral, God-fearing
nation. In the late 1960s, groups like MOMS (Mothers Organized for
Moral Stability) had sprung up in conservative communities to fight
against the dissemination of birth-control information in their children's schools. Self-published anti–sex education books such as *Is the
Schoolhouse the Proper Place to Teach Raw Sex?*, distributed by the
Christian Crusade, became best sellers in conservative religious circles.[47] Social conservatives believed that parents had the right to control their children's sexuality and to limit their exposure to sexually
explicit information. Many religious conservatives believed the Bible
damned homosexuality and adultery. For many conservatives, liberals' open acceptance of homosexuality and the rise of a mass movement in behalf of gay liberation were almost unimaginable blows to
the nation's moral and spiritual health.

This issue came to a head in 1977 when officials in Dade County,
Florida, passed a gay rights ordinance. Several dozen other communities, almost all of which had active gay civil rights movements, had
already done likewise. But in this case, local resident and national

celebrity Anita Bryant—a former Miss America, pop singer, and Florida orange juice spokesperson—decided to fight back. She started an anti–gay rights organization, Save Our Children, to repeal that ordinance. Schlafly, Reverend Jerry Falwell, and other conservative figures flocked to southern Florida to support Bryant and her group. Schlafly vowed to fight what she referred to as the "perverts." Falwell issued a somewhat bizarre jeremiad: "So-called gay folks [would] . . . just as soon kill you as look at you." And in an only slightly more temperate tone, the erudite conservative columnist George Will declared the gay civil rights ordinance "the moral disarmament of society."[48] Bryant and her well-known supporters made the Dade County fight a national symbol for the culture wars that were breaking out all over the United States.

Bryant used language similar to that of the anticommunist crusade of prior years to attack the gay rights movement. Speaking to the anti-gay fears of many contemporary Americans, she warned: "As a mother, I know that homosexuals cannot biologically reproduce children; therefore, they must recruit our children." She hit a strong nerve. Dade County voters responded to the charge by overwhelmingly voting in favor of a referendum that overturned the gay rights ordinance. The Save Our Children movement expanded and with its allies rolled back gay civil rights ordinances in several other states.

As was true of the ERA battle and the school textbook battles of the 1950s and early 1960s, the issue of gay rights resonated with many mothers and fathers who feared that liberals' relatively new spirit of tolerance and expansive notions of equality were putting their families at grave risk. Government-mandated equal rights—first for African Americans in the 1950s and early 1960s and then for women and homosexuals in the late 1960s and 1970s—had become a major American battleground. Mostly, those who favored such rights understood that they were liberals and those who opposed such forms of legally mandated rights saw themselves as conservatives. When it came to the issue of gender equality, Schlafly, as much as anyone, had helped to draw that line and create that political war.

By 1980, Schlafly was just one general among many. Other committed conservative, religiously driven cultural warriors dedicated to returning Americans to their God-given moral verities, as they interpreted them, helped lead the charge. In 1977, Dr. James Dobson began Focus on the Family. Its mission was "[t]o cooperate with the Holy Spirit in sharing the Gospel of Jesus Christ with as many people as possible by nurturing and defending the God-ordained institution of the family and promoting biblical truths worldwide."[49] Two years later, Beverley La Haye, coauthor with her husband of a best-selling guide to a rewarding Christian marriage and an ardent anti-ERA activist, formed Concerned Women for America. Its charge was similar to that of Focus on the Family: "The vision of CWA is for women and like-minded men, from all walks of life, to come together and restore the family to its traditional purpose. . . . We believe it is our duty to serve God to the best of our ability and to pray for a moral and spiritual revival that will return this nation to the traditional values upon which it was founded."[50] Much more forthrightly than Schlafly, members of these groups and of many other similar organizations, demanded that public policy follow Christian verities as they understood them. Moral order—the bedrock of American society, they believed—must be based on the inerrant word of the Bible, which, they asserted, condemned homosexuality and feminist precepts.

These culture wars taught millions of Americans that they were conservatives. The equal rights battles and the oft-linked struggles over homosexuality were directly connected, as well, to other massive changes in American mores and legal rights. Most important, the 1973 Supreme Court's ruling in *Roe v. Wade* that gave constitutional protection to women's right to choose to have an abortion widened the gap between liberals and conservatives. While many Americans opposed abortion because they believed, in keeping with church teachings, that life began at conception, the debate over abortion also fit into the liberal-conservative versions of discipline and order. For liberals, who believed that the state should protect individuals from the dangerous unpredictability and uncertainty of life in a modern, capitalist society, women's legally guaranteed right to have an abortion made sense. For conservatives, who believed that people needed to be held responsible for their bad choices and that only a strong, religiously based moral code could produce a stable and good society, abortion was a moral abomination that placed the right to individual sexual pleasure above society's need to protect the family, and most especially the family's most vulnerable members. The Catholic Church, operating through the National Conference of Catholic Bishops' Family Life Division, responded almost immediately to the legalization of abortion by forming the National Right to Life Organization. For many Catholic conservatives, abortion replaced anticommunism as a singularly important and galvanizing political issue. Soon many Protestant-led conservative organizations joined the fight, as well. The conservative-liberal battle over abortion would only sharpen at the cusp of the 1970s and 1980s, giving ever-greater salience to the cultural issues conservatives had been championing for decades. Phyllis Schlafly, who had come to national prominence fighting the communist threat and whose Republican Party had spurned her in the post-Goldwater anticonservative witch hunt, had helped lead conservatives to a new battleground where they fought on favorable terrain. To earn victory, however, they would need to find another hero for the cause.

FIVE

RONALD REAGAN

The Conservative Hero

BEFORE RONALD REAGAN, the greatest champions of modern American conservatism were naysayers who proffered fear and even doom. They did so, in large part, because each, in his or her own way, believed in the power of evil in the world, the fallibility of human nature, and the inability of human beings to divine God's will. As a result, they emphasized the perils of social and political experimentation and the need to respond to sin, sacrilege, and threat with massive force, be it rhetorical or military. Thus, Barry Goldwater tried to win over voters by warning that he might well have to set off a few nuclear bombs to stem the ever-surging communist tide. Phyllis Schlafly gave one of her best-selling, antiliberal screeds the Halloween-spooky title *The Gravediggers*, and told Americans that liberals wanted to assault their families and send their daughters off to foreign wars to be raped and killed. Robert Taft, cheerful as any mortician, had a hard time saying something positive about most anything. William Buckley did his best to break the conservative mold by smiling a lot and demonstrating that he knew how to have fun. But his essential message was that as long as Americans continued to allow liberals to rule they all were surely going to hell in a hand basket, and deservedly so.

Ronald Reagan could be scary, too, when he believed the occasion called for it—but there was not a pessimistic, misanthropic bone in his body. Reagan pictured conservatism as a forward-looking, optimistic, sunny political crusade. In the 1980s, even as he advocated almost everything in which Taft, Buckley, Goldwater, and Schlafly believed, Reagan did his best to make conservatism the party of hope. Such happy faith in the goodness of man and the certainties of progress made him an odd conservative but also the most successful of them all.

Like other conservatives, Reagan believed in discipline. He rose to political power in the mid-1960s, chastising those whom he characterized as unruly, riotous, and undeserving—along with the liberals he blamed for cosseting such misbehavior. He was, in the parlance of the times, a law-and-order man. But in 1980, Reagan ran for president as an emancipator who would unleash Americans from liberalism's restraining hand. At the beginning of the decade, when a majority of Americans feared that the country's greatest days were a thing of the past, Reagan promised them economic recovery and global leadership in the war on communism.

Reagan's America was born in liberty and came of age as the richest and most powerful nation on earth. The nation's success was proof of its virtue. Its failings were indications only that people (liberal politicians, federal bureaucrats, cultural elites) had strayed from that which had made America great. As Reagan explained in speech after speech,

America was a divinely blessed producer's republic, founded on principles of liberty and freedom for all, built by small-businesspeople,
farmers, entrepreneurs, workers, and economic risk-takers and reliant on the virtuous bonds of family, church, and community. Government policy, he said, had to promote those values, reward those
people, and protect those institutions. During an era in which the
federal government had become the guarantor of equal opportunity,
provider for the poor, protector of the environment, and regulator
of the marketplace, Reagan insisted that big government—what liberals offered the American people—was the enemy of the citizenry.
Those political systems that seek to take away individual liberty and
national virtue, most malignly Soviet communism but also misguided
American liberalism, must be stopped. Reagan crafted his conservative principles and foundational policies in the 1950s and early 1960s
and never (or, as we shall see, almost never) fundamentally altered
his core beliefs. Thus it is worth examining the process of this political development carefully.

Reagan's American success stories worked best when others told
tales of woe and demanded, even violently, dramatic national change.
The sixties were made for Reagan's brand of conservative politics. He
was first elected California governor when leftist dissidents, white and
black, insisted that America was racist, had failed the poor, and needed
new values and public policies to produce a just and equitable nation.
Not so, said Reagan; it was the dissidents and troublemakers who were
failing America with their cult of victimhood, their culture of com-
plaint, and their disdain for law and order. When legions of liberals
and their allies on the Left flagellated the United States for the deaths
of millions in Southeast Asia and for siding with third-world dictators
in the name of anticommunism, he berated them for their lack of faith
in flag and country and, looking back, insisted that the Vietnam War
was, in fact, "a noble cause." The power of Reagan's positive thinking, as
well as his well-worded contempt for those who criticized the United
States or saw themselves or others as victims of circumstances beyond
their individual control, won him massive support from Americans
who rejected the politics of economic redistribution, government-
mandated equality, and a culture of "blame American first."

Reagan was elected president in 1980 after his opponent, President Jimmy Carter, having failed to turn around the U.S. economy or demonstrate American global power, urged Americans to recognize national limits. Reagan chuckled at Carter's pessimism. He responded to the dire economic news of the late 1970s and early 1980s and the uncertain efficacy of his own policies in winning fashion, first by urging Americans "to stay the course" and then by affirming in his 1984 reelection campaign: "It's morning again in America." Reagan convincingly portrayed conservatism as a forward-looking, optimistic faith in the American way of life—as he defined it. His good-natured faith and his refusal to recognize domestic poverty, racism, and inequality infuriated liberals, many of whom ridiculed him as a failed Hollywood "B" actor who "found out who he was through the roles he played on film" and then confused real life challenges with Hollywood dreamscapes.[1] Liberals underestimated Reagan. When he won the presidency in 1980, he had spent years reading, writing, and thinking hard about the Cold War struggle with communism, economic policy, and political leadership. Such intellectual dedication did not make him a platonic king. Like many an autodidact, he had massive blind spots; many issues, especially newer ones, simply did not capture his interest, leaving him ill-prepared to respond to them. And even more than most politicians, he often failed to differentiate, in his own mind and in the telling, between the empirically verifiable and the anecdotally compelling. By the time Reagan was president, his intellectual curiosity had disappeared, and on occasion the critics were right: sometimes scenes from movies did invade and even supplant his recollection of real-life events. Then, too, at nearly seventy, Reagan was the oldest person who had ever become president, and by time he left office in January 1989 he was far from the man he had been intellectually thirty years earlier. Sometimes it showed painfully. But more than his political enemies acknowledged, Reagan had worked out his own political philosophy and had studied the major public policy questions that interested him. More obviously, and here critics, cronies, and supporters agree, Reagan knew how to take what he believed and communicate it to a hungry audience. For decades, he had made his living persuading people to trust in what he was telling them. Americans responded to his well-honed message and his impressive ability to deliver that message by making him the first full-two-term president since Eisenhower. By 1988, at the end of President Reagan's second term, for the first time since such polling data existed, more Americans identified themselves as conservatives than as liberals.

When Ronald Reagan ran for president as a conservative Republican in 1980, the liberal political order that Franklin Roosevelt had set into motion nearly a half-century earlier was broken, and liberals did not know how to fix it. Under President Jimmy Carter—arguably, a liberal only in contrast to the man who would defeat him in 1980—the national Democratic Party had become the congeries of disappointment, pessimism, and a backward-looking faith. Carter's attempts to lead the American people through a difficult time looked more like those of the dour Herbert Hoover than the jaunty Franklin Roosevelt. Carter's failures were not just his own. Liberals, the historian Judith Stein explains, had no answers for the economic ills of the United States in the late 1970s: "liberalism lacked an economic blueprint to match its social agenda."[2] And while the election year of 1980 was no match for misery with the Great Depression year of 1932, the times in America at the tail end of the 1970s were very bad. Ronald Reagan, the political outsider and anti-incumbent, the change candidate, was lucky to be running at such time. But he had always been lucky. And conservatives were extraordinarily lucky to have Reagan available to them in 1980, when a great many Americans believed that the old liberal order had failed them.

Reagan liked simple sayings that reflected big truths, such as people can make their own luck. Robert Taft's father had been president of the United States, and young Bob had been assured of going to Yale, in essence, since he was born. That is luck of one kind. Reagan's luck was of another kind. His parents had not graduated from high school. His father was an alcoholic, small-town shoe salesman. Young Reagan, known then as Dutch, had no chance of going to Yale. It could be said that he was a man of poor beginnings, fated to a cramped life. But he never saw his circumstance or himself that way. Ronald Reagan made his own luck by embracing the world as he found it. His luck, above all, was in his ebullient character. His own life story gave proof that anything was possible in the United States of America.

In 1928, when Ronald Reagan began working his way through tiny Eureka College, no political party or creed had a corner on the rhetoric of uplift or belief in personal advancement. Democratic presidential aspirant Al Smith had grown up poor in the Irish Catholic immigrant neighborhoods of New York's Lower East Side and become one of New York's most successful governors. His Republican opponent, Herbert Hoover, was an orphan who had made a fortune as a mining engineer and then achieved international honor administering food programs that saved a starving post–World War I Europe. Both men in their respective campaigns insisted that they would maintain an America in which their rise from penurious obscurity to national honor remained an American birthright. Reagan, who spent his childhood reading uplifting tales of boyhood adventure, believed in that dream.

By the time he graduated from Eureka in 1932, the United States had become a very different place. A quarter of all American workers had lost their jobs, including Reagan's own father, who eventually found employment with the New Deal's Work Relief Administration. Most Americans had lost the kind of faith in the free market that had prompted President Calvin Coolidge to remark just a few years earlier, "The man who builds a factory builds a temple; the man who works there, worships there." Franklin Roosevelt stepped in to offer a new and different faith. Optimistically, he told Americans that "the only thing we have to fear is fear itself," and he and his administration began forging the machinery of the New Deal, which sought to use government power to protect American workers and middle-class wage earners from the punishing blows of an unrestrained free market.

Young Reagan, just old enough to vote in 1932, supported Franklin Roosevelt and the New Deal. He saw, firsthand, how perilous the American economy had become. Just out of college, he had almost become another statistic in the economic downturn as he lost his hoped-for job as a department store junior manager in his hometown of Dixon, Illinois. But Reagan made his own luck. He found a small-time job in Davenport, Iowa, broadcasting college football games.

Talented, he almost immediately moved to a much bigger station in Des Moines, where he made a name for himself announcing the Chicago Cubs's games. Far from Wrigley Field, he had an uncanny ability to take the bland facts of the game, transmitted to his broadcast studio in Iowa by telegraph, and turn them into colorful play-by-play reporting. Five years later, he fulfilled his boyhood fantasy. He was in Hollywood, a movie actor. Without capital or connections, in the darkest days of the Great Depression, Reagan proved that the American dream lived on.[3]

Reagan had made it, but he did his best to remain loyal to those who had not. Four times he voted for Franklin Roosevelt, later writing that he was "a New Dealer to the core."[4] His enthusiasm for the New Deal was much less a faith in any particular policy or program than it was a sense that President Roosevelt was doing everything in his power to restore the American dream. Reagan was also a stalwart union man. As soon as he arrived in Hollywood, he enthusiastically joined the Screen Actors Guild. Unlike Taft, Buckley, Goldwater, Schlafly, or George W. Bush, all of whom came of political age as conservatives and never looked back, Reagan began his political journey as a liberal and a card-carrying union member. It would take him nearly thirty years to say good-bye to the Democratic Party.

From the late 1930s through the early 1950s, Reagan was a liberal Democrat in one of the few places in the United States where his liberalism put him in the political center: Hollywood. Reagan was a movie star but never quite made the first tier. Perhaps his most memorable role was in *Knute Rockne All American* (1940) in which he played Notre Dame football star George Gipp, who succumbs to pneumonia—but not before uttering the iconic words "win one for the Gipper" (a phrase President Reagan loved to recycle in the 1980s). But if Reagan never became a Clark Gable or a Jimmy Stewart, he did rise to the front ranks of his profession in another fashion: from 1947 to 1952 and again from 1959 to 1960, he was president of his labor union, the Screen Actors Guild (SAG). He also became a major Democratic activist, joining a range of organizations and campaigns affiliated with the liberal cause. "An actor," Reagan wrote in his autobiography, "spends half his waking hours in fantasy." Reagan wanted more out of life and he got it: "I came out of the monastery of movies into the world."[5]

How then did Reagan, the Hollywood liberal, become the avatar of modern American conservatism? It happened slowly and then all at once. In the beginning, there was the anticommunist cause. In the late 1940s, most liberals were just as anticommunist as most conservatives. Reagan, from the liberal side, was one of them. His SAG leadership, as well as his intense interest in politics, put him in the middle of the battle. There really were communists in the movie industry, struggling to establish a "nerve center," as one of them later stated, in America's dream machine.[6] Reagan took on those communists, blasting them for their secret maneuvering, their antidemocratic ideology, and their allegiance to the totalitarian Soviet Union.

Reagan's fight was public, and it was fierce. In the midst of an internecine labor union battle, a communist-led group, the Conference of Studio Unions, called a strike and demanded that all actors join them in shutting down the film industry. Reagan told his fellow SAG members to reject the demand. In return he got a phone call telling him that "[y]our face will never be in pictures again." Reagan got a gun, police protection, and a hard attitude about communist-run labor unions. He was also discovering that communists in Hollywood played by different rules. Much of their activity was secret; they conspired to take over organizations and to manipulate noncommunists who unwittingly joined such organizations. Reagan had joined one such group, the elaborately—and it turned out, ironically—named Hollywood Independent Citizens' Committee of the Arts, Sciences, and Professions. He did not appreciate being played for a dupe. When the FBI, already deep into the hunt for communist subversives, called on him to stay in the organization in order to inform on the communists' plans, he did so, earning the code name T-10.

Still, Reagan was not an anticommunist zealot. He saw himself as a liberal doing his best to control the communists' dangerous but not deadly conspiracies. In 1947, when the House Un-American Activities Committee (HUAC) launched its headline-seeking investigations of "Reds" in Hollywood, Reagan appeared as a friendly witness, but he believed he could put out the fires of hysteria, not stoke them. In words that echoed those of liberal intellectual Arthur Schlesinger, he insisted, "I believe that, as Thomas Jefferson put it, if all the American people knew all of the facts that they will never make a mistake. . . . I never as a citizen want to see our country become urged, by either fear or resentment, to compromise with any of our democratic principles."[7]

Reagan's animated anticommunism, at first, drove him only deeper into the liberal cause. He was a national board member of the quintessential Cold War liberal anticommunist group, Americans for Democratic Action. But even early on, Reagan was disappointed by the reticence of many of his liberal allies in taking on the communists more aggressively. Too often, he felt, their sympathies for some of the communists' goals, such as an end to racism and better lives for American workers, and their concerns about destroying people's lives based on a naive or foolish political act, blinded them to the mendacity and malevolence of the Soviet-led Communist Party. Too many liberals, he feared, fought communism with one hand tied behind their backs—worst of all, they had fettered themselves.

By the early 1950s, Reagan's commitment to the anticommunist cause had deepened, driving him to embrace harsher measures against Hollywood "Reds." He championed a measure in the SAG constitution that outlawed Communist Party members. And while he, as SAG president, formally opposed the "blacklist" banning communists from the movie business that Hollywood studios created in response to the political pressure they feared, he did nothing to fight it. He wrote to one actress who faced blacklisting, ". . . if any actor by his actions outside union activities has so offended public opinion that he has made himself unemployable at the box office, the Guild cannot and would not force any employer to hire him."[8]

Reagan's suspicions about liberals' long-term commitment to the anticommunist cause and his movement to the political right were given further substance by a book. It was the same book that had so impressed William Buckley. In *Witness* (1952), the ex-communist Whittaker Chambers, the man who had worked with then Congressman Richard Nixon to reveal the high-ranking government official Alger Hiss as a tool of the communists, argues that all parties of the left, whether they call themselves communist, socialist, or liberal, are allied, even if unwittingly. All, Chambers deduces, have fallen prey to the "totalitarian temptation," having rejected the absolute necessity of individual liberty in a free society for the false promise of a statist utopia. American liberals, in their expansive regard for government solutions to all social problems, pave the way for the communist take-over even of the United States. Over the course of the 1950s, Reagan's encounters with Hollywood communists and his close reading of *Witness* and other books, including Friedrich von Hayek's attack on liberal political economy, *The Road to Serfdom*, pushed Reagan away from the anticommunist liberalism in which he had swum in the late 1940s and toward the deeper waters of the conservative cause.[9]

Anticommunism was not the only source for Reagan's move away from the New Deal liberalism of his younger days. After a breakout role in the 1942 dramatic tearjerker *King's Row*, in which the Reagan character wakes up a double amputee and gasps, "Where's the rest of me?" Reagan began to make big money. Too much of that money, he felt, was being siphoned off by the tax man. What was the point in working hard if the government was, as Reagan bitterly joked, his "senior partner"? Reagan's astute biographer Lou Cannon believes that it was Reagan's frustration with liberal policymakers' love affair with high tax rates for the wealthy, more than any other single factor, that propelled him from Democratic liberalism into Republican conservatism.[10] It was not just self-interest that moved him. High taxes, the future president observed, made any man less likely to put in more hours at work, and that could not be good for the overall economy. Reagan the New Dealer, once focused on protecting the "little guy" from the "economic royalists," had begun to look at the economy from the perspective of a self-made millionaire. In 1952, for the first time ever, Reagan voted Republican in the presidential election, quietly supporting the probusiness Eisenhower.

Reagan's walk away from liberalism accelerated in the 1950s as his career took a new turn. Like many other male movie stars, he had served in the army during World War II making training films; Reagan was a captain in the First Motion Picture Unit. He continued to make films after the war, but as his youthful good looks faded, so did his career. By the mid-1950s, with decent roles becoming rare, he needed work. At the end of 1954, he left the glamour of the movie business for the upstart television industry. He signed on with General Electric to host *General Electric Theater*. Film critic Richard Corliss believes the unwelcome switch helped develop the talent Reagan would later use so well: "A movie star typically projects danger and a TV star comfort and familiarity. Reagan had this domesticated appeal—bred into him, perhaps, but also hammered into him by all those roles in which he essentially played the sensible master of ceremonies. . . . This steadiness, combined with a voice suggesting homespun wisdom, made him a welcome, authoritative TV figure and a superb politician."[11] Reagan's contract with GE did more than extend his acting career and hone his talent. It directly contributed to his growth as a conservative political figure.

To round out the television contract, GE also paid Reagan to spend some of the downtime from the TV show touring GE's many plants, entertaining the employees. The company pretty much left it up to Reagan to work out his palaver with the workers, and at first he gamely offered them humorous anecdotes about celebrity life in Hollywood. Reagan enjoyed the storytelling, but as his reading grew deeper and his own interest in trading on his old life grew fainter, he began to mix in more and more commentary about national politics. Taxes played a major part in those speeches. Reagan was speaking to GE employees across-the-board, trying to persuade hourly workers, as much as their well-paid managers, that high taxes hurt everyone. He was trying to make the anti-tax message a populist one, and he was pitching it over and over, perfecting his ability to take a dry political subject and find a way to connect with his audience.

Reagan worked eight years for General Electric. Driven by his readings and, he said, by his many conversations with GE employees, he became ever more convinced that the federal government, fed by its insatiable hunger for tax revenues, had become a malign force "encroaching on liberties we had always taken for granted."[12] Reagan the onetime New Dealer was talking a great deal like Roosevelt's adversary, the economic liberty–loving Senator Robert Taft. Dedicated to the anticommunist cause, appalled by the confiscatory nature of the federal progressive income tax system, and informed by working for one of America's most successful business corporations, Ronald Reagan had become a champion of unregulated capitalism.

By the early 1960s, Reagan was again looking for work. General Electric had decided (after Reagan had begun attacking one of its biggest customers, the Tennessee Valley Authority, which he saw as a big government experiment run amuck) that he should stop talking so much about politics and go back to lighter fare in his company-sponsored appearances. Reagan said no, and that was that. By 1962, he was dedicated to the conservative political cause; he just was not sure what he would do with that commitment.

Despite the short-term loss of a steady paycheck, Reagan was a happy man in the early 1960s. After a shattering divorce—for him— in 1949 from the movie star Jane Wyman (she accused him of mental cruelty, by which she meant that Reagan insisted on constantly talking about politics around the breakfast table), he had married Nancy Davis in 1952. He had found his soul mate and another source for his growing conservatism; Davis's wealthy stepfather, a prominent surgeon, was an outspoken archconservative. Reagan had also become much less reliant on his acting earnings; wealthy friends in the film industry and elsewhere had helped him to invest in Southern California real estate, and he was a rich man in his own right, further attuning him to the concerns of the investing class. In 1962, he had at last finally and formally left the Democratic Party. Reagan, whose eight years touring GE plants had made him a remarkably successful speaker, was also in big demand on the anticommunist, pro–free enterprise lecture circuit. He had come a long way from Dixon, Illinois, and his 1932 vote for Franklin Roosevelt.

In 1964, Reagan was co-chair of Barry Goldwater's campaign in California. He spoke out frequently in support of Goldwater's brand of conservative Republicanism. But Reagan's big moment in the campaign, the event that would put him on a trajectory for the White House, came by accident. Shortly before the November election, Goldwater canceled a major Los Angeles fund-raising speech. The organizers asked Reagan to fill in. Reagan, though tailoring his remarks to promote Goldwater, gave the same basic speech he had been honing for years. However, few Americans outside of GE plants or what Reagan self-mockingly called the "mashed potato" lecture circuit had ever heard it. The crowd of bigwig Republican donors was starstruck by Reagan's performance. Especially as compared to Goldwater (but really as compared to any contemporary political figure), Reagan was, as soon would be said everywhere, a great communicator. A group of the wealthy men asked Reagan to repeat the speech on national television. They would buy the airtime.

Reagan's speech hit the nation's television screens a week before the election. It was titled "A Time for Choosing." "The Speech," as his supporters came to call it, laid out the principles he had been developing for years. Reagan would speak to those same principles—and use some of the same phrases—for years to come, all the way to the White House. He began by harkening back to his Democratic Party roots. Yet he called not on Roosevelt but on 1928 Democratic presidential candidate Al Smith, who was a founding member of the pro–property rights, anti-Roosevelt group, the American Liberty League: "Back in 1936, Mr. Democrat himself, Al Smith, the great American, came before the American people and charged that the leadership of his party was taking the party of Jefferson, Jackson, and Cleveland down the road under the banners of Marx, Lenin, and Stalin." Reagan chastised the Democratic Party for its embrace of big government. In behalf of a liberty-loving people, he denounced mandatory Social Security taxes, chastised Lyndon Johnson for his planned program of mandatory health insurance for the elderly, and denounced the wasted money that went to dependency-creating welfare payments for the undeserving poor. And as for liberals' demands that billions be spent on food and nutrition programs for the hungry, Reagan just shook his head: "We were told four years ago that 17 million people went to bed hungry each night. Well, that was probably true. They were all on a diet."

Much of the speech was a pro-Goldwater, anti-tax, anti–big government broadside. His melodious delivery moved from engaging to inspiring—even electrifying—when Reagan took after the communist threat and spoke of what it meant to be a true American in a time of such peril. Liberals, he warned, have proven that their only response to the brutality and the dangers of communism is appeasement. Such cowardice runs against everything Americans believed in. The liberal, he said, claims it is better to be "Red than dead." The liberal admits "he would rather 'live on his knees than die on his feet.'" With his thin lips held tight, Reagan intoned, "those voices don't speak for the rest of us. You and I know and do not believe that life is so dear and peace so sweet as to be purchased at the price of chains and slavery." He then called out, "should Moses have told the children of Israel to live in slavery under the pharaohs? Should Christ have refused the cross? Should the patriots at Concord Bridge have thrown down their guns and refused to fire the shot heard 'round the world?" The conservative legions had found their answer to the cool fire of John Kennedy and the passionate religiosity of Martin Luther King Jr.[13]

Reagan's televised speech produced an outpouring of donations to Goldwater's campaign. None of it—neither speech nor the money it produced—was nearly enough to save Goldwater from his crushing defeat a few days later. But it did convince a powerful group of wealthy conservative businessmen in California that they had found a champion. They asked Reagan if he would like to be the next governor of the state. Reagan the citizen-activist was ready to become Reagan the citizen-politician. His run for governor in 1966 put him smack dab in the middle of the political and cultural explosion Americans have come to call simply "the sixties."

At least in some senses, the sixties hit California harder than anywhere else in America. The Bay area was the hothouse for much of it: the Berkeley-based free speech movement helped create the radical student movement, the Black Panthers originated in Oakland, and San Francisco's Haight-Ashbury was the sanctum sanctorum of the "hippie" counterculture. But the largely segregated and racially polarized environs of Southern California had a place of honor, as well; the first major race riot of the era, the 1965 conflagration in the Los Angeles neighborhood of Watts, broke out there. Other breakdowns in law and order that ranged from a pandemic of illegal drug use to a vertiginous rise in violent crime to an embrace of a politics of vandalism and civil disobedience erupted all across the California landscape.

No simple answer explains why California was in so many ways the epicenter for the sixties. However, Reagan's own journey from

Dixon to Hollywood explains part of it. California, especially from the 1920s through the 1960s, was where Americans went to reinvent themselves. Millions had taken that path, making California the home of more nonnative born residents than any other state. The massive World War II–era build up of California's economy brought large numbers of African Americans and Latinos to the state, all eager to take advantage of the glut of good-paying jobs. Not all of them found the prosperity they sought; many found only the hard hand of prejudice and discrimination. California, in the postwar years, was a land awash in confrontation, reinvention, frustration, and possibility. An energetic and sometimes feverish anticommunist movement had boomed there, as had a tidal wave of church building and evangelical revivalism. In the 1960s, those conservative movements would be met head on by a multifaceted movement on the Left. Swirling around both groups would be a great many uncertain Californians whose mixed emotions were open to political negotiation. That was the electorate that Ronald Reagan mastered.

Reagan expected to run for governor in 1966 on the issues he had laid out so eloquently in The Speech: anticommunism, lower taxes, and less government. Running on those issues would have made him, in essence, a more genial, better communicating, (much) less scary, and smarter Barry Goldwater. His opponent, the two-term incumbent governor, Edmund "Pat" Brown, was in many ways a quintessential liberal; he was an experienced politician who had made big government look good in California by building highways, water systems, universities, and by simply presiding over a high-growth state economy. Given the results of the 1964 presidential election and Brown's shellacking of Richard Nixon in the 1962 governor's race ("You won't have Nixon to kick around anymore"), the outcome seemed predictable. Certainly Governor Brown saw it that way. Brown enjoyed telling voters "that he had been solving California's problems while Reagan was making Bedtime for Bonzo, a 1951 film in which a chimpanzee plays the title role."[14]

Whether Reagan would have defeated Brown running as he had planned will never be known because, in the face of a new set of issues (most spectacularly of all the outbreak of protests at California's flagship university but also growing racial tensions), Reagan unveiled a new campaign. In particular, he ran against the student protesters and the entire challenge they—and he identified that "they" broadly—were making against the social order and political system in which Reagan and, it turned out, a great many Americans fervently believed. Reagan, in his 1966 campaign and throughout his subsequent two terms as California governor, brought to the conservative cause a new moral appeal against the political and cultural dissidents of the 1960s. He was far from alone in making this case; Richard Nixon would deploy a similar appeal in both of his successful campaigns for the presidency. But Reagan, as much as anyone, made the crackdown against the leftist social change movements of the sixties a core aspect of conservative politics. This popular cause brought a great many "traditional" Americans, appalled by the breakdown in law and order, as they saw it, to the conservative cause.[15]

Reagan expressed his dismay with student radicalism in a shotgun fashion that often spoke more to the cultural experimentation of the students than to any particular political issue they had raised. He rarely spoke directly to questions students were raising about racial justice or the Vietnam War. Instead, he told spellbound audiences about a party held at the University of California: "The hall was entirely dark except for the light from two movie screens. On these screens the nude torsos of men and women were portrayed, from time to time, in suggestive positions and movements. . . . The smell of marijuana was thick throughout the hall. . . . There were indications of other happenings which cannot be mentioned."[16] Reagan understood the cultural politics of the era.

Governor Brown had no clue about how to respond to this kind of politics. Like many a liberal, he was generally cheered in the early to mid-1960s to see young people fighting for racial justice, expressing their intellectual curiosity, and passionately committed to exercising their democratic rights. After a series of nonviolent student protests in the early 1960s, Brown had avuncularly praised "this new, impatient, critical crop of young gadflies."[17] He *had* ordered a mass arrest in 1965 following the free speech protests at UC Berkeley, but he was clearly uncomfortable in that role and steered clear of politicizing the campus protests and student culture of the mid-1960s. On that reticence Reagan feasted. Voters cheered him on.

William Buckley had made his name attacking campus radicalism back in 1951 in *God and Man at Yale*. Reagan, with a bigger canvas to work on, took after the issue in much the same terms but with a more effective populist bite. Like Buckley, he bemoaned the ways in which "academic freedom" was used to excuse any and every kind of subversive behavior on university campuses. He told the men and women whose taxes helped fund higher education in California that "the campus has become a rallying point for Communism and a center of sexual misconduct."[18] In 1966, Reagan had found a way to link conservatives' long-standing fears about domestic communism to liberals' tolerance for social and cultural experimentation—and he could do it in one sentence.

More diffidently, Reagan took on the other great issue roiling California voters: racial justice. In the years between the 1964 presidential election and the 1966 gubernatorial contest, race politics in California had exploded. On August 11, 1965, thousands of black residents in the Watts neighborhood of Los Angeles responded to the arrest of an intoxicated black motorist by a white policeman and decades of racial oppression by rioting. Just days before the 1966 gubernatorial election, racial violence again broke out, this time in San Francisco. White voters were appalled, and often scared, by the mayhem. Liberals in California responded, in part, to the state's fierce racial divisions by trying to treat what they saw as the primary cause of black anger—systemic racial discrimination. Housing discrimination was near the top of the list.

As in the rest of the United States, a great many white Californians had used every means at their disposal, including violence, race-based mortgage-lending, and racially prescribed real estate practices to keep housing racially segregated throughout the state. Mainly, whites simply exercised their individual right to sell their property to whomever they pleased: other whites. Liberals in California responded to this endemic racial segregation by pushing for a Fair Housing Act that would end Californians' right to racially discriminate when selling a home or apartment. Governor Brown supported this measure.

Reagan condemned the Fair Housing Act. He was not a racist, he said. He had been raised by his family to respect black people and had stood up for black individuals against racial discrimination several times in his life. But he believed absolutely in people's right to sell their home to whomever they wanted. According to Reagan, the government had no role to play (even though, of course, the government played a great many roles in the housing market, providing low-cost mortgages, mortgage insurance, and tax exemptions, none of which he opposed).

Whites overwhelmingly opposed the Fair Housing Act. In California, as in most parts of the United States, overt public racism was rare. But a great many whites, fearing above all for their property values but also anxious about the safety of their families, practiced a different kind of racial prejudice. Whites treated potential black neighbors differently than they would whites. At best, most white homeowners saw a black neighbor, no matter how wonderful an individual, as a harbinger of racial turnover, and that racial turnover represented an unacceptable financial and personal gamble. Reagan, believing that economic property rights trumped equal housing opportunities, sided with the majority of whites and supported their racial fears. Principle clearly played a role. Reagan, like Barry Goldwater, opposed the 1964 Civil Rights Act and the 1965 Voting Rights Act as inappropriate big government interventions in local affairs. His opposition to government-mandated racial equality was consistent with his larger principles, but it was also, without question, the politically winning move not only in the Deep South but in California in the 1960s.

Reagan, like Phyllis Schlafly, never found anything to praise about the civil rights movement and, like her, he generally did his best to steer clear of the politics of racial justice. He never openly advocated racist practices, but he also never condemned them. In his breakthrough speech, "A Time of Choosing," given at the height of the civil rights revolution, he never mentioned the issue of racism or racial equality. Reagan was by all accounts not a racist. The question of racial justice, as compared to anticommunism or economic liberty, just did not much interest him—which was a shocking self-indulgence for a man seeking elected office in the midst of the civil rights movement.

Though Reagan was much better read than his critics assumed, his reading did not extend to the multitude of new works detailing the black experience with slavery, segregation, or systemic discrimination. Race was one of his blind spots, and he did not much think about what it meant to be a black American in "the land of the free."[19]

In 1964, Goldwater had lost California by more than three hundred thousand votes, not surprising in a state in which registered Democrats outnumbered registered Republicans by a ratio of 3 to 2. So it was quite an upset when Reagan won the governorship by more than a million votes. He retained the state's active conservative bloc, but he also won over large numbers of blue-collar Democrats, who responded enthusiastically to his get-tough rhetoric and his racially infused homeowners' rights stance. Governor Brown and California's liberal Democratic establishment were shell-shocked; they would not be the last liberal Democrats to be outsmarted by Ronald Reagan.

Reagan was governor of California from 1966 through 1974. During those years, he became one of the nation's best-known opponents of the social change movements sweeping the country. Usually, though not always, his hard rhetoric raced ahead of his actual policies. And as governor of the nation's most populous state, with an economy bigger than all but a handful of nations in the world, Reagan also learned a great deal about governance, policymaking, and the practice of politics. Though he almost always spoke as an unalloyed conservative, he governed more pragmatically.

Following Barry Goldwater's 1964 defeat, Reagan had made the case in the *National Review* that if conservative politicians meant to win future elections, they had to show American voters that their own beliefs were in fact conservative. During his years as governor, Reagan used campus protests to do just that. Because most liberals were "soft" on student protests—by 1968 liberals, too, marched against the Vietnam War and believed that racial justice demanded major changes in American life—California's leftist protestors became Reagan's best illustration in his case for conservatism. His attacks on student radicals were matched by many other political figures on the right, ranging from the populist, self-proclaimed conservative George Wallace to the master politician of resentment, Richard Nixon. But Reagan had two advantages: first, as the governor of a state with highly visible protests, he faced the issue directly, and second, his rhetorical style was unmatched by any other major figure (though Richard Nixon was no slouch on the topic).

At the rhetorical level, Reagan could be fierce on the subject of radical protesters. But he could also keep the mood light. When Alabama Governor George Wallace ran for president in 1968, he loved to brag in front of crowds that if a protester tried to stop his motorcade with some kind of sit-in demonstration, it would be the last demonstration that hippie ever lived to try—he would run him over and never look back. Generally, Wallace's audiences cheered, but such scary talk did not tend to sit well over the long haul. Reagan took the story of the radical protester in a different direction. He told his audiences that he had recently seen an antiwar demonstrator waving a "Make Love Not War" placard, but he was pretty sure the demonstrator was incapable of either act: "His hair was cut like Tarzan, and he acted like Jane, and he smelled like Cheetah."[20] Reagan turned the dangerous into the comedic, the radical into a laugh line about a Tarzan movie. It was populist genius. He did not need to kill the enemy; he simply mocked it. During his run for governor, as noted earlier, Pat Brown had tried to ridicule Reagan as the has-been actor who had played second lead to a chimpanzee in *Bedtime for Bonzo*. Reagan turned it around; it was the fancy-talking student radicals and their liberal professors at California's elite university who were the chimps.

Those same voters cheered, too, when Reagan showed the iron fist in the velvet glove to the student radicals. In 1969, when Berkeley protesters tried to stop university administrators from building on a vacant piece of property counterculturalists had turned into "People's Park," Governor Reagan ordered National Guardsmen to join the local police in restoring order. In so doing they released military-grade tear gas over swaths of Berkeley. Guardsmen bayoneted to death one bystander, blinded another, and sent dozens of people to the hospital. University administrators were horrified, liberals decried the action, and so did a broad range of observers and investigators. Reagan dismissed their concerns, stating that he had done what was necessary to restore law and order.

The California electorate, reflecting national surveys, overwhelmingly sided with their governor.[21] In the intellectually disciplined pages of William Buckley's *National Review*, the necessity for order in a civilized society had been carefully and repeatedly stressed throughout the 1960s; Ronald Reagan put flesh to those words. During this era liberals tried desperately to solve what they believed were underlying problems that had created so much disorder and criminality in America. Conservatives simply said that disorder and criminality were dangers that must not be countenanced. In the eyes of the majority, conservatives had the better of the argument. A sizable number of Americans, when it came to the issue of law and order, were learning that what they believed in was called conservatism.

Governor Reagan had much on his plate besides radical students, Black Power militants, and an epidemic of violent crime. In governing California he tried to implement his conservative principles, but he also learned about the difficulties of governance and the limits of executive power. Three issues, during those years, stand out: taxes, welfare reform, and the politics of abortion. Reagan's number one priority as governor was to *cut* state taxes. His first major act in office was to call for the largest tax *increase* in California's history. Over his eight years as governor, he raised the sales and income tax by some 50 percent. He had no other viable option; his liberal predecessor had overseen rapid economic growth but had left the state government in financial crisis. Reagan cleaned up the mess by doing what he most hated. Given the sacred status of tax cuts for the conservative movement, the irony here is substantial; but Reagan had done what he felt he must, and by 1973 he had moved the state budget from red to black.

Reagan wanted no other governor or the taxpayers of California to face a similar budgetary fiasco. He asked the nation's preeminent antigovernment, pro–free market economist, the brilliant Milton Friedman, to help him solve the problem. With Friedman's assistance, Reagan and his gubernatorial team drafted a state constitutional amendment that would limit state spending and state tax increases. Reagan explained his thinking to supportive businesspeople: "You can lecture your teenagers about spending too much until you're blue in the face, or you can accomplish the same goal by cutting their allowance. We think it is time to limit government's allowance—to put a limit on the amount of money they can take from people in taxes. This is the only way we will ever bring government spending under control."[22] Reagan threw everything he had into the fight, but many Californians found the measure too confusing and, for some, too restrictive, and voted it down. As a tax cutter, Reagan had failed in California. But his war on "tax and spend" politics had just begun.

Reagan had greater success in the battle over welfare. Conservatives had long been arguing that government handouts to the poor were big government paternalism at its worst: government welfare payments only hurt the poor by luring them into a lifetime of spirit-breaking dependency. In 1965, even one of President Johnson's advisers (and later Democratic senator), Patrick Moynihan, had worried that the federal welfare system was contributing to a rise in black families headed by unmarried women, damning them and their children to a culture of poverty.

Reagan believed that some desperate people truly needed government assistance, but he worried that far too many were simply taking advantage of taxpayers' generosity. "The state constitution says that you have to be a resident for five years in order to run for Governor," Reagan stated in his inimitable fashion, "But you have to be here only 24 hours to get on welfare." Many welfare recipients, he argued, did not need the money; they were welfare cheats, illegally enrolled in the program, who used their handouts at the racetrack and the liquor store. The rhetoric was strong, but the facts were simple: in 1963, 375,000 Californians received welfare payments from Aid to Families with Dependent Children, and in 1970 some 1,566,000 did. Working with the Democratic state legislature Reagan devised a compromise that reduced welfare rolls by three hundred thousand people (his goal) while increasing payments for most of those who remained (liberals' goal). The 1971 law also began a pilot program that made some welfare recipients with older children work in exchange for their public assistance. It was breakthrough legislation, and it was popular with voters. Reagan had found another winning issue that showed taxpayers that the solutions they favored were conservative ones.

During his years as governor, on some issues that would become vital to social conservatives in the 1970s, including abortion, Reagan was still working out his principles and his willingness to compromise. Conservatives were by no means of one mind on a great many social issues. The aforementioned Milton Friedman, the epitome of an economic conservative, was very much a libertarian on every kind of social issue: he believed marijuana should be legal, as should prostitution and gambling. He believed Americans should have access to whatever kind of birth control they wanted and that women should have the right to abortion. Friedman was consistent; he opposed almost all forms of government regulation of individual behavior, economic or otherwise, as long as that behavior did not directly harm another individual. Barry Goldwater, though he had kept quiet about all of these issues during his presidential run, had a good deal of sympathy for this kind of libertarian conservatism; years later he would come out in support of gay rights and the decriminalization of some illegal drugs.

Reagan, too, had his libertarian side. When an initiative came up in California, pushed hard by a faction of social conservatives, to ban all homosexual teachers from California's public schools, Reagan helped to defeat it. He did not want to see the government peering into adults' bedrooms to examine their sexual practices. But unlike his anticommunist, free market faith, newly elected Governor Reagan had not really thought through where his anti–big government conservatism ended and his social order conservatism began. Thus, the abortion issue blindsided him.

When Reagan took office in 1966, the issue of legalized abortion had yet to become a major dividing line between liberals and conservatives. The Catholic Church had long opposed abortion, just as it opposed the use of every form of "artificial" contraception. On the other side, the newly minted feminist movement insisted that all forms of birth control, including abortion, should be made available to women, and they began a political campaign to make abortion legal; the practice had been made illegal through state legislation, generally, in the late nineteenth century. Many health-care providers and family planning advocates also supported legalized abortion. At the time, a majority of Americans, including most evangelical Protestants and such famous ministers as Billy Graham, were ambivalent about the issue. As with so many controversies during this time, California was among the first states in which the question came to the fore. In 1967, the California state legislature passed a bipartisan measure, the Therapeutic Abortion Act, which would allow a woman to terminate a pregnancy in the case of incest, rape, or if a doctor determined that her health was at risk. The measure also allowed a woman to have an abortion if the fetus showed signs of serious abnormalities.

When the bill came to him, Reagan was not sure what to do. At a press conference, he displayed "total confusion" about the legislation. Instinctively, Reagan opposed the bill. He was not, at the time, able to articulate exactly why he was made so uncomfortable by it—and it is worth repeating that many conservative religious Protestants shared that unarticulated discomfort but had not yet made abortion a major issue either. Finally, he took a stand, demanding that the legislature delete the provision that allowed a woman to abort a fetus on the grounds that if it came to term it would have major birth defects. That was the kind of law Hitler would approve, he said. That one provision was stripped from the bill, and Reagan then signed it into law. Thanks to Ronald Reagan, six years before the Supreme Court made "a woman's right to choose" a constitutionally protected individual liberty, Californian women had greater access to legal abortions than women in all but a handful of states in the country.[23] Governor Reagan had been willing to compromise on abortion; it would take a political movement to stiffen his spine on this issue.

After eight years as governor, Reagan had received an education in governance and economic policymaking. His conservative ideology had been tempered by political realities. Most obviously, he had been forced to raise taxes to fight the state's budget deficits. But in other ways, small and large, he had moved California politics to the right: he had restricted welfare benefits; he had sided with the state's big agricultural interests in their battles with farm workers; he had worked with the lumber lobby against redwood-conserving environmentalists; and he had supported every effort to fight crime, preserve law and order, and expand property rights. Ironically, Reagan was able to do little as governor in the political struggle that most mattered to him: fighting communism. He had been able to exercise that muscle in the satisfying battles against student radicals, anti–Vietnam War protestors, and Black Power militants, but that was not quite the same as taking on the Soviet Union. Reagan had much unfinished business, and he had decided early on in office that he was not ready to retire with California governor as the last line on his impressive résumé.

Reagan flirted with running for the presidency in 1968 when he went to the Republican convention as the favorite-son candidate of the California delegation. Remembered for his speech in behalf of Goldwater and admired for his get-tough approach toward California's leftist dissidents as well as his anti–civil rights stance, Reagan was a favorite with conservatives, especially in the South. But after South Carolina's Strom Thurmond rallied southern delegates in behalf of Nixon, Reagan realized he could not win and quickly turned over his delegates to the front runner, who had backed away from some of his earlier liberal domestic positions and made the issue of law and order his battle cry. Reagan loyally supported him in the election and in Nixon's 1972 reelection bid. That loyalty did not carry over to the man who replaced Nixon after the unpleasantness of Watergate. Reagan had been unhappy with Nixon's failure to embrace the GOP's conservative causes; he was even more disappointed with President Ford's continued trek, à la Eisenhower, to the moderate middle of the political spectrum. Reagan knew, too, that conservative activists all over the country were furious with Ford for selecting Nelson Rockefeller, the liberal champion of East Coast Republicanism and their bitter enemy in 1964, as his vice president. Reagan decided to run hard for the 1976 GOP nomination against the incumbent, albeit unelected, president of the United States.

Taking the nomination away from the incumbent was a long shot. President Ford had all the power of his office to line up support, as well as the gratitude of his party for serving the nation honorably after Nixon fled the White House in disgrace. On his side, Reagan had the power of a swelling conservative movement, as well as his own gifts. In the end it was shockingly close, as Reagan lost the nomination fight by just 117 delegates. To defeat Reagan, Ford had been forced to move to the right. He repudiated the policy of détente engineered by Richard Nixon and his own secretary of state, Henry Kissinger, and he amped up the volume of his anti-Soviet, anticommunist rhetoric. To appease conservative delegates, Ford jettisoned Nelson Rockefeller and selected as his running mate the midwestern conservative, acid-tongued Senator Bob Dole. The conservatives had shown their muscle in 1976, but they had not been able to put their champion Ronald Reagan over the top. It was a gallant try, but many thought that would be the last they would see of the "Gipper" on the national stage. Reagan was sixty-five years old.

Reagan was not worried about his age; he still wanted to be president. As soon as Jimmy Carter defeated Ford in November 1976, he began to organize for the 1980 election. Between 1976 and 1980 the strands of the conservative movement coalesced in support of his candidacy. Against the dark times of the late 1970s, that movement expanded and strengthened. It brought Reagan money, ideas, volunteers, and victory. In the late 1970s, from every direction on the political map, Americans demanded change. Jimmy Carter had ridden the first wave of that demand to the White House. The former one-term governor of Georgia campaigned against President Ford as an outsider, untainted by the stink of Watergate, the horrors of Vietnam, and the substantive failures of the Washington policymaking community. "I will never lie to you," he said to the American people. That message, above all, won Carter the presidency. It certainly helped, too, that he was a proud southerner and an avowed evangelical Christian. And in 1976 he did not just run against his Republican opponent but also against traditional Democratic Party politics, easily beating his more liberal competitors for the presidential nomination. In 1976, a majority of Americans were ready for a change, and the outsider, nonideological, religious southerner Jimmy Carter seemed to offer America something different.

Unfortunately for President Carter and the American people, he was unable to deliver on those hopes. He genuinely was an outsider, and even once he was ensconced in the White House, he stayed that way—lambasting Washington insiders for their politics-as-usual ways. That might have been good campaign rhetoric, but it made working with the congressional old boys, even of his own Democratic

Party, nearly impossible. Such political missteps were only a small part of the problem. Carter inherited a bevy of economic problems when he took office: growing trade deficits, high unemployment, inflation and slow growth (a.k.a., "stagflation"), declining productivity, and record-high energy prices. During his presidency almost all of those economic problems worsened. Carter tried. He broke from the liberal economic policies of the past, most particularly by deregulating several key American industries. But it was not enough. At the advent of the 1980 presidential campaign, the economy was reeling, and Americans were again demanding change.

Making matters worse, Carter also found himself in the midst of international security crises. The most obvious disaster was the takeover of the American embassy in Iran by Islamic militants supported by the new revolutionary theocracy headed by the Ayatollah Khomeini. Sixty-six Americans were taken hostage on November 4, 1979, and nearly a year later, in the weeks leading up to the presidential election, more than fifty remained captive. The hostage takers put up a banner on the embassy wall: "CIA, Pentagon, Uncle Sam, Vietnam Wounded You; Iran Will Bury You."[24] At Christmas 1979 the Soviet Union invaded Afghanistan, increasing fears in the United States that the communists were again on the march, taking advantage of an American foreign policy establishment paralyzed by the Vietnam War "syndrome." In the face of these threats, the United States military, too, remained in a post-Vietnam funk, underfunded and facing major difficulties recruiting quality personnel. In answer to this litany of woes, Carter offered the American people calls for sacrifice in an age of limits. In his 1980 State of the Union message he scolded the American people, quoting the pundit Walter Lippmann, "You took the good things for granted. Now you must earn them again. . . . There is nothing for nothing any longer."[25] Ronald Reagan, the conservative movement's sunny optimist, had found his moment.

Reagan faced a pride of challengers for the Republican presidential nomination, chief among them George H. W. Bush, but now he was the favorite, and he beat them all. His speeches inspired and in debates he sparkled. Any questions about his age were dispelled by the energy and obvious delight he brought to his campaigning. And this time, Reagan had the money and the wholehearted support of a vibrant conservative movement behind him. He and the burgeoning conservative movement were ready to run for the presidency and win.

Reagan was a gifted candidate. As his victories in California proved, he had a rare ability to connect with voters. But in the 1980 election, Reagan did not have to carry the load alone. The conservative movement had come a long way since the 1964 Goldwater campaign. If he had only lived to see the day, Senator Robert Taft would have been flabbergasted by the breadth and depth of the activist base that stood behind Reagan's White House run. In Taft's day, the only political action committee had been run by organized labor, and campaign donations for GOP candidates tended to come in big checks but from relatively few people. Religiously oriented groups played no role, and except for business associations, few narrowly focused organizations had a hand in elections. Those were different times.

Reagan ran at a time of extraordinary politicization of civil society. For a number of years, the public had been most aware of liberals' successes, in this regard. By 1980, liberals had a vast network of issue- and group-based politically focused organizations. Feminist groups, civil rights groups, environmental organizations, public interest legal organizations, organized labor, and a multitude of other advocacy groups dedicated to using government resources to protect rights, foster equality, and regulate the private sector abounded. Others had arisen as watchdog organizations to reveal corrupt relationships between Washington politicians and big business as well as to lobby against the raw, secretive power of the "military-industrial complex" and the "national security state." A great many of these groups had their start in the 1960s or saw their memberships increase dramatically then or during the early 1970s. In the presidential election almost all could be counted on to support the Democratic Party candidate.

By 1980, conservatives were well prepared to beat back that effort. William Buckley, as vital as ever, had been preparing this battleground in the intellectual realm for better than a quarter of a century. He was joined by legions of other intellectuals and policy advocates trained in the hothouse atmosphere of right-wing think tanks sponsored by wealthy conservatives. In the 1970s, Phyllis Schlafly had mobilized an army of women to fight government-supported gender equality and the secular culture that feminists and their allies promoted. She and her "Eagles" were 100 percent behind Reagan, as were an army of anti-abortion activists. So, too, was an extensive network of highly motivated rich businesspeople.

Some of these business leaders, both self-made millionaires and inheritors of great wealth, had been active literally for decades; they had first gotten involved in conservative politics fighting the New Deal. But joining them were a great many of more recent vintage. Like Reagan, they were furious with high taxes that they believed were taken from them to fund welfare and pay for the liberals' zealous efforts to bring equality to every group that claimed to be oppressed. People who ran successful but not large-scale businesses were frustrated, too, by the seemingly endless regulations federal bureaucrats produced at the behest of liberal politicians to ensure a safer, fairer, nondiscriminating, nonpolluting, consumer-friendly private enterprise system. Big corporations could handle the regulatory costs, but for smaller businesses they could be a terrific drain of capital, time, energy, and profit.

Donating vast sums to the Reagan cause, through direct donations but more often through the sponsorship of political action committees and other independent political organizations, were a hardnosed crew of multimillionaires. They included beer baron Joseph Coors, oil man Nelson Bunker Hunt, and Gulf Oil's Richard Mellon Scaife. Their deep pockets helped fund the giant conservative political action committees that swamped the airwaves and helped pay for the effort to put Reagan into the White House. Joining their megaefforts were literally millions of small contributors. A remarkable number of them had been solicited through pathbreaking direct-mail efforts led by Richard Viguerie. He had gotten his start in the conservative cause in the early 1960s with the Young Americans for Freedom and then, using a mailing list of contributors to the 1964 Goldwater campaign, he had developed an unprecedented fund-raising machine for the conservative movement. PAC money was no longer just labor money, as it had been in Robert Taft's day. Indeed, the United Auto Workers warned that Viguerie's direct-mail efforts, alone, could raise as much money for a political candidate or issue as all of the labor movement combined.[26] Thanks to the right-wing millionaires, Richard Viguerie's direct-mail genius, and other conservative activists, the three largest PACs in the country in the 1979–1980 campaign year were all a part of what the mass media had begun calling the New Right.

Joining those giant right-wing PACs were hundreds of new business PACs. In 1974, only eighty-nine corporate PACs existed, but by 1980 more than one thousand were operating, almost all of which supported the Reagan campaign.[27] After forty years of liberal big government policies that aimed to safeguard Americans from the ferocious risks and vicissitudes of the free market, big business and big money were betting tens of millions of dollars that their time was, once again, at hand.

Among the best-known contributors to the Reagan campaign, in large part thanks to the fascination and only partly masked disdain of the mass media, was the Moral Majority, founded by the Lynchburg, Virginia–based fundamentalist Baptist Reverend Jerry Falwell and other devout Christians. Falwell had received his political calling in the mid-1970s, when his disgust with feminism, homosexuality, and what he perceived to be a general moral degeneracy overrode his long-standing, oft-declared belief that ministers should save souls, not preach politics. Falwell had bluntly stated that ministers should not be involved in the secular struggle for black equal rights. However, when it came to struggles for equal rights for women and gays, he saw it differently. It was his religious duty as a minister, he explained, to fight such perversions of God's word, which he blamed on Americans' acceptance of "secular humanism."[28] According to Falwell, "Satan had mobilized his forces to destroy America. . . . God needed voices raised to save the nation from inner moral decay."[29] The secular mass media enjoyed publicizing such sentiments by Falwell, assuming that they indicated his outré marginality.

The mass media were wrong. In 1980, the United States was by most measures the most religious society in the industrialized world; about half of all Americans told survey takers that they prayed every day, and 80 percent believed in heaven.[30] And even as many of the more liberal Protestant denominations were losing congregants, the more fundamentalist-oriented and evangelical denominations such as the Assembly of God and the Southern Baptist Convention, as well as the Church of Jesus Christ of Latter-day Saints, were gaining adherents who were looking for a spiritual anchor that would hold their families safe against the rising tide of moral relativism. As Phyllis Schlafly had proved, many deeply religious people were appalled by liberals' campaign to mandate equality for women and homosexuals, and they were angry enough to do something about it.

Some religious people's general concern over what Reverend Falwell called "moral decay" was given greater political urgency in 1978 when the Internal Revenue Service, supported by the Carter administration, threatened to take away the tax-exempt status of whites-only Christian private schools unless they permitted black students to attend them. These academies had arisen in large numbers in the South as a response to the court-mandated desegregation of public schools that followed the *Brown v. Board of Education* decision. Some two hundred thousand people wrote to the IRS demanding that they rescind this policy, which they argued was purposely anti-Christian. Big government, they argued, had no right to interfere in how a Christian school chose to run its affairs.

The Moral Majority was joined by dozens of other conservative religious organizations, creating what the mass media dubbed "the Religious Right." This Religious Right reached its constituents, not only through the pulpit and direct-mail solicitations but also through its extensive "electronic ministry." Just as the Christian anticommunist crusade had taken to the radio waves in the 1950s, so too did the Religious Right take advantage of an extensive radio and television network set up primarily for evangelical purposes. Falwell had a popular radio show, *The Old Time Gospel Hour*, which was aired all over the nation. Pat Robertson, whose father had been the United States senator from Virginia, created the Christian Broadcasting Network and hosted the *700 Club*, a lively television show that freely intermixed faith healing and an ardently conservative take on the daily news. While not all televangelists threw their resources behind the Reagan campaign, many did. Liberals had nothing to match this kind of living-room outreach.

Reagan did not need to rely just on the organized forces of the Religious Right and the business community to win over voters. His main message was that high taxes to support big government were morally and economically wrong. In 1980, that was a winning message. Historian Bruce Schulman argues that even with all the other efforts of conservative activists throughout the 1970s, "the right needed a match—something to ignite a grass-roots chain reaction. Conservatism would find it with the tax revolt of the late 1970s, and the economic turmoil of the era would provide the tinder."[31] Reagan himself had tried to ignite that movement in the early 1970s in California but had not quite pulled it off. By the late 1970s, hyperinflation hammered home the tax issue for millions of Americans. Because of inflation, many saw their incomes rise but their purchasing power stay the same; similarly, their homes appreciated in price but not really in relative value. But even as Americans felt as if they were running faster and faster just to stay in the same economic place, their tax burdens kept going up. Many, with good reason, were angry. In response, in 1978, voters in Reagan's California passed a referendum, Proposition 13, slashing taxes. Thirty-seven other states followed, cutting property taxes. Twenty-seven slashed state income taxes. It was an avalanche pouring down on liberals' big government ideology. Reagan was on top of the mountain, hurling down the boulders.

If the tax issue put Reagan on the high ground, he was also willing to go into the swamps or, as Barry Goldwater put it in 1964, to go hunting where the ducks are. After formally winning the Republican presidential nomination, Reagan chose to open his general election campaign in Neshoba County, Mississippi. In national terms—and ones that most civil rights activists remembered—Neshoba County was infamous for one of the most evil acts perpetrated by white supremacists. It was there that local law enforcement conspired with Ku Klux Klansmen to torture and murder three young civil rights workers. In December 1979, the GOP national committeeman for Mississippi had recommended that the Republican presidential candidate come to the Neshoba County Fair to solicit what he labeled "George Wallace inclined voters."[32] Reagan, in other words, knew he was going to Neshoba to woo racist white voters. And in his speech there, he used the watchwords of the anti–civil rights, pro-segregation cause. "I believe in states' rights," Reagan proclaimed. He said nothing about the nightmare events that had put Neshoba County into the headlines back in the 1960s; he said nothing about moving past old racial divisions; he said nothing about racial justice. He simply gave the audience what it wanted; he hoped they would give him their votes. Carter, the white Southern Baptist, had won Mississippi in 1976. Reagan was only hoping to make the state competitive in 1980.

For Reagan, such a blatant appeal to racist whites was rare. And while he was willing to use this claim in the racist backwater of Neshoba County, his campaign team believed such moves were generally counterproductive and unnecessary. Richard Nixon, beginning in 1968 had shown that a Republican could win southern whites' votes, and the votes of many other whites throughout the United States, with less racially explosive but still racially resonant appeals. Reagan had himself similarly won over whites opposed to mandatory civil rights laws back in 1966 when he had rejected the California Fair Housing Act. Rather than use old-fashioned code words such as *states' rights* to appeal to racist sentiments, Republicans could, as Robert Taft had done back in the 1940s, simply make a principled stand in favor of individual property rights.

In other words, conservative Republicans could oppose liberal solutions without having to speak in favor of segregation, discrimination, or racism. They could oppose measures unpopular in the white community, such as government-mandated school busing programs, by speaking of local communities' right to self-determination; they could reject affirmative action programs by calling for color-blind policies. And while some whites, North and South, would be drawn to these stands for blatantly racial reasons, others would support them because they believed in free market principles, individual liberty, and merit-based equal opportunity. Reagan did not need a "southern strategy" based on racist appeals to win over whites opposed to government racial justice programs. He could accomplish the same thing with a Sun Belt strategy based on racially neutral conservative principles.[33] While liberals in 1980 would accuse Reagan of making racially-loaded appeals to white voters and of ignoring the impact of America's racist history, Reagan generally steered clear of the race issue. Race just muddied the water. He knew that white voters who worried, for whatever reasons, about liberals' mandatory racial equality policies would be drawn to his conservative stand. And Reagan did not think in very sophisticated terms about race. Perhaps he did not think much about race at all. As he suggested, somewhat whimsically, during his presidential debate with Jimmy Carter, back in the good old days when he was young, "this country didn't even know it had a racial problem." Carter, the antiracist, white southerner, was appalled. "Those who suffered discrimination," he said, ". . . certainly knew we had a problem."[34]

The 1980 presidential race made clear that Reagan had gaps in his knowledge. It made even clearer that he had conservative answers to some of America's major problems. He promised to fix the economy by cutting taxes and reducing government regulation and to increase America's global role by rebuilding U.S. military might and by challenging Soviet expansionism. He would restore traditional values and give the American people the leadership they deserved. Reagan easily won the 1980 election. He received about 51 percent of the vote (a third-party candidate, liberal Republican Congressman John Anderson, siphoned off about 7 percent). Reagan won every region of the country, taking forty-four states and 489 electoral votes. Surprising even his own campaign staff, he won the entire South except for Carter's own Georgia. Reagan picked up one in four registered Democratic voters. A plurality of white union members, rejecting their leadership, voted for Reagan. White Catholic voters, long a staple of the Democratic Party, went narrowly for Reagan, led by Irish Americans and Italian Americans. Voters with only a high school education, reliable supporters of the Democratic Party, turned to Reagan. Jimmy Carter, the first avowedly "born-again" Christian president, lost the white evangelical Protestant vote by a 2 to 1 margin, receiving 25 percent less of this vote than he had in 1976 before the Religious Right organized against him. While political scientists still debate the exact role the Moral Majority played in this turn, it is likely that the organization helped Reagan win several closely contested races in the South. Overall, both men and women voted for Reagan over Carter, but Reagan did much better among men; he lost some women voters over his anti-ERA stance and others because they believed him to be too warlike in his stated policies. Reagan had opened up an electoral gender gap. The politics of sexuality and gender mobilized women on both sides of the partisan divide.

The New Deal coalition that had created the long-lasting liberal Democratic hegemony in Washington had broken apart. Only two groups from the old coalition stayed true to the Democratic Party: Jewish Americans and African Americans (about 85 percent of black voters supported Carter). Hispanics, in 1980 a relatively small constituency, also voted overwhelmingly for Carter. While polls showed that some 38 percent of the electorate said the main reason they voted for Reagan was simply because "It's time for a change," the president-elect could rightly claim that he had won an electoral mandate. Not only had he taken the presidency, but he, and the general conservative turn, had brought in a Republican Senate as well, netting twelve seats, knocking out several prominent liberals, and ending twenty-six years of Democratic majorities. In the House, too, Republicans had scored major upsets and had picked up thirty-three seats. All over the United States, numerous liberal officeholders had run on the defensive while conservatives had tooted their ideological horn. The result: Congress had moved a long way to the right. At the top of the ticket, Ronald Reagan had run as an avowed conservative; he had won as a conservative; and he intended to govern as such.[35]

President Reagan gave a powerful signal to his supporters when he took his oath of office. He placed his hand on a Bible opened to 2 Chronicles 7:14: "If my people, which are called by my name, shall humble themselves, and pray, and seek my face, and turn from their wicked ways; then I will hear from heaven, and will forgive their sin, and will heal their land."[36] Reagan would do his best to make conservatives' commitment to moral order, faith in the free market, and belief in a militarily strong, militantly anticommunist America his ruling principles. His successes in turning those principles into law and policy made him the modern conservative movement's greatest hero. And at least some of those policies and laws propelled him to a landslide victory in his reelection bid in 1984. Reagan had eight years to make over the American polity into a conservative realm.

Reagan's presidency is the stuff of numerous memoirs, journalistic accounts, and policy studies. Debates still rage over the range, depth, and meaning of what his supporters call the "Reagan Revolution." What is clear is that on every issue Reagan took the conservative side. His was an ideological administration—though, as was true of his governorship, pragmatism often warred with purity of principle. And on several issues of major importance to the conservative movement, such as rolling back federal civil rights policy, freeing industry of environmental controls, shrinking federal spending on social welfare programs, banning abortion, and instituting greater religiosity in public life, public opinion or powerful interests were not with the Reagan administration, and only small changes in policy ensued. Much of Reagan's personal fire was aimed at cutting federal taxes, deregulating the economy, and increasing U.S. military might to fight the Cold War against Soviet communism. Still, Reagan did do his best to fight liberals over social issues. He believed himself to be in a culture war, and he worked hard to be a leader in restoring Americans' confidence in what he believed to be the eternal truths of the American way of life.

Reagan's major domestic policy successes came in the area of economics. In some ways, he was pushing against an open door. Most everybody in 1980 conceded that the New Deal economic policies that had governed the United States since the 1930s were not working. Liberals were running scared. President Carter had already begun deregulating key transportation industries, and a bipartisan Congress chipped in by deregulating the banking industry, which inadvertently destroyed the savings and loan industry, resulting in a costly government bailout. Dramatic change was already afoot when Reagan took office. Given such an opportunity, he acted boldly.

Tax cutting had been at the core of Reagan's message since he announced his candidacy: "The key to restoring the health of the economy lies in cutting taxes." Cut taxes, he said, and America will have restored "individual initiative," and by so doing, greater economic growth will follow.[37] Reagan had been making this case in general terms since the early 1950s, when confiscatory tax rates on high incomes had made him reluctant to take on new acting jobs. By the early 1980s, he did not have to argue his case anecdotally. Conservative think tanks, journals, and newspaper editorialists had dressed up, blessed, and widely disseminated the tax-cutting message. Reagan, who followed the conservative movement's debates about the form and substance of tax policy, had explicitly signed on to the version of tax cutting that went under the broad heading of "supply-side" economics. Specifically, he backed a policy aggressively marketed by the charismatic New York Congressman Jack Kemp, who like Reagan had been a star (quarterback of the Buffalo Bills) before he had become a politician.

Kemp pushed for supply-side economics. New Dealers and those who followed their Keynesian approaches focused almost exclusively on macroeconomic tools that would stimulate aggregate demand. Kemp and the new supply-side advocates "shifted attention back to the problem of productivity and how to raise it," to measures that would promote investor and business confidence in the economy, and to increasing "the incentives for individuals to work, save, and invest." In other words, rather than using a government stimulus to keep consumers employed and spending, the supply-siders argued that the government had to make sure capitalists felt rewarded so that they would keep investing and taking the risks with their money, which would expand the economy—which in turn would provide jobs and keep consumers spending. Some supply-side advocates (rarely the ones with PhDs in economics) argued that big cuts in capitalists' taxes would so incentivize wealthy people's propensity to invest in the economy that those tax cuts would, counterintuitively, actually raise government revenues. Liberal critics—and some plain-vanilla economists—just called the whole thing "trickle-down" economics and warned that big tax cuts for the wealthy would produce some economic stimulation but little or no increase in income for working people. And without big reductions in government spending, supply-side tax cuts would also produce massive federal budget deficits.[38]

Even as the debate went on, Reagan got what he wanted from a skittish Congress. The Economic Recovery Tax Act of 1981 cut income taxes across the board and reduced the tax scale for wealthiest Americans from a top rate of 70 percent to 50 percent. Some of

Reagan's advisers, following the tenets of supply-side economics, had urged him to cut rates only for the wealthy. They argued that only the rich could use their tax savings to make productive economic investments; cutting taxes for less well-off Americans would produce little investment capital but risked creating federal budget deficits. Reagan often left much of the actual policymaking to his advisers, but in this case he took the lead, telling them, "I don't care." All taxpayers, he believed, deserved lower taxes. And Reagan was ever optimistic that supply-side principles would result in so much economic growth that budget deficits would take care of themselves. Reagan the savvy politician also believed that cutting taxes for middle-income Americans could help turn "Reagan Democrats" and millions of other voters into committed Republicans.[39] Across-the-board tax cuts were a popular, and even populist, measure. That's not to suggest that Reagan forsook traditional Republican interests for the formerly-Democrat masses. Tax cuts overwhelmingly favored the wealthy. And the Reagan administration offered businesses a host of incentives as well. "Reaganomics," as the pundits dubbed the overarching package, was off to the races.

Congressional passage of Reagan's cherished Tax Act was assured by a near tragedy. Less than two months after the inauguration, President Reagan was shot by a mentally-ill young man who hoped that killing the president would, somehow, win him the heart of a famous actress. A bullet—called a Devastator—nicked Reagan's lung and lodged just below his heart; the seventy-year-old president was bleeding internally, and his blood pressure was plummeting; a doctor gasped, "Think we're going to lose him." Despite the gravity of his wound, the president remained calm and, remarkably, joked with everyone around him, keeping *them* calm, as well. As he was prepared for emergency surgery, he looked at his doctors: "I hope you're all Republicans," he said.[40] As Americans kept vigil for their president, word spread of Reagan's grace, courage, and good humor. He recovered much more quickly than anyone had predicted—except for Reagan himself. Americans were heartened by their president's character. The Democratic Speaker of the House, Tip O'Neill, stated the obvious: "the President has become a hero. We can't argue with a man as popular as he is." The president had been lucky that the bullet had missed his heart, the rest of his luck he made himself.

Reagan needed the goodwill of Congress and the American people for the other major piece of economic policymaking aimed at ending the "stagflation" that had gripped the nation. The tax cuts were supposed to fight economic stagnation by prompting investment, but before people felt confident enough in the American economy to make the long-term investments that would create strong growth, inflation had to be beaten back. To defeat rampaging inflation, the Federal Reserve Bank, with Reagan's strong encouragement, dramatically tightened monetary policy. The "tight money" policy threw the American economy into a short-term tailspin, causing unemployment to rocket upward. Rather than give in to the political pressure caused by the economic downturn—the recession of 1981–82 was the worst since the dreadful days of the 1930s—Reagan used all his communication skills to convince the American people that they must "stay the course" and take the pain. By the end of 1982, the tight monetary policy had done its work, and inflation had been tamed. Given a more stable economic environment, tax cuts, and other incentives, investors began investing, and businesses began expanding. The economy began to grow again.

Reagan had told the American people in his inaugural address that "government is not the solution to our problem; government is the problem." In line with his fellow conservatives, he believed that the federal government did too much, spent too much, and regulated too much. Translating that belief into policy, however, was not something Reagan had thought a great deal about. His own feelings on the subject were somewhat contradictory. And while many Americans, in the abstract, supported the idea of cutting the size of the federal government, not so many wanted to see any programs they favored face the budget axe. George Will, the nation's eagle-eyed conservative pundit, cheered Reagan's desire to cut government spending but offered an ironic warning: "Americans are conservative. . . . What they want to preserve is the New Deal."[41]

In January 1982, as his administration struggled to cut federal spending and Reagan faced a great deal of criticism from the multitudes of

Americans who benefited from that spending, ranging from farmers to businesspeople to senior citizens to advocates for the poor and the disabled, the president wrote privately of his frustrations: "The press is trying to paint me as trying to undo the New Deal. I remind them I voted for FDR four times. . . . I'm trying to undo the Great Society."[42] At the same time, even as Reagan grumbled about his loyalty to FDR, he made a striking symbolic attack on the New Deal. He ordered the removal of a portrait of Harry Truman from the Cabinet Room of the White House, and in its place he had hung a stern painting of the last unsullied, tax-cutting pre–New Deal champion of the almost unregulated free market system: President Calvin Coolidge.

Reagan's champion would have found plenty of places to cut federal spending, damn the public outcry, but the Reagan administration, led by their pragmatic and non-detail-oriented leader, had a much harder time. Taking off the table the various New Deal and popular post–New Deal entitlement programs such as Social Security and Medicare left much less spending to cut from the federal budget, even as the administration took after the various antipoverty programs that had grown in the 1960s. Budget cutting was further complicated, to say the least, by Reagan's commitment to huge increases in military spending and national security programs. Big spending cuts would not be a significant aspect of Reagan's conservative legacy to federal policymaking; the opposite actually held true.

Since the late 1950s, conservatives had been insisting that the United States military establishment was being outspent by the Soviet Union. Goldwater had made this concern one of his 1964 campaign mainstays, and Phyllis Schlafly had labeled liberals "gravediggers" for their supposed refusal to match and better Soviet military expenditures. Reagan had made similar claims, arguing that the Soviets had engineered "the biggest military buildup in the history of man."[43] He insisted that he would end Americans' vulnerabilities to Soviet aggression and achieve "peace through strength." Here, Reagan was as good as his word. Over the course of his presidency, he demanded that Congress produce massive increases in military spending, and he got them, with more than $2 trillion dollars appropriated. The result of his extraordinary spending increase, limited spending cuts in other government programs, and the failure of supply-side economics to deliver the increases in tax revenues its more optimistic proponents promised resulted in the largest peacetime budget deficits the United States—or the world—had ever seen, creating a huge national debt that generations of Americans would have to pay off. Some political analysts argue that Reagan knowingly took on huge budget deficits in order to handcuff future politicians' ability to instigate big new federal programs. The evidence is out on that debate, but Reagan did willingly accept the cost of his gigantic military buildup: "Defense is not a budget item. You spend what you need."[44]

Throughout much of the 1970s, especially in the immediate post–Vietnam War years, American policymakers, including Presidents Nixon, Ford, and Carter, had focused on improving relations with the Soviet Union, pursuing a policy of détente that included nuclear arms control treaties. As a partial result, all three presidential administrations had tried to limit the number of big-ticket new weapons systems, and until the last years of the Carter administration, the defense budget had grown quite modestly. Nixon had ended conscription, which had largely been in effect during peacetime as well as during times of war since 1940, and created a smaller, all-volunteer military force, but neither Ford nor Carter provided the military with sufficient pay and benefits for service to keep quality and morale up, especially in the army.

Reagan turned around all of these trends. Servicemen and women, whose pay had seriously declined as compared to the civilian job market, saw big improvements. Unprecedented sums went to defense contractors—many of them, it is only fair to say, located in California and other Sun Belt states that had supported Reagan—for military equipment of every kind, both conventional and strategic (nuclear weapons), including billions for research into weapons systems that Reagan hoped would eventually be capable of shooting down enemy missiles aimed at the United States: the strategic defense initiative, a.k.a. "Star Wars." Reagan hated the fact that so-called mutual assured destruction—in other words, a nuclear holocaust—was America's only military defense against a Soviet nuclear attack. Most of all, he rejected détente with the Soviet Union and, instead, went on the offensive, at least for a while.

When Ronald Reagan took office, the Cold War between the United States and the Soviet Union was nearly thirty-five years old, and since the 1950s, Americans had been living under the shadow of the mushroom cloud. President Richard Nixon, whose anticommunist credentials were iron-clad, had surprised many, and infuriated conservatives, when he chose to open up relations with the People's Republic of China and de-escalate tensions with the Soviet Union. Nixon worked closely with his national security adviser, Henry Kissinger, one of the conservative movement's least-favorite individuals. Conservatives believed, with good reason, that Kissinger was indifferent to the Soviet's moral deficiencies and interested only in establishing a global balance-of-power that locked in the Soviet's control of their own sphere of influence in exchange for more peaceful relations between the superpowers. The Nixon-Kissinger détente policy seemed to implement that worldview.

Reagan had long decried détente with the Soviets. In one of the radio addresses he gave regularly before the 1980 campaign began, he joked bitterly, "détente—isn't that what a farmer has with his turkey—until Thanksgiving Day?"[45] Reagan did not trust the Soviets. He believed that they intended to aggressively expand their influence wherever and however they could and that the presidencies of Nixon, Ford, and Carter had strengthened the Soviet's global reach. Reagan's commitment to increasing America's military strength was the clearest proof of his concern, but it was not his only one.

For the first years of his presidency, Reagan launched a war of words against the Soviets. In speech after speech he condemned the Soviet Union and warned its leaders that its days were numbered. In one of his most famous speeches, delivered to the British Parliament on June 8, 1982, he listed the Soviets' sins against humanity: the ongoing brutality of the Berlin Wall, the attacks on East German anti-Soviet demonstrators in 1952, the 1956 slaughtering of Hungarian Freedom Fighters, the crushing of Prague Spring in 1968, and the attempted destruction of Poland's Solidarity labor movement. He warned the Soviets "that the very repressiveness of the state ultimately drives people to resist, if necessary, by force." Nine months later he spoke to a convention of evangelical Christians and in biblical tones lambasted the Soviet Union as an "evil empire" and urged his audience to "pray for the salvation of all of those who live in totalitarian darkness—pray that they will discover the joy of knowing God." Then Reagan stated, "But until they do, let us be aware that while they preach the supremacy of the state, declare its omnipotence over individual man ... they are the focus of evil in the modern world." The historian John Paul Diggins appreciatively concludes, "The old era of polite, soft diplomacy aimed not to offend the Kremlin as the United States continued policies of containment and détente," but "[l]ike an old prophet, Reagan could do no other than to rage against hypocrisy and mendacity."[46]

Reagan's war of words and his billions for military defense were not his only weapons against the communist adversary. Fulfilling conservatives' long-standing hopes, his administration took to the offensive. Following up on a Carter initiative, the Reagan administration began providing large-scale support for the Islamic rebels fighting the Soviet occupation of Afghanistan. Reversing the Carter administration's focus on supporting human rights in the third world, Reagan's national security team began looking for additional places to fight the communists and to support anticommunist allies. In this struggle, Reagan was personally influenced by a November 1979 article he had read in *Commentary* magazine, whose editor, Norman Podhoretz, was a well-known member of a group of intellectuals who called themselves neoconservatives.

Most of these neoconservatives had started their political journey in the pre-1960s era on the Left but as strong opponents of Soviet communism. Almost all of them had supported John Kennedy–style, liberal anticommunism, but during the later 1960s they fell away from liberalism and eventually from the Democratic Party out of disgust with its failures to maintain sufficient rigor in the anticommunist cause and to promote American global leadership. One of these figures, Jeanne Kirkpatrick, authored the seminal article, "Dictatorships and Double Standards," that captured Reagan's attention. She wrote: "We seem to accept the status quo in Communist nations (in the name of 'diversity' and national autonomy) but not in nations ruled by 'right-wing' dictators or white oligarchies."[47] Kirkpatrick warned that to demand that nations transform themselves quickly into democracies was a fool's errand, likely only to produce explosive conditions contrary to American anticommunist interests. Iran was her major case in point. She concluded by arguing that whereas communist totalitarian nations would never transform themselves into more benign political systems, what she called authoritarian nations—noncommunist dictatorships—would do so, on their own, if given plenty of time.

This intellectual argument fell in nicely with Reagan's own sentiments and those of many of his national security team. In accord, Reagan reversed Carter's anti-apartheid South Africa policies, welcomed to the United States the dictators of South Korea and the Philippines, provided plentiful support to the murderous but anticommunist regime in El Salvador, and gave financial support to Lebanon's brutal Phalangist Party, which in a complicated set of actions resulted in the deadly terror bombing of a U.S. Marine Corps deployment in Lebanon. Human rights, except in the Soviet bloc, were out in the Reagan White House. Fervent anticommunism was in.

Leftist regimes in America's own backyard gave opportunity for direct confrontation. The small island of Grenada afforded the chance for what President Teddy Roosevelt might have called "a splendid little war" to showcase America's growing military strength and confidence. The despotic left-wing government of Grenada had allied itself with communist Cuba. The Reagan administration, claiming that the Cubans were preparing a major military base there, stormed the island and overthrew the leftist regime. With the war won, Reagan told the American people that Grenada "was a Soviet-Cuban colony being readied as a major military bastion to export terror and undermine democracy. We got there just in time."[48] While a CIA secret report concluded that this claim was wholly inaccurate, a majority of Americans were pleased to see the American military perform its mission so well, and few, including Grenada's neighbors and most Grenadians, had any regrets over the demise of Grenada's brutish and incompetent government.

The Reagan administration launched a much more controversial and extended campaign against Nicaragua's leftist government. In 1979, the Sandinistas had overthrown a pro-American dictatorship that had been propped up, directly and indirectly, by American support for decades. Carter, in accord with his antidictatorship, pro-human rights policies, had accepted the regime change. Reagan, disgusted by the Sandinistas' open alliance with Cuba and a host of other left-wing regimes and groups around the world, did not. Reagan's aggressively anticommunist CIA director, William Casey, began a multipronged effort to overthrow the Sandinistas by training and funding a group dubbed the Contras and promoted by Reagan as "freedom fighters." They were more accurately a largely mercenary force that one CIA agent described as "animals . . . the Hells Angels of Central America."[49] Congress explicitly outlawed this effort. Zealous officials in the Reagan administration operated a secret, byzantine—and unlawful—program that used profits made from illegally selling weapons to the Iranian theocracy (in a secret effort to free American hostages in Lebanon) to illegally fund the Contras. This particular brainstorm, exposed first in a Lebanese newspaper of all places, led to the Reagan administration's lowest moments, the so-called Iran-Contra scandal, in which several top administration officials were found guilty of breaking various laws. In so many ways, Reagan's attempts to confront communism in the third world did not represent his finest hours in office. In an ironic defense of many of the administrations' misdeeds and miscues, the master investigative reporter of the Reagan years, Bob Woodward, recounts that Ronald Reagan had little knowledge (or interest) in foreign affairs other than those that had to do directly with the Soviet Union.[50]

Reagan did have a great deal of interest in the Soviet Union, even if he did not actually know much about its people, culture, or history. What he knew was that the Soviet regime was built on the slaughter and persecution of its own people and that its systematic destruction of personal freedom was antithetical to every principle on which he believed the United States stood. Thus, the "evil empire" rhetoric, the military buildup, the fervent and even feverish anticommunist activities in the third world. Given such an ideological base and set of policies, Reagan's move to negotiate an end to the arms race with the Soviet Union seems counterintuitive and to run against the whole thrust of conservatives' approach to fighting communism. Basically, it was.

Hard-line conservatives, including many of President Reagan's closest advisers, did not want him to reach out to the Soviet Union—in any fashion. These counselors had helped Reagan put his anti-communist feelings into words and deeds throughout much of his first term in office. But toward the end of that first term, Reagan began to have some second thoughts. As was often true with the president, a movie played a role in his mental process. One night in October 1983, Reagan watched *The Day After*, a made-for-television movie that imagined what would happen in Lawrence, Kansas, in the event of a nuclear war with the Soviet Union. The movie, Reagan wrote in his diary, "left me feeling greatly depressed." That depression was given greater urgency, a month later, when Reagan learned that Soviet officials had seriously considered launching a preemptive nuclear strike against the United States. Some of those Soviet officials had come unglued watching a NATO war game, Abel Archer 83; they feared that the game was a trick, masking a genuine attack on the Soviet Union. Reagan was shocked to learn that at least some people in the Soviet Union actually believed that the American president's fierce anticommunism and strident rhetorical attacks against their country were leading to an actual military confrontation. He began, if only marginally, to ponder how to use the military strength and demonstrations of national resolve he had overseen not to attack the Soviet Union but to reduce the threat of nuclear war that had long haunted him. His commitment to building some kind of anti-missile defense system was a part of that effort, as was his entire "peace through strength" strategy. But the real turn in President Reagan's thinking came in 1985 after Mikhail Gorbachev became the leader of the Soviet Union.

Gorbachev, rejecting the hard-liners in the Kremlin, believed that the Soviet Union had to defuse the Cold War hostilities with the United States. Gorbachev reached out to Reagan. And Reagan reached back. Cheered on by the more pragmatic members of his administration, especially his far-seeing Secretary of State George Shultz—as well as his wife, Nancy—Reagan began to offer a hand to those in Soviet Union who were genuinely interested in reducing the chances that the United States and the Soviet Union would end the world in a nuclear holocaust. He began meeting with the new leader of the Soviet Union.

Reagan could not have found a better partner. Gorbachev wanted desperately to turn his country away from its expensive and draining Cold War with the United States. Unlike the Central Intelligence Agency or the rest of Reagan's national security team, Gorbachev knew that the Soviet Union was dying; decades of economic rot, corruption, and inefficiency were destroying the communist state from within. The "containment" policy, which every president from Harry Truman onward had embraced, had done its work. The Soviet's own communist system was a cancer. There was no need for any outside power to go to war to defeat the Soviet Union; it would kill itself. This is exactly what the architect of the containment policy, George Kennan, had argued in the immediate post–World War II years.

Gorbachev hoped that he could redirect his society toward massive economic and political reform, and he knew that less threatening relations with the United States would give him more economic resources and a more stable domestic platform from which to begin remaking the Soviet system. By the end of 1987, Reagan, America's most fiercely anticommunist president, had signed a treaty with the Soviets' most daring reformer to begin actual reductions in nuclear weapons. And this was just the start. Reagan had argued that peace would come through strength. In his negotiations with Gorbachev, at least, his way had worked. Reagan, the onetime hard-liner, had successfully reduced the catastrophic threats of the Cold War.

Not even Reagan knew (or could have hoped) when he signed the 1987 Intermediate Nuclear Forces Treaty that the Soviet Union was on its last legs. Gorbachev failed to reform the Soviet Union; instead he unhappily oversaw its demise. The once-mighty communist state had failed. While scholars will long debate exactly what role President Reagan played in bringing the Cold War—and the Soviet Union—to its end, he was the president in office when Soviet communism began its death rattle. Just lucky?

Reagan's surprisingly pragmatic and winning negotiations with the Soviets earned him accolades from other world leaders and a broad spectrum of Americans. Ironically, many of his old, conservative, hard-liner allies felt that Reagan had been duped—only the fall of the Soviet Union in 1991 helped bring them around. While the Iran-Contra scandal and several of the Reagan administration's other adventures in the third world, as well as the massive deficits accrued by the herculean defense buildup, gave liberal critics ample ammunition for battling Reagan's conservative national security legacy, the American public, by and large, believed in Reagan's big picture: America was the world's "indispensible" superpower. And most Americans were pleased that Ronald Reagan had made the country so overwhelmingly strong again. Liberals would still argue that conservatives placed too much value on military strength, foreign policy belligerency, and unilateral actions, but Reagan's presidency gave conservatives a national security platform they were thrilled to build on.

Conservatives had more mixed emotions about Reagan's efforts to restore the social, cultural, and religious beliefs that they (and he) felt were the heart and soul of a virtuous American republic. More than he is often given credit for, Reagan did try to fulfill the agenda of the Religious Right and other social conservatives. But on many of the issues about which these supporters felt most deeply, Reagan faced major obstacles, sometimes splits in his own conservative movement but more often large-scale divisions in public opinion. In addition, on the most contentious social issue—abortion—"pro-life" activists were so focused on total victory that they often seemed to forget how committed Reagan had become to their cause. It is true that his first priorities were cutting taxes, increasing military spending, and fighting world communism. But through his government appointments, executive actions, policy commitments, and selections for the federal judiciary, Reagan moved the country decisively to the right on social issues. He was himself a religious Christian and was a careful reader of the Bible. During his presidency he pondered the coming of endtimes and at one point shared his thoughts with a Jewish lobbyist: "You know, I turn back to your ancient prophets in the Old Testament and the signs foretelling Armageddon, and I find myself wondering if we're the generation that's going to see that come about."[51] Reagan shared much with the New Right.

Reagan, of course, opposed the Equal Rights Amendment, but he vocally and energetically supported two very different constitutional amendments through his presidency. He championed an amendment that would give public school officials the constitutional right to provide organized prayer sessions to students. He also asked Congress to pass a constitutional amendment that would make abortion illegal in the United States. Both amendments were aimed specifically at overturning Supreme Court decisions and more generally toward the liberal cultural turn that sanctioned most every form of public and private sexual expression even as it restricted institutional forms of religiosity. As Reagan stated in his 1983 address to the National Association of Evangelicals, "For the first time the Congress is openly and seriously debating and dealing with the prayer and abortion issues— and that's enormous progress right there."[52] Still, despite Reagan's unequivocal support, both efforts failed.

However, in numerous ways Reagan moved the polity on these very issues. In every case, he appointed key officials in his administration who supported greater religiosity in American life and who opposed abortion. Wherever his executive power allowed, he instigated regulations that forbade abortions or the funding of abortions, and he worked with conservative members of Congress, especially the Senate's leading antiabortion champion, North Carolina Senator Jesse Helms, to deny foreign aid money of any kind to any organization that provided abortion services or abortion counseling, even if no federal money was ever used in that effort. Moreover, Reagan supported every effort by his executive appointees and conservatives in Congress to ban or limit federal funding of sex education (except abstinence programs) and sexual contraceptives. In his appointment of some three hundred judges to the federal bench, the issue of abortion was considered in the selection process. He did not fulfill the hopes of his most zealous social conservative followers, especially on either the issue of prayer in schools or abortion, but his commitment to "turning back the clock" to the values that had governed America when he was a young man was heartfelt. Despite setbacks, Reagan assured that those issues remained central to the conservative movement he had come to embody.[53]

Ronald Reagan ended his presidency on a wave of popularity equaled in the twentieth century only by his former idol, Franklin Roosevelt. A leading expert on the American presidency, Stephen Skowronek, places Reagan in the rich company of the presidents who transformed the United States: Thomas Jefferson, Andrew Jackson, Abraham Lincoln, and Franklin Roosevelt. Skowronek writes, "No president in recent times has so radically altered the terms in which prior governmental commitments are now dealt with or the conditions under which previously established interests are served."[54] Reagan took the dreams and ideas of the conservative movement that had been in the works for decades and made them, in many cases, the law of the land—and, just as telling, conventional wisdom. By no means did all Americans accept his conservative plan for the United States. At the end of his presidency, Reagan's social policies remained enormously divisive, and in many cases a majority rejected his attempts to rollback the government-assisted struggles for racial justice, gender equity, and equal opportunity in American life. Liberals believed his indifference to the plight of the poor and to growing economic inequality in the United States were terrible wounds in the body politic, and they vowed to heal them. Reagan transformed American politics, but he also contributed to the growing polarization of the American people. When he left office, just as when he gained it, liberals despised him. But conservatives, even more, loved him for what he had accomplished. Reagan's electoral coattails remained long. Reagan's vice president, George H. W. Bush, who had once scorned Reaganomics as "voodoo economics," had refashioned himself as a Reagan acolyte and won the 1988 election. Much of what Reagan had created would be continued.

Reagan was almost seventy-eight when he departed the White House. John Adams solemnly observed that at the end of George Washington's presidency the once-vibrant leader "seemed dazed and wholly scripted at certain public ceremonies, like an actor reading his lines."[55] Reagan, the actor who had become president, was an intellectually ailing man at his political end, but he had done what he had set out to accomplish. He was ready to step off the stage. He knew, as did his supporters, that he had left the conservative movement far, far stronger than he had found it.

GEORGE W. BUSH

The Conservative Calling and the Great Crack-up

WHEN GEORGE W. BUSH BEGAN HIS RUN FOR THE PRESIDENCY at the end of the twentieth century, he inherited a massive, confident, and powerful conservative movement. Though Bush's father, a late-blooming conservative fellow-traveler, had lost his bid for a second term to Bill Clinton, the Democratic Party political wunderkind and master of a postliberal triangulated politics that attempted to satisfy both liberal and conservative voters, the Right had only grown stronger in the 1990s. Ronald Reagan had become a national icon. Conservatives owned the Republican Party. They dominated Congress and the policymaking landscape. As William Buckley had dreamed nearly half a century earlier, conservatives had forged a public culture in which conservative voices and personalities filled the airwaves, bookstores, magazines, and the emergent digital empire of public opinion. This multifaceted power did not mean that most Americans called themselves conservative in the year 2000; about half of America's voters claimed the middle ground, describing themselves neither as liberal nor conservative but just plain moderate. But in the election year of 2000, liberals remained diffident while a confident conservative movement was proudly assertive about its vision for America.

While liberals struggled to reinvent their creed for a new century, their presumptive leader, President Clinton, had made an ideological retreat—if only to salvage what he could in order to fight another day. Reeling from a conservative Republican takeover of both houses of Congress in 1994, Clinton veered to the right. During his 1996 State of the Union address, made as he began his campaign for reelection, Clinton solemnly announced, "We have worked to give the American people a smaller, less bureaucratic government in Washington. And we have to give the American people one that lives within its means. The era of big government is over." Under his leadership, Clinton announced, fewer Americans were receiving food stamps and welfare checks. And in rhetoric that could have come straight from Ronald Reagan he intoned, "I believe our new, smaller government must work in an old-fashioned American way, together with all of our citizens through state and local governments, in the workplace, in religious, charitable and civic associations." Then, in words that would have cheered Phyllis Schlafly if she had trusted Clinton even a little bit, he paid homage to the family: "Family is the foundation of American life. If we have stronger families, we will have a stronger America." In a Buckley-esque turn, he reprimanded the producers of American popular culture for sullying the virtue of America's youth and asked Hollywood executives to make movies and television shows "you'd want your own children and grandchildren to enjoy." And in one more bid to reassure Americans that he understood the new politics of a post-Reagan America, Clinton promised to support legislation that would end the federal welfare entitlement that the 1935 Social Security Act had established.[1] Clinton would keep that promise, signing the conservative-driven Personal Responsibility and Work Opportunity Act in August 1996. He also advanced the deregulation of America's financial sector, continuing the work of the Reagan administration, by signing the 1999 Financial Services Modernization Act. Led by archconservative Texas Senator Phil Gramm, this act repealed a major aspect of the New Deal's regulation of the banking industry.

Clinton was no conservative. Despite his bows to an increasingly conservative electorate—and his embrace of Wall Street's demands for a freer hand in accumulating wealth and profits—Clinton saw many uses and many needs for an activist federal government. And the egalitarian family ideal he supported was not the one the most zealous anti-ERA activists had insisted on. Nonetheless, he believed with good reason that running for the presidency in 1996 as a liberal, New Deal or otherwise, was political suicide. So he ran as he had against Bush in 1992, as a "new" Democrat, respectful of the conservative political hurricane that had blown across great swathes of the United States. Clinton won his second presidential term, but he did so only by tacking into that wind. Clinton the Democrat was in the White House at the end of the twentieth century, but liberalism was, even still, in the doghouse.

So, in 1999, when George W. Bush went to Iowa to announce his presidential candidacy, he did so confident that he should and could run as an avowed conservative. In words that echoed those of Barry Goldwater, in the simple, emotive, and occasionally disjointed sentences that would become his trademark, he told a small crowd: "I make decisions based on a conservative philosophy that is engrained in my heart." He ticked off the elements of that philosophy: "Understand that private property is the backbone of capitalism. Fight for American interests and American workers in the world. Know the importance of family and the need for personal responsibility. These are principles from which I will not vary."[2] In my heart, Bush said, I am a conservative like you.

Bush was an unusual conservative leader. He had not come of age intellectually in conservative institutions or organizations, nor was he well-schooled in the conservative intellectual tradition. His conservatism came from a different set of experiences. It was roughly forged in his disgust with the left-wing, sixties campus political culture he endured as an undergraduate at Yale University. While others protested the war in Vietnam and struggled for racial justice, young George embraced the conventional role of hard-drinking, fun-loving fraternity boy. And though born to one of the most cosmopolitan and powerful families in the United States, with roots deep in Northeast bastions of clubby sophistication, and though graduated from three of America's most elite schools, he embraced his own proudly provincial life-course in Texas, where his father, in pursuit of oil riches, had moved the family when George was just two and where young Bush chose to return after his Ivy League education to make his business and then political career. Finally, and unlike Ronald Reagan, Bush found the core of his conservative values not in his readings in free-market economics or anticommunist treatises but, he said, in the words of God as revealed in the Bible. Like Barry Goldwater, Bush was an instinctual conservative. More than any other democratically elected conservative profiled here, Bush found his conservative anchor in his spiritual and not his intellectual life. That spiritual life had brought order to his troubled soul, and Bush believed that a religiously infused public life was a vital ingredient in bringing order and moral discipline to American society.

During Bush's eight years as president of the United States this self-described "compassionate conservative" and immensely confident leader pursued the modern conservative political agenda with a fiery certainty. He revered and promoted the tax-cutting, probusiness, anti–government regulation, pro–wealth creation policies President Reagan had made the new American common sense. He fought to make the antiabortion, pro-life position government policy in every way he could. He regularly demonstrated his own commitment to

Christianity and worked to instill a religious perspective into the American cultural fabric. Most fundamentally, in 2001 after the murderous 9/11 attacks on the United States by followers of al-Qaeda, President Bush and his administration convinced the American people to embrace what he described as a war against evil. Proclaiming that the world was divided between the forces of good and those of evil, he unleashed the dogs of war.

Just as William Buckley, Phyllis Schlafly, and Barry Goldwater had demanded decades earlier in the struggle against the communist foe, after 9/11 President Bush cast aside those cultural and legal norms that he believed handcuffed America in its battle against "evildoers." In search of a restoration of order, security, and international control, the president selectively dismissed the Bill of Rights and international agreements such as the Geneva Conventions in order to keep suspected terrorists captive and without legal recourse, crossed whatever borders were necessary to capture and imprison others suspected of terrorism, and used torture to try to discover what those who were captured and imprisoned might know about plans and individuals who meant the American people harm. Bush agreed with the claims William Buckley had made in his defense of McCarthyism in the 1950s: rules made for civilized people and civilized times should not be mindlessly applied when faced with enemies who were themselves extraordinarily evil. Moreover, Bush argued, when the United States used extreme measures against its enemies or those suspected of being its enemies, it was not the same as when other nations used torture or other such measures. The United States, he believed, was inherently a moral nation that only sought to safeguard its people and its principles against evil. As a result, its use of exceptional measures was moral, because a moral nation had used them under threat from immoral people.

Despite such logic, most liberals opposed these measures. They argued that breaking treaties, breaking laws, and breaking the code of simple human decency made the United States a broken nation, less respected abroad and less honorable at home. Fighting evil with evil means, they argued, carried too many costs—and displaying their pragmatic core, they often added that using such extraordinary

means, including torture, often failed to provide actionable intelligence and instead worked as a recruitment tool for the terrorist
enemy. Liberals were joined in their protests by a minority of self-
described conservatives who added that, by their principles, morality
could not be situational. But a vast majority of conservatives sided
with their president. Their embrace of harsh disciplinary measures
in the "War on Terror" was in keeping with conservatives' overwhelming disgust for procedural safeguards that protected criminal
suspects and prison inmates and with their support of capital pun-
ishment, long prison sentences, and, in general, harsh treatment for
miscreants, law breakers, and others who abrogated the rules that,
in their minds, kept society safe, secure, and orderly. A great many
nonideological Americans, at least in the case of suspected terrorists,
agreed with the conservative position, accepting the commonsense
dictum that sometimes you had to fight fire with fire.

In 2003, when President Bush chose to go to war against Iraq in
a preemptive strike, he followed the path Robert Taft had mapped
in the early days of the Cold War struggle against the Soviet Union.
Rejecting the strategy of collective security liberals had long
embraced, Bush insisted on the right of the American government to
act unilaterally and decisively in the face of a perceived threat against
the United States. Similarly, Bush's strategy in attacking Iraq echoed
that of conservatives in the 1950s and early 1960s who had argued
that America needed to "rollback" communism in eastern Europe in
order to liberate such people who, once freed, would then embrace
democracy and the principles of economic liberty. The United States,
Bush believed, as had his conservative forebears, was the embodiment of such universalist principles. The country was, as President
Reagan often said, a "city upon the hill," an exemplar for the rest of
the world. Thus, when the United States launched a preemptive war
against Iraq, it did not finally matter that the Bush administration, to
be generous, had misrepresented or manufactured the evidence it had
used to convince the American people that an Iraq ruled by Saddam
Hussein represented a clear and present danger to the nation. More
important, President Bush explained, regime change in Iraq not only
would stop an enemy from endangering the American people and its

allies in the region, but it would also ensure that a liberated Iraqi people could emulate the United States and form a democratic nation, thereby inspiring others in their region to do likewise.

This version of unilateral action taken both as a form of national defense and as a strategy for creating democratic nation-states around the world was not what Senator Taft had in mind when he opposed Franklin Roosevelt's attempts to involve the United States in the fight against Nazism. And a few conservatives in the days leading up to Bush's war against Iraq opposed his mission of democratic state building in Iraq and around the Middle East. Cultural traditions, they believed, were not so easy to change; it was liberals, they argued, who believed that government-driven social engineering could quickly bring about social good. Bush himself had made similar arguments against President Bill Clinton's foreign policy strategy during the 2000 presidential election campaign. But after 9/11, Bush embraced a variant of President Reagan's optimistic version of conservatism: bad governments, not bad cultures or even bad citizens kept people from enjoying their inalienable rights and from exercising their democratic desires. Liberate people from bad regimes and good societies would follow, almost automatically. Bush, like Reagan, was a sunny-side-of-the-street conservative.

By the time President Bush left office in 2009, the conservative political movement he had led was in disarray. The war in Iraq had become a long, painful slog, even as the low-intensity conflict in Afghanistan against the al-Qaeda-supporting Taliban worsened and spread to Pakistan. The president had justified the Iraq war by arguing that Saddam Hussein's regime possessed weapons of mass destruction that would likely be used against the United States and that Saddam Hussein was in secret cahoots with the al-Qaeda terrorists. These claims proved to be untrue. A majority of Americans—though only a small majority—knew that the Bush administration had misled them. And despite the claims of administration officials, voiced most boldly by Vice President Dick Cheney, that the war would be won easily and cheaply, in large part because the Iraqis would welcome U.S. troops as liberators, Iraq had become a long-term sinkhole, draining American blood and treasure, as well as its international reputation.

The liberal Democrat Barack Obama, the man who would replace President Bush in the White House, first energized his campaign by running against the war in Iraq and against the conservative, unilateralist, bellicose foreign policy that undergirded President Bush's decision making.

But, in a turn of events that almost no one predicted in late 2007 when Obama began his presidential campaign, the economy, not the War on Terror and the Iraq War, became the main issue of the campaign. The Taftian-Reaganesque conservative economic policies that Bush had embraced and assiduously implemented during his presidency had, in the months before the 2008 election, catastrophically failed. A nearly unregulated capital market, driven by America's fabulously rewarded bankers, financiers, and speculators had imploded, taking down trillions of dollars in Americans' assets and nearly destroying the American-led global financial system. The American political economy, based for nearly thirty years on conservative economic principles, had crashed. Americans saw the value of their homes plummet; millions could no longer pay their mortgages. The stock markets lost nearly half their value. Life savings and pensions plunged in worth. Venerable American corporations were on the chopping block. Millions of Americans lost their jobs. George Bush, the conservative movement, and Republican presidential candidate Senator John McCain had been overtaken by a new political reality.

Barack Obama, portrayed in conservative attack advertisements as the most liberal senator in the United States, suddenly had a powerful campaign weapon: conservative economic policies had failed the American people. The people needed help and, like Franklin Roosevelt, Obama promised to use the federal government to bring discipline to the nearly unregulated financial markets and fix what decades of obstreperously pro–free market conservative policies had wrecked. The presidential election was his, and Obama was joined in victory by dozens of new liberal members of Congress. A black man who championed equal rights and rejected all the forms of social hierarchy that conservatives had historically accepted and in some cases embraced was president of the United States. In 2009, under President Barack Obama, liberals were back in control of American policymaking and politics. On George Bush's watch, the conservative political movement, once so mighty, had taken a great fall.

THE BIOGRAPHY OF GEORGE W. BUSH, especially as presented by those who tended to prefer his various political opponents, goes something like this: baby George was born in Connecticut in 1946 to one of America's most prominent and wealthy families; that is, he was born with a silver spoon in his mouth. Grandfather Prescott Bush was a Yale Skull and Bones man (as had been generations of Bush men before him) who became a Wall Street banker and then Connecticut's U.S. senator. He played golf with Ike. Prescott's second son, George Herbert Walker Bush, the father of George W. and the man who would become the forty-first president of the United States, was a golden boy with a storybook life: war hero, Yalie, self-made millionaire, and entrenched member of the American ruling class.

Little George, on the other hand, the first-born son of George H. W. and the indomitable Barbara Bush, was kind of a screwup and most certainly a cutup; he was more interested in having a laugh than studying or working hard. After skating his way through the schools male Bushes had long attended, Phillips Academy and Yale University (class of 1968), he dodged service in Vietnam through some string-pulling and spent a minimal time in the Texas Air National Guard. During these years, as student and then young man, nobody ever accused him of being driven by intellectual curiosity, the desire to challenge authority, or a concern for social justice. He missed, willfully, the sixties. In an age of marijuana, he stayed the course with alcohol. Despite his academic limits and party-hearty attitude, and maybe because of his rejection of the causes and concerns of many of his classmates, he earned an MBA at Harvard.

Soon after, he returned to Texas, where his father had moved the family when George was but two years old. This Bush never embraced the East Coast preppie style his family ties and schooling might have suggested. He was and would remain a Texan. He dipped snuff. Back home, he used family connections to begin working in the oil business.

His endeavors therein never made money, but those same family connections made sure he profited anyway. In 1977, after a whirlwind courtship, he married Laura Welch, a Midland, Texas, girl and graduate of Southern Methodist University who had been a second-grade teacher and then a librarian. She helped settle him down. Bush found the Lord, gave up drinking, helped his dad run for president. With dad in the White House, he was offered a small piece of the Texas Rangers ballclub and became a managing director of the team. He made millions off the deal. In 1994, with the help of his daddy's name and the political Svengali Karl Rove (more, later), he became governor of Texas. In 2001, despite his intellectual limits, his inarticulateness, and his unfamiliarity with much of the world but blessed by his family name, the zealous support of both wealthy economic and masses of socioreligious conservatives, the bad taste left by Bill Clinton's dalliance with a young intern, and the help of the U.S. Supreme Court, George W. Bush became president of the United States.

This version of the conventional biography has much truth to it, but it hides a great deal, too. There are reasons beyond the changing structure and size of the conservative movement that allowed George W. Bush to follow in his father's giant footsteps and become a conservative president of the United States even as the more cerebral and hard-working Robert Taft failed a half-century earlier in his bids to follow *his* father into the White House. Bush had an array of skills of exactly the right kind for his rise to the presidency under the banner of modern conservatism.

George W. Bush, despite the fancy family name and super-elite schooling, had the common touch. And it was genuine. He was, in that sense, the opposite of the wooden and patrician Robert Taft. Nor was he like Ronald Reagan (or Franklin Roosevelt), who was unsurpassed in connecting with an audience or amusing a small crowd but who had little genuine interest in individuals or personal intimacy. Bush liked people and they liked him. He was naturally inclusive and gregarious in a towel-snapping, acid-tongued, locker-room kind of way. In the early days of Bush's run for the Republican presidential nomination, journalists at the *Washington Post*, in a series of in-depth biographical reports on the then Texas governor, seized on this aspect of Bush's personality and gave an enduring boyhood gloss to it that is almost ritualistically repeated in subsequent profiles and biographies.

At the Phillips Academy, the *Post* reported, other boys were in awe of the Texan in their overwhelmingly East Coast, refined, WASP midst. Bush was no brain nor was he a gridiron hero, but he was "cocky and irrepressible." Through "sheer force of personality," he had become a big man on campus. An anecdote serves as explanation: rather than compete on the usual terrain, Bush laid claim to his own, where he could be king. Actually, he made himself "commissioner." Bush convinced his classmates to turn an informal game of stickball into an arena of goofy competition in which he made up the rules and established teams. Unlike the traditional sports played on campus, Bush's stickball league was open to all, regardless of the degree of their athletic coordination. Bush made sure everybody had fun.[3] Compare Bush's stickball inventiveness to poor, stiff Robert Taft's laborious attempts during his boyhood to teach himself how to hit a baseball.

Bush went to one of the nation's most elite prep schools and then onward to Yale, but just as Reagan had no ounce of pessimism in his soul, Bush affected no sense of snobbery or exclusivity. People—voters—could see that in him. He was a josher not a judger. And like Bush's prep school peers, they seemed almost to forget that his comfortable swagger and jokey ease was bred in his aristocratic bones, as much as it was formed in the rough and tumble of his Midland, Texas, boyhood.

Just as Bush trumped his politically suspect elite pedigree with his winning persona, so too did he turn his troubled years of early adulthood into a politically compelling narrative of spiritual uplift. And he was politically savvy enough to hang a lantern around the most visible of his onetime troubles. For a few years—twenty or so—Bush drank too much. He was no alcoholic, but regularly enough, he got drunk. He had been arrested for driving under the influence of alcohol. Hangovers were a part of his life. The drinking was hurting his marriage and his family life. As Bush told the story about himself, it took Jesus to save him from his personal failings.

In 1985, with his dad serving his second term as vice president, George Bush joined the Community Bible Study group in Midland,

Texas. He was thirty-nine years old. His search for spiritual strength and religious succor had begun earlier that year when Bush, troubled and unsure of where his life was leading him, had taken a stroll, at his father's home in Maine, with evangelical leader Billy Graham. As Bush later recalled, "It was the beginning of a new walk where I would recommit my heart to Jesus Christ." Bush had left behind the country-club, quiet, Episcopalian faith of his father and embraced the firmer stuff of Methodism.

At the CBS, a small group of Christian men would meet weekly and work their way through a chapter of the gospels. There was nothing out of the ordinary about such a group in Midland. As one of the leaders of the group said, "[T]he atmosphere in Midland is wonderful. There's a desire to introduce people to who Jesus is on a local level and on a national level. And there's a confidence there that God can use me to do that. I don't have to go to seminary. I don't have to be the smartest person in the world. I just have to be a man who's yielded to the Lord. And he will use me in the way that he uses so many of those people from Midland."[4] Bush participated regularly, committed himself to Jesus Christ, and from then on read the Bible every day. Through the CBS he learned to apply his faith to his life. That faith, he told the American people, allowed him to stop drinking the day after his fortieth birthday and dedicate himself to his family. That faith became his bedrock, the foundation on which he built his life.

The discovery of that faith also gave Bush and his political allies a way to narrate his life, to give an appealing arc to the relatively undistinguished record—given that he was the first-born son of George Herbert Walker Bush—of his accomplishments up until his midlife crisis. Thus in 1999, when Bush was preparing to launch his bid for the presidency, he published an autobiography meant to introduce him to a wider circle of voters. *A Charge to Keep* did not dwell on his family's pedigree and wealth, his "legacy" status at Phillips Academy, Yale, and Skull and Bones, or his connections to a great many very rich and powerful individuals. Rather, the emotional centerpiece of the book, the seeming inner-look at the real Bush, emphasized instead his onetime problems with alcohol and his life-transforming embrace of Jesus. That it was true made it no less studied a vantage point.

In all of his runs for public office, after his religious turn in the mid-1980s, first during his Texas gubernatorial campaign in 1994 and then in his 2000 bid for the presidency, Americans regularly heard George Bush refer to his Christian faith in explaining himself and his principles. At the third debate among the Republican candidates for the presidential nomination in 2000, when asked what philosopher he most admired, he spoke without hesitation: "Christ, because he changed my heart." During his stump speeches he referred to his experience walking with Billy Graham and told audiences "my relationship with God through Christ gives me meaning and direction."[5] Church-going evangelical Christians overwhelmingly approved, and so did many other religious Americans.

Bush's embrace of Jesus Christ as his personal savior helped to turn around not only his family life but his political fortunes. In 1978, well before he began his daily Bible reading and when he was still casting around for direction, Bush had run for Congress in Texas's Nineteenth District. Based in Midland, he campaigned against the Carter administration's oil policy (not pro-oil enough); his TV commercials showed him on his daily run, fit and ready to lead. His opponent, a Texas Tech–educated Democratic state senator named Kent Hance, shared Bush's economic views but ran far to his cultural right. Hance's coup de grâce came just a few days before the election, when some Bush supporters put on a political rally that featured free beer. Hance's campaign used the beer bash against Bush. A letter went out that began, "Dear Fellow Christians," and then went on to lament that the Yale-educated Bush was using "his vast sums of money" to bribe young Texans into voting for him by offering them alcoholic beverages. Voters were equally disconcerted by the commercials showing Bush running in the Texas heat. A local voter observed, "if a guy is jogging in Dimmitt, somebody is after him."[6] Bush had run that campaign with great stores of personal energy and the financial backing of a host of well-to-do supporters, but it was not enough. In a relatively benign echo of George Wallace's failed Alabama campaign two decades earlier, Bush had been out-Texan'd by his rival. Never again.

By the time Bush ran for Texas governor in 1994, he had a new image to offer voters. Since 1989, he had been the managing director of the Texas Rangers baseball team. He had become a Bible-reading, born-again Christian and was an honest-to-God family man. He campaigned in cowboy boots and kept his daily run out of his commercials. Then, too, Texas had changed in the sixteen years since he had run for Congress. The "good old boy" culture was by no means a thing of the past, but the state had far more Hispanic voters, and it also had an energized liberal-progressive bloc that had gained statewide power. Bush's opponent, the incumbent governor, Ann Richards, represented that progressive bloc, and she did so with a scathing populist wit. Bush had to be more than an exemplary old-school Texan to win the governorship, and he knew it.

Richards had won the Texas governorship in 1990 by beating Clayton Williams, an immensely wealthy, conservative oilman and rancher. Williams made himself out as a proud exemplar of old school, white Texas masculinity. From the perspective of the national press, this made him both a humorous subject and a formidable force for the governorship. A fourth-generation rancher, he campaigned in a "gray Resistol hat and black ostrich-skin boots" and promised voters that he would bring more jobs to Texas, never raise their taxes, "fight drugs from every direction," and "introduce [drug pushers] to the joys of bustin' rocks."[7] Besides being tough enough to lead his men on the annual cattle roundup at his forty-three-square mile Happy Cove ranch, he also thought of himself as a country-boy wit. That wit did get him into trouble in the eyes of some Texans, as when, upon observing an incoming storm, he laughingly told a large group of reporters that bad weather was just like rape: "You can't do anything about it, so you might as well lay back and enjoy it."[8] Richards's upset victory proved that even in Texas, by the mid-1990s, a great many voters could only stomach so much oil man money and good old boy humor. Women flocked to Richards and proved, once again, that even in a state where liberals were far outnumbered by conservatives, many voters could be turned in one political direction or another by the power of campaign particulars, inspirational rhetoric, and individual personalities.

Richards had a lot of personality, as George W. Bush knew full well as he prepared to square off against her. Her national reputation and path to the Texas governorship had been set in 1988 when the

Democratic Party, somewhat desperate to get a persuasive woman's face on camera at their presidential nominating convention, had turned to Richards, who was then the little-known Texas state treasurer. She lit up the night. First she made a pitch for more women leaders: "But if you give us a chance, we can perform. After all, Ginger Rogers did everything that Fred Astaire did. She just did it backwards and in high heels!" And she zinged the occasionally inarticulate Republican presidential candidate, George H. W. Bush: "Poor George. He can't help it. He was born with a silver foot in his mouth!" But her speech that night added up to far more than those humorous one-liners. At a time when liberals had been ground down by years of failed policies and the great popularity of Ronald Reagan, Richards had let loose a liberal battle cry.

Calling on her rural Texas background and her childhood in the midst of the Great Depression, she asked what had happened to American values of fair play, equal rights, and dignity for all. "This Republican Administration," she said, "treats us as if we were pieces of a puzzle that can't fit together. They've tried to put us into compartments and separate us from each other." Blue eyes blazing, she raged, "They told working mothers it's all their fault—their families are falling apart because they had to go to work to keep their kids in jeans and tennis shoes and college. And they're wrong! They told American labor they were trying to ruin free enterprise by asking for 60 days' notice of plant closings, and that's wrong. . . . No wonder we feel isolated and confused. We want answers and their answer is that 'something is wrong with you.' Well nothing's wrong with you. Nothing's wrong with you that you can't fix in November!"[9] Richards had seized the national stage that night, and liberals all over the United States cheered for her and her message. Alas for the 1988 Democratic presidential candidate, Massachusetts Governor Michael Dukakis, there just were not enough of those cheered-up liberals among the American electorate.

In 1994, fortunately for George W. Bush, who had not forgotten Richards's verbal dig at his father in 1988, her record as governor had not equaled the power of her rhetoric. She had few achievements to showcase after nearly four years in office. Still, Bill Clinton had taken down George H. W. in 1992 using rhetoric much like that deployed by Richards, although Bush's unfocused response to the economic contraction of 1991–92 and his reneging on a campaign promise to never raise taxes had at least as much to do with his defeat. While 1994 turned out to be a very good year nationally for conservatives, led by Congressman Newt Gingrich, Bush could not know that when entering into the race. Richards expected to beat George W. Bush just as Clinton had beaten George H. W. Bush just two years earlier.

Guided by the best political mind in Texas, the campaign consultant Karl Rove, Bush ran a carefully modulated race against Richards. He positioned himself as a different kind of conservative. He ran for governor without a deep commitment to any one conservative principle—though a conservative he fully believed himself to be. This was in part owing to historical circumstance: some of the conservative movement's best issues were not available to the Bush-Rove effort. Thanks to a forty-year commitment by Democratic and Republican politicians to a policy of containing international communism and the internal contradictions of the Soviet Union, the Berlin Wall had fallen, eastern Europe had lifted the dead hand of Soviet-style Marxism, and the "evil empire" itself had imploded. The hunt for domestic communist subversives, long a staple in conservative Texas politics, was as a result a dead letter. And Bush chose to tread lightly around the racial land mines that still lay buried just under the surface of Texas politics.

Still, a few old-style, conservative positions were available, and Bush, coached by Rove, seized on them, creating a recipe that was equal parts something new and something old. Taking a page from Ronald Reagan's long ago 1966 California campaign, Bush ran against welfare cheats and, as conservatives were wont to say, the whole dependency-producing system of welfare payments. National Republicans, led by the insurgent Georgia Congressman Newt Gingrich, were that same year playing the same card. The electorate, in Texas and in most other places, liked it, even as some liberals continued to claim it was a racially charged attack.

To the delight of the business community, Bush seized on a relatively new issue in the conservative playbook: tort reform. The idea here was to take the deregulation movement that the Reagan administration had successfully used to unleash the financial sector of the economy (as well as a host of other industries) from firm government oversight and re-jigger it to apply to the American civil justice system. Under that system, American juries, as well as judges, had erected expansive and expensive measures to protect and compensate individuals from harm done by others, ranging from dangerous products to deadly work environments. Since those others often were businesses with deep pockets, conservatives argued that tort law had become an unfair, unnecessary, and mollycoddling structure that dragged down the free enterprise system by penalizing successful businesses that rarely had done anything seriously wrong. Too often, conservatives argued, individuals were given huge monetary rewards when a little common sense would have prevented any problem from occurring. Individual responsibility, they continued, was being trashed by a civil justice system that rewarded the incompetent while punishing successful entrepreneurs and companies. While tort reform did not ignite a massive electoral brushfire, it did garner a lot of campaign contributions from those businesspeople who felt themselves prey to plaintiff lawyers. Bush made tort reform one of the principal issues of his campaign, and it would become a staple conservative cause. In a more popular appeal—and in partial response to his father's famous presidential retreat from his "read my lips" pledge about not raising taxes—Bush promised Texas voters that he would lower their state property taxes.

Bush ran most successfully, and with the most personal passion, on two other issues. The first, surprisingly, was education. He declared that his number one priority was the schoolchildren of Texas. Bush promised to reform the state's education system by making schools accountable. In practice, that meant regularly testing students to measure their achievements in key academic skills like reading and mathematical calculation and then sanctioning low-performing schools. Bush also promised to increase funding to schools to pay for the testing and to assist schools in improving. To make schools better, Bush was demanding greater state oversight and was even willing to increase state spending to help them do better. Government, in this case, was part of the solution—not typical conservative fare. If not for the fact that teachers' unions, overwhelmingly Democratic

Party partisans, distrusted and even despised the accountability measures—in part, because they feared that some teachers who failed to improve students' test scores might be fired—there was nothing particularly conservative or liberal about this hard-nosed policy. For more traditional conservatives, Bush did also call for competition among schools; he advocated outside-the-bureaucracy, state-supported charter schools, and he also supported a voucher program that would allow parents to use state money to help pay for private schools, which, in practice, would overwhelmingly be Christian academies. Still, Bush demonstrated with his school policies that he was not a dogmatic conservative; a picture he would seek to refine when he ran for the presidency.

Bush's other major policy priority was to harden the state's juvenile justice system. Like a good many other states, in the early 1990s Texas had experienced a fierce rise in crimes committed by young teenagers, a disproportionate number of whom were African American and Hispanic. Many in the state felt that young criminals were on the rise because too often they were getting away with murder—sometimes literally. Bush promised that he would find tougher ways to handle kids who had gone bad. In making this pitch for a harsher juvenile justice system, Bush took a page from Barry Goldwater's *Conscience of a Conservative*. Being hard on people who had done wrong, Bush said, especially young ones, was not about being mean-spirited or hard-hearted; it was the opposite. In his gubernatorial debate with Ann Richards, he explained, "We understand in Texas that discipline and love go hand in hand."[10] It was a perfect conservative formulation, but it was a rare conservative politician up until then who used the word *love*, even if it was tough love, when talking about dope pushers, auto thieves, or robbers, even if the lawbreakers in question were fourteen or fifteen years old.

Guided by campaign manager Karl Rove's expert hand, Bush stayed relentlessly on-message, sticking to his talking points and four policy priorities. His campaign discipline stood in sharp relief to that of Governor Richards, who loved a snappy one-liner just a little too much. At one point during her governorship she had mocked Texans who were demanding the right to carry concealed handguns by offering them a compromise: they could carry a gun on a chain around their necks so "everyone would know who's packing, 'Oh-uh, look out for that one—he's got a gun.'"[11] Bush promised to support Texans' right to carry concealed weapons so that they could protect themselves. Ann Richards was a true daughter of Texas, but Bush out-Texan'd her. He won in a romp.

In Bush's first term, he accomplished almost all of his campaign promises and more. Gun owners got their right to carry a concealed weapon, and (shades of Reagan) Bush found a way to fulfill his pledge to cut the state property tax. He moved forward on state tort reform and evidenced his disdain for business regulation by relaxing enforcement of various environmental laws. Bush talked up the idea of reducing the size of government by privatizing public services, even the University of Texas. He also began looking into turning some social service programming, like drug addiction counseling, over to "faith-based" organizations. For Bush, this policy was personal; he had reason to believe that religious faith and lessons learned from the Bible could help people make better lives for themselves.

A big majority of Texas voters liked what George Bush did as governor. He easily won a second term in 1998, raking in a record-setting 69 percent of the vote. Bush had also confounded liberals by picking up substantial Hispanic support. He had worked hard to learn some conversational Spanish and respected the traditions and customs of his Hispanic constituents, most especially their religiosity—and he let them know it. Bush straightforwardly rejected the patronizing and often hostile attitudes toward Hispanics that had historically been de rigueur for most Anglo conservative politicians in Texas. Bush, like several other conservative politicians of his generation, was forthrightly breaking with the race-baiting and direct appeals to ethnic or racial prejudice that had long characterized the conservative movement. A majority of Hispanic voters responded by giving him their votes. Still, the overall picture Bush presented to Texas voters was a traditional one. At the state Republican convention that nominated him to run for that second term, the official campaign film featured the governor alone in a bass boat, fishing. He catches a good one and demonstrates that he knows how to hook 'em, and hold 'em up by the gills for the camera. Bush, the film explains, is the embodiment of the "Texas culture of faith and values."[12]

Even before Bush had his Texas bona fides validated by the state's voters for a second time, he had begun exploring a presidential bid. He was the son of a president with all the national name recognition that guaranteed; he had governed a major state; and he had a rock-solid electoral base in Texas that gave him the credentials to run strong throughout the Sun Belt. Also, he had personal and family connections to a big-money network of contributors that ran from Wall Street to big oil, and because no obvious front-running Republican leader had staked out the presidential race, major contributors were there waiting to be courted. Still, Bush had not spent a lifetime preparing for or dreaming of being the president, nor was he driven by some fiercely held set of beliefs that he wanted to make national policy. But George Bush did have the self-confidence to believe that he could be the president of the United States, and he did have the willingness, especially after watching eight years of the Bill Clinton presidency, to give it a go and see what happened.

In April 1998, he traveled to California to try his hand at a little out of state fund-raising and, more important, to meet with some of the wise men of Republican administrations past. George Shultz, who had done it all, including serving as secretary of state under Ronald Reagan, hosted an intimate luncheon for Bush. Bush listened and asked smart questions as Shultz, conservative economists, and policy experts such as Martin Anderson and Michael Boskin, as well as Stanford University provost and rising star in foreign policy circles Condoleezza Rice, laid out the big issues of the day: budget and tax policy, international relations, and entitlement programs like Social Security. Bush proved to this extraordinarily brilliant circle that, despite his own self-effacing comments about his lack of academic achievement and a reputation for intellectual narrowness, he was presidential timber. George Shultz took him aside and told him that nearly twenty years earlier he had hosted a similar event for the former governor of California, Ronald Reagan. After that meeting, doubts assuaged, he and the others had joined Reagan's crusade for the presidency. Now, Shultz told Bush, we are ready to join yours.[13]

Bush was no Reagan. He had a different skill set, a different back-ground, and the times were quite different, as well. Reagan, of course, was at his best when talking to a crowd. Bush was at best a medio-cre public speaker; he often tangled his syntax, and his years of rela-tive indifference to international relations and domestic policy issues showed when reporters moved him away from his prepared talking points and asked him tough, specific questions about public affairs (here, he shared ground with Reagan). Sometimes when Bush read a prepared speech, he was dreadful. But he did connect well with voters, and like-minded people thought he was a good man. Before becoming president, Reagan had been developing his conservative ideology for decades, reading, talking, and writing about political ideas and first principles. Bush had never gone through that process of refining his political and ideological beliefs. But he was a man of certain religious faith, which grounded his moral sense, and he did believe strongly in a few core conservative beliefs, in particular lower taxes, less government, and more reliance on the private sector and individual discipline. And by the year 2000, because most of conser-vatives' biggest issues, such as battling communism and restraining big government, lacked the saliency they once had, a different kind of presidential campaign between some sort of "new" Democrat and some sort of conservative Republican was likely anyway. The stark divide between an old-school liberal and a fiery conservative was an unlikely scenario for the 2000 campaign. Bush had the advantage of not being the kind of "scary," dogmatic conservative who pushed away too many middle-of-the-road or independent voters, who often liked their politics to be nicer and less divisive sounding. Bush made sure that voters understood that he was a new kind of conservative.

As Bush geared up for his presidential run, his father's 1992 loss to "new" Democrat Bill Clinton haunted and inspired him. Bush knew that Clinton was a once-in-a-generation politician, a man of extraor-dinary talents tailor-made for the electoral arena. And he knew that his dad was a less-gifted politician, a patrician who was mocked when he tried to pass himself off as a regular fellow and who had lost a chunk of voters because he had memorably promised—"read my lips!"—not to raise Americans' taxes and then did so anyway (because he believed it was the right thing to do to strengthen the economy). And Bush knew that his father, the incumbent, was blamed for the 1992 economic recession that seemed to crowd out the many victories the president had won, including the extraordinary 1991 battlefield triumph over the army of the Iraqi dictator Saddam Hussein. But Bush also knew that his father's 1992 losing campaign of reasoned, principled, conservative policies had been badly tarred by the "pitchfork" rhetoric of the more ferocious elements of the conservative movement that battled for control of the Republican Party.

Pat Buchanan had done a good deal of that tarring. In 1992, Buchanan had run against George H. W. Bush for the Republican presidential nomination. Buchanan was, to use William Buckley's term, a veteran conservative "publicist." He had supported Goldwater, had been a member of the Young Americans for Freedom, had worked for Richard Nixon, had written widely and appeared regularly on television, and had served as communications director for President Reagan. Buchanan had long believed that the majority of Americans were repulsed by the social and cultural changes liberals had supported since the early 1960s. He believed that Bush was a moderate who did not understand those social and religious passions that animated the masses of conservative voters. So he ran on cultural conservative issues against his party's incumbent president for the 1992 nomination, garnering some three million votes before conceding the race to the far-better-financed and established George H. W. Bush campaign. Though he lost, Buchanan's primary vote totals, Republican leaders decided, earned him a prime-time address during the Republican National Convention.

In that speech, Buchanan pulled out the stops, raging against "the discredited liberalism of the 1960s and the failed liberalism of the 1970s." Shades of Phyllis Schlafly, he targeted Bill Clinton's wife, Hillary Clinton, for her "radical feminism." He warned America against the agenda of "Clinton and Clinton": "abortion on demand, a litmus test for the Supreme Court, homosexual rights, discrimination against religious schools, women in combat units." He then declared war on feminists, gay people, environmentalists, secularists, and liberals in general: "There is a religious war going on in this country. It is a cultural war, as critical to the kind of nation we shall be as the Cold War itself. For this war is for the soul of America. And in that struggle for the soul of America, Clinton & Clinton are on the other side, and George Bush is on our side." With the Republican delegates roaring their approval, he concluded, "[B]lock by block, my friends, we must take back our cities, and take back our culture, and take back our country. God bless you, and God bless America."[14] Pundits referred to this heated rhetoric as the "culture war" speech, and while it inspired many religious conservative activists who had worried about Bush's dedication to their issues, its vehemence frightened wobbly independent and less–culturally conservative Republican voters who feared that this Republican Party seemed to want to tear the nation apart.

In 2000, George W. Bush did not want voters to fear him or his brand of conservatism. Just as Bill Clinton had used conservative catchphrases and religious language to sometimes advance a more liberal agenda, Bush sought to soften the sometimes harsh, exclusionary language of the modern conservative movement to reach uncertain and less-ideological voters. In 1988, his father had actually done much the same in his successful run for the presidency, telling Americans, "I want a kinder and gentler nation." Bush called his approach "compassionate conservatism." He hallmarked his "compassionate" conservative approach in his acceptance speech at the 2000 Republican convention in Philadelphia. Rather than chastise "welfare cheats" as Ronald Reagan had done or use images of a black criminal to scare white voters as even own father had done in the 1988 election, Bush asked the people listening to him that night to understand what it was like for "single moms struggling to feed the kids and pay the rent; immigrants starting a hard life in a new world; children without fathers in neighborhoods where gangs seem like friendship or drugs promise peace, and where sex sadly seems the closest thing to belonging." Even Bill Clinton, who had sometimes been mocked for his empathy-laden turns of phrases ("I feel your pain"), had not been so expressive in discussing the challenges facing tens of millions of Americans. "We are their country too," Bush reminded the Republicans sitting in the hall that night. "When these problems are not confronted, it builds a wall within our nation. On one side are wealth, technology, education and ambition. On the other side of that wall are poverty and prison, addiction and despair. And my fellow Americans, we must tear down that wall."

But if Bush was insisting on compassion for the downtrodden, even going so far as to compare that struggle with Ronald Reagan's hallowed call to tear down the communists' Berlin Wall, he was also insisting on conservative solutions to do so. To the cheers of the delegates, he intoned, "Big government is not the answer, but the alternative to bureaucracy is not indifference. It is to put conservative values and conservative ideas into the thick of the fight for justice and opportunity."[15] Exactly what that meant in policy prescriptions would have to wait for another day—and it would be a long wait. But the tone, for sure, was strikingly different. And if the tone was not backed up by specifics, it was supported by powerful imagery.

Unlike any previous Republican convention, African Americans played a major role at Bush's. Colin Powell, the first African American to serve as head of the military's Joint Chiefs of Staff, gave the opening speech. Condoleezza Rice, an African American who served as Bush's chief foreign policy adviser, also gave a major address. Laura Bush was surrounded by a sea of black schoolchildren, and numerous black singers and choral groups performed from the stage. The *New York Times* African American editorialist, Brent Staples, noted that only a tiny percentage of the actual delegates to the Republican convention were black and that the Bush campaign knew that it was likely to win only a miniscule percentage of black votes. Most African Americans, he observed, dismissed the parade of black faces on the stage as nothing more than "minstrelsy" and a brazen attempt to erase the party's recent history of race-baiting "by dressing up in blackface." But he understood, too, that the Republican Party was not actually seeking black voters; it was "directing its [racially inclusive] entreaties to the white, moderate suburbanites who abandoned the party in the last two elections to vote for Bill Clinton. The ploy of cosmetically colorizing the G.O.P. could work."[16]

Bush was no racist. And in his Texas electoral contests he had a proven record of winning over, if not African American voters, at least a sizable percentage of the important Hispanic vote. Bush was not willing to change his policies to win minority voters, nor would he reach out to longtime organized opponents of conservative politicians such as the National Association for the Advancement of Colored People, but he did genuinely want to turn the page on the kind of race-baiting, blatant and coded, that a good many conservatives from the time of Barry Goldwater forward, including Ronald Reagan and his own father, had allowed and at times played a direct hand in. Thirty-two years after the martyrdom of Martin Luther King Jr., Bush meant to move his party and his conservative followers forward on the issue of racial prejudice.[17]

Bush was well-intentioned on the issue of race, and his campaign team knew that in the year 2000 essentially no votes could be gained (the Republican Party already had those kind of voters)—and plenty could be lost—with a racially charged campaign. And given the ugliness of the 1992 Pat Buchanan-led culture wars rhetoric, few on the Bush campaign team were looking to launch a holy crusade against feminists or even gay men and women, though both issues still stirred up the passions of many ardent conservative voters, often referred to, by that time, as the mass electoral base of the Republican Party. In part, Bush could skip these targets, and thus avoid antagonizing a certain sort of more culturally progressive voter, because he had a better one: Bill Clinton. Bush could run as the candidate of moral virtue and religious rectitude—and thus stir the hearts of what pundits had come to call "traditional values" voters—by reminding Americans voters that he was not the kind of man who would ever commit adultery in the Oval Office. It was like shooting fish in a barrel. Though Bush's actual opponent was the wholeheartedly monogamous and true-blue family man Al Gore, Bush had no qualms about tarring poor Gore with the same brush that ran so smoothly over the rough hide of Vice President Gore's two-term boss.

Bush made Clinton's character, as well as his own, a major theme throughout the campaign. Matching his call for "compassionate conservatism" with a declaration that he would "lead this nation to a responsibility era," he assured Americans that he knew "that [the] president himself must be responsible." In direct reference to Bill Clinton's Oval Office misbehavior with a young White House intern, he proclaimed, "So when I put my hand on the Bible, I will swear to not only uphold the laws of our land, I will swear to uphold the honor and dignity of the office to which I have been elected, so help me God." As Bush and his supporters saw it, Bill Clinton's sexual misconduct was the product of baby boomer Clinton's embrace of the hedonistic cultural relativism that, conservatives believed, the sixties era had unleashed on the American people. Bush rejected those times and those precepts. His verities, he said, came from a more distant time and from a far greater authority: "I believe in tolerance, not in spite of my faith, but because of it. I believe in a God who calls us not to judge our neighbors but to love them. I believe in grace because I've seen it, and peace because I've felt it, and forgiveness because I've needed it."[18] In an age of moral uncertainty, Bush promised to bring his disciplined faith to the Oval Office. That faith, he assured Americans, was the rock on which his presidency would be built.

Throughout the presidential campaign, Bush's character became a key issue. Liberals argued that Bush was at best a hypocrite. For decades, they said, he had been a heavy drinker. The mass media unearthed his drunk-driving arrest in Maine. Bush had admitted that he was not much of a student. And until he had become governor just six years earlier, his critics complained, he had accomplished relatively little on his own merits. How could this flawed man claim that his character was a worthy credential for the presidency? When liberals looked at Bush they saw the second-rate son of an extraordinarily privileged and wealthy family who was given every kind of advantage, who learned little from his education and sophisticated background, who partied his way through his youth and much of his adulthood, and then through connections and family name became governor. Now, they argued, he sought the presidency in order to punish people whose backgrounds did not protect them from their mistakes and to reward privileged Americans like himself.

Bush's supporters, most especially those who shared his kind of religious faith, saw a completely different man. They saw a person who was almost destroyed by the cosmopolitan life he had been provided by his family's wealth, his Ivy League education, and the sixties lifestyle to which so many of his generation, they believed, had fallen prey. But Bush, they said, rose above his background. After many difficult years, he found his personal Savior and was able to regain his moral compass through the good works of his loving wife and a forgiving religious community. George Bush's conservative followers embraced a variety of ideological principles, but in the music of self-redemption and the possibilities of individual responsibility his political coalition became an orchestra of many instruments and voices.

Bush ran hard on his character, insisting that Americans needed a change from the traumatic, X-rated years of Clinton and Gore: "This is not the time for third chances; it is the time for new beginnings." But he ran even harder on Taft-Reagan economic principles. Tax cuts were the centerpiece of his policy promises. He would cut income taxes, he would abolish the inheritance tax, and he would make sure Americans could invest their own Social Security savings instead of just paying their money into the government's coffers. People had to be free to look after their own property, and government, he said, had to get out of the way of hard-working, entrepreneurial, risk-taking Americans.

Because the Clinton "new" Democratic years had been economically good ones for a great many Americans, Bush had a challenge on his hands. In particular he had to address one of the minor miracles of the Clinton years; the liberal Bill Clinton had managed to turn around the massive annual government deficits the conservative administrations of both Ronald Reagan and George H. W. Bush had produced. Clinton had not only balanced the federal budget but through careful stewardship of federal spending had actually achieved budget surpluses! Conservatives had a hard time accusing the Clinton-Gore team of being "tax-and-spend" liberals. Still Bush tried to turn this extraordinary accomplishment into a major failing. "The surplus," he intoned, "is not the government's money; the surplus is the people's money." The rhetoric came straight out of the Reagan playbook. If voters made him president, he promised to end years of surplus by cutting taxes.

The presidential race between Gore and Bush was extraordinarily close. Gore's campaign had a lot going for it. Gore, a studious man, was clearly much more informed about both domestic and international policy issues. More important, the Clinton-Gore years had produced, more or less, nearly eight years of peace and prosperity. Income inequality, after years of widening, had actually closed during their years in office. Like Clinton, Gore confounded his conservative opponent by running against big government liberalism. During one of his debates with Bush, he informed viewers that during the Clinton years the federal government had shrunk, while in Texas, under Bush, state government had grown.[19] Gore promised that he would oversee a "smaller, smarter government." Like Clinton, Gore ran away from the liberal label that Presidents Roosevelt, Truman, Kennedy, and Johnson had trumpeted.

But Gore had problems, too. Clinton's extremely well-publicized sexual peccadilloes that had led to his impeachment and nearly resulted in his removal from office shadowed the Gore campaign. And Gore was a stiff and lugubrious candidate. To attack Bush's economic policies, particularly the privatization of Social Security, he repeated over and over . . . and over and over that a Bush presidency would be "risky." He told Americans that he, unlike Bush, would safeguard their Social Security and Medicare payments by placing them in a "lockbox." His sonorous repetition of that odd word was tailor-made for mockery. In polls, voters indicated that folksy Bush just was more likable; intellectual Gore came across as arrogant. Of such things are close elections sometimes determined.

The 2000 election demonstrated that American voters were almost perfectly split between the economically and socially moderate, zig-zagging "new" Democratic politics of Clinton-Gore and the avowedly conservative, yet "compassionate" views offered by George W. Bush, at least insomuch as voters actually paid attention to the issues and not just the personalities of the two candidates. Gore won about 543,000 more votes than did Bush. But after the conservative-dominated Supreme Court ruled 5 to 4 that Florida could not recount its astonishingly close election results, Bush won that state by some 1,600 votes and, thus, a 271 to 266 majority in the Electoral College (one elector chose to abstain). The election was only decided on December 13, almost five weeks after the American people had voted. Gore's supporters were left bitter and angry. George W. Bush was the president.

The conservative coalition formed in the Reagan years mainly held. Bush had won every southern state and every western state except for the heavily Hispanic New Mexico. Gore won the Pacific Coast states of California, Oregon, and Washington. Gore also won the entire Northeast, except New Hampshire, and most of the Midwest. According to exit polls, white voters preferred Bush to Gore 55 percent to 42 percent; white Protestant voters went for Bush over Gore by 62 percent to 35 percent; and white evangelical voters, cheered on by leaders of the Religious Right, gave Bush a massive 38–percentage point advantage over Gore. Voters with household incomes over $100,000 preferred Bush 55 percent to 43 percent. On the other side, about 90 percent of black voters and about 62 percent of Hispanics voted for Gore, and households with incomes under $50,000 also sided with the Democrat.

Election day exit polls indicated that 20 percent of American voters identified themselves as liberal and 29 percent as conservative. After eight years of Bill Clinton, a resounding 50 percent of voters called themselves moderates.[20] That divided electorate also produced a Senate that was evenly split, with fifty Democrats and fifty Republicans—the Democrats had picked up four seats. The House, which had been in Republican hands since 1994, stayed Republican, though by a narrower margin. Regardless of how close the election had been and what those ideological labels meant to the electorate, the American people would have a proudly self-avowed conservative as their president beginning January 20, 2001.

President George Bush ran as a conservative, intended to govern as a conservative, and believed that throughout his presidency he stayed true to his conservative principles. Not all conservatives agreed with him. His critics from the Right pointed out that as president Bush quickly reversed the Clinton federal budget surpluses by creating massive deficits and that Bush used the federal government to intervene forthrightly in American life. Some unhappy conservatives labeled his approach with the deliberately oxymoronic phrase "big government conservatism." And Bush sometimes contradicted even his own notions of what good conservative policy meant. He had run for the presidency castigating President Clinton's military interventions in the Balkans, Haiti, and elsewhere as a misguided liberal policy of "nation building." Yet, Bush ended up as the greatest champion of nation building since the ultraliberal President Lyndon Johnson. Despite these problematic turns, overwhelmingly Bush did dedicate his presidency to advancing the conservative cause that had been growing, in ever-mutable form, since Robert Taft had taken on Franklin Roosevelt's New Deal.

Unlike his father, Bush kept his promise on taxes. His greatest legislative victory came early. Less than five months after taking office, Bush signed the Economic Growth and Tax Relief Reconciliation Act of 2001, which reduced the amount Americans paid in taxes by some $1.3 trillion. All people who paid income taxes saw their rates go down and their tax breaks go up. Critics argued that the super-rich benefited most of all, and they did. But as George Bush explained, rich people paid most of the tax bill, so it only made sense that they got most of the benefits. At the bill's signing, a jubilant Bush spoke: "The message we send today: It's up to the American people; it's the American people's choice. We recognize, loud and clear, the surplus is not the Government's money. The surplus is the people's money, and we ought to trust them with their own money."[21] Two more major tax-cut laws would follow.

Bush walked triumphantly down the path Ronald Reagan had laid. And like Reagan, Bush seemed to believe that the massive deficits his tax policies created would force, over the long haul, a reduction in federal spending, even if Bush himself, again, like Reagan, was unwilling to do almost any of that cutting. President Reagan, in the words of his shell-shocked budget chief, had rung up deficits "as far as the eye can see," thereby doubling the national debt. Bush made Reagan look like a piker; his tax-cut and big-spending policies added at a minimum $3.35 trillion to the amount of money the American government—a.k.a., the American people—owed to creditors.[22] The nation of China was the largest among them. The ironic humor of the world's largest communist, or at least quasi-communist, nation owning the biggest share of the world's largest capitalist nation's debt, while governed by a free market–loving conservative president, was lost on most Americans, whether they were liberal, conservative, or somewhere in the murky middle.

Tax policy was only one piece of the Bush administration's fealty to the free market and respect for capitalism's big winners. Big oil and other traditional energy businesses achieved major victories, too. Given Bush and Vice President Cheney's long-standing ties to the industry, and the immediate appointment of dozens of other people associated with the conventional energy producers, the administration's respect for the wishes of oil, gas, and coal companies surprised no one who followed politics. Cheney, who had stepped down as CEO of the Halliburton Corporation, a giant oil and gas services company, to join the Bush team, chaired a task force that met behind closed doors with industry representatives to chart a new course for the administration. Environmental restrictions on the energy sector were systemically dismantled, and new areas were opened up for oil drilling with more, including the Arctic National Wilderness Area, heartily recommended. Other extractive industries like timber and mining enjoyed the same relief from Clinton-era regulations and restrictions. Bush explained his thinking: "This new approach is based on the common-sense idea: that economic growth is key to environmental progress, because it is growth that provides for investment in clean technologies."[23] Translated into simple prose, this meant that the private enterprise system, not government regulation or federal support, would provide Americans with the environmental protections and future energy alternatives they needed. In the Bush White House, traditional energy and extractive industries were in the catbird seat, and government regulation–seeking environmentalists and alternative energy advocates had no place at the table.

Bush also dedicated himself to the religiously inspired policies he had openly advocated as a candidate. His appointments included many men and women drawn from the Christian Right, including his attorney general John Ashcroft, a speaking-in-tongues disciple of the Assembly of God, who thrilled like-minded audiences by telling them that in the United States there was "no king but Jesus" and that upon taking his major political offices he had followed the teachings of the Bible by anointing himself with oil as had King David. In the Bush administration prayer circles became commonplace in the corridors of power and the president frequently talked about the power of prayer and its sustaining force in his life and in the life of the nation. Bush quickly established an Office of Faith-Based and Community Initiatives, in an effort to channel social welfare funds to religious organizations that relied on prayer, proselytizing, and other forms of spiritual faith to help people in need. One of Bush's first acts as president was to demonstrate his allegiance to the right-to-life movement. He overturned President Bill Clinton's international family planning policy, returning to the restrictions created by the Reagan administration: any organization that condoned, performed, or even informed women about their legal right to have an abortion was ineligible for American funding; this ruled out almost all of the most well-established international programs. Later, Bush appointed as chief of federal family-planning programs a man who had served at a Christian pregnancy counseling center that declared "that the crass commercialization and distribution of birth control is demeaning to women, degrading of human sexuality and adverse to human health and happiness."[24] Most controversial, Bush decided to forbid most federal funding of stem cell research, arguing that taking the cells from frozen embryos, even though the embryos were scheduled to be discarded after fertility treatments, was essentially the same as abortion. Bush spoke to the American people on the subject: ". . . human life is a sacred gift from our creator. I worry about a culture that devalues life, and believe as your president I have an important obligation to foster and encourage respect for life in America and throughout the world."[25] Bush regularly consulted with evangelical Christian leaders and announced that he supported the antievolution movement, telling Americans that if science students were instructed in evolutionary biology they should also be taught the religiously inspired belief that life forms were created by "intelligent design." Likewise, he supported a constitutional amendment to ban gay marriage, a measure fervently supported by many of the president's conservative Christian adherents. In ways that were symbolic but also programmatic, Bush often rejected scientific experts' advice and committed his presidency to the conservative religious values in which he and many of his most ardent supporters believed.

Bush's first term was running along predictable, and not terribly exhilarating conservative lines right through September 10, 2001. Then, on September 11, for George Bush, at the very least, everything changed.

After the 9/11 attacks on New York City and Washington, D.C., the Bush presidency became almost singularly focused on fighting what the president called a Global War on Terror. Immediately after the attacks, the nation was paralyzed. Nearly every American had viewed the strikes on television. They watched as each of the two main towers of New York's World Trade Center was rammed by a hijacked commercial airplane, caught on fire, and then collapsed, killing thousands, including hundreds of firefighters and police officers who had gone to rescue the men and women trapped in the buildings. They watched the Pentagon burn, also hit by a hijacked airplane, as bodies were pulled out of the rubble. The nation learned that another hijacked plane, probably headed for the U.S. Capitol, had crashed in Pennsylvania, downed as passengers fought the terrorists for control of the plane. Even thousands of miles away from the attack sites, even in small towns and cities, people feared for their lives. It was irrational, but millions of people needed to be reassured.

At the very first President Bush had appeared uncertain about what to do, and in a nationally televised speech that evening he had failed to deliver the words Americans needed to hear. Two days later, he had gone to "Ground Zero" in lower New York City, and he began to find his footing as the nation's leader. Over a bullhorn, in brief, prepared remarks, he tried to simply thank the rescue workers and tell them that Americans were praying for "the people whose lives were lost here." It was pretty uninspirational stuff. People shouted that they could not hear what the president was saying. Suddenly Bush came alive: "I can hear you! The rest of the world can hear you. And the people who knocked these buildings down will hear all of us soon."[26] Bush was becoming a different kind of president.

Three days after the attacks, the American people observed a "National Day of Prayer and Remembrance," and President Bush gave a major public speech at the pulpit of Washington's National Cathedral. In what many have called his best post-9/11 speech, he explained his understanding of what had happened and what the United States must do in response: ". . . our responsibility to history is already clear: to answer these attacks and rid the world of evil. . . . They have attacked America because we are freedom's home and defender." He concluded by calling on "God's love. May He bless the souls of the departed. May He comfort our own. And may He always guide our country. God bless America."[27]

America had faced such moments before. Roosevelt had steeled the nation after Pearl Harbor. John Kennedy, in his inaugural address had insisted that the Cold War demanded similar resolve. Both of those presidents had spoken with fervor and moral certainty. Roosevelt: "No matter how long it may take us to overcome this premeditated invasion, the American people in their righteous might will win through to absolute victory. . . . We will not only defend ourselves to the uttermost, but will make very certain that this form of treachery shall never endanger us again." Kennedy: "Let every nation know, whether it wishes us well or ill, that we shall pay any price, bear any burden, meet any hardship, support any friend, oppose any foe to assure the survival and the success of liberty. This much we pledge— and more."[28] But Bush had sounded his trumpet with even greater vigor, telling his fellow Americans and people everywhere that the United States would not just "answer" the attacks and defeat a specific enemy as had Roosevelt and Kennedy. Bush would "rid the world of evil." No liberal had ever framed America's enemy in that way. Here was an extraordinary call to arms.

Bush repeated this religiously inflected conservative formulation again and again. By one count, Bush used the word *evil*, almost always as a noun, some one thousand times in public remarks made during his first year and a half as president.[29] In a moving speech given at the United States Military Academy, he categorically rejected the kind of cultural relativism and situational ethics secular liberals had long used to explore the moral particularities of a given situation. In assessing 9/11, Bush saw no moral ambiguities: "Moral truth is the same in every culture, in every time, and in every place. . . . There can be no neutrality between justice and cruelty, between the innocent and the guilty. We are in a conflict between good and evil, and America will call evil by its name."[30] In the months after the 9/11 attacks, Americans, by a large majority, were exhilarated by Bush's fiery certainties and moral absolutes.

Some on the Left tried to muddy the waters, rumbling about the United States's many provocative interventions in the Middle East and reminding Americans that the Reagan administration had supported the very same Islamic fundamentalist mujahidin during the anti-Soviet war in Afghanistan who were now being called evil-doers and terrorists. And around the world, even as most people in almost all nations sympathized with the American people, many found Bush's moral absolutism absurd; these international critics believed it was the United States that had often used violence and coercion to take what it wished from other nations and to impose its will on other cultures. They responded to 9/11 by lecturing the United States: "The U.S. imperium policy has caused too much injustice in the world because the U.S. has grown to be a huge country with huge consumption needs," said a leading Indonesian Muslim intellectual. "It is like a giant that needs too much."[31] And closer to home, many well-respected voices in Mexico argued that the United States had only gotten what it deserved, a position stated most bluntly, perhaps, by the Catholic bishop of Chiapas who observed, "Now they harvest what they have sowed."[32] Few liberals in the United States accepted such hard-hearted indictments, even as some, at least, were made uncomfortable by Bush's religious formulations and by the moral absolutism that informed his policymaking. But, by and large, leading liberal politicians kept quiet except as to support the Bush administration's War on Terror.

American intelligence agencies quickly ascertained that the 9/11 attacks had been devised by the shadowy Jihadist group, al-Qaeda, led by Osama bin Laden. Al-Qaeda was part of a larger movement of Islamists, some of whom likewise embraced violent methods, and a great majority of whom did not, that meant to create theocratic governments based on *Sharia*, or Islamic law. These groups were overwhelmingly opposed to the consumerist-oriented, individual rights–based, secular lifestyles they associated with the West. They wanted the West out of the Middle East; they wanted Israel destroyed;

they rejected gender equality; and they wished to make all people live under the codes of behavior, as they understood them, that had been established by the Islamic caliphate well over a thousand years earlier. Such views made the differences between American conservatives and liberals seem almost trivial.

Al-Qaeda was based in Afghanistan under the protection and support of the Taliban, the rulers of that nation's Islamic theocratic government. On September 20, 2001, Bush appeared before a joint session of Congress and issued an ultimatum to the Taliban: turn over the leaders of al-Qaeda to the United States, close all terrorist training camps, arrest all terrorists in Afghanistan, and allow the United States to enter Afghanistan to police compliance. As the Taliban sought to negotiate with the Bush administration, the American people overwhelmingly supported the president's firm stand. While tens of thousands of Americans did stage antiwar protests in the days after Bush's threat of war, tens of millions approved of his call to arms. On October 7, as the Taliban continued to equivocate, the United States, supported by the United Kingdom, launched Operation Enduring Freedom, which was aimed at toppling the Taliban government and capturing or killing the al-Qaeda terrorists based in Afghanistan. By mid-November, the Taliban government had collapsed, and al-Qaeda terrorists were killed, captured, or on the run. Several key leaders of the Jihadist organization, including the group's leader, Osama bin Laden, did escape, almost surely into the tribal areas of southeastern Pakistan. Despite that setback, the Afghan war had seemed successful; few Americans realized how tenuous the American-led victory over the Taliban was. As a result, according to polls, Americans approved of the job their president was doing by an extraordinary 90 percent.[33]

Well before the Bush administration launched Operation Enduring Freedom and even before the September 11, 2001, attacks, key administration officials, including the president, had begun to target another enemy: Iraq. Bush had made his concerns clear to the American people. In his January 29, 2002, State of the Union address, he warned of an "Axis of Evil," which included the nations of North Korea, Iran, and Iraq. These nations, he warned, all sought "weapons of mass destruction" which they "could" then give to terrorists to use against the United States. "[T]ime is not on our side," warned the President, but he also offered Americans his assurance: "I will not wait on events while dangers gather. I will not stand by as peril draws closer and closer. The United States will not permit the world's most dangerous regimes to threaten us with the world's most destructive weapons."[34] Like Barry Goldwater, President Bush envisioned a world in which American might cleansed the world of evil regimes so that the American people could live out their days in peace and security.

Over the next months the drumbeat toward war intensified. In June, before the graduating class of the United States Military Academy, President Bush declared, "Yet the war on terror will not be won on the defensive. We must take the battle to the enemy, disrupt his plans, and confront the worst threats before they emerge. (Applause.) In the world we have entered, the only path to safety is the path of action. And this nation will act. . . . Our security will require all Americans to be forward-looking and resolute, to be ready for preemptive action when necessary to defend our liberty and to defend our lives." Bush and his administration had begun to urge the American people to accept "preventive" war as a new necessity in the Global War on Terror.

Bush believed that the American war against "evil-doers" served a purpose far greater than that of basic security. "For too long," he told the American people, "our culture has said, 'If it feels good, do it.' Now America is embracing a new ethic and a new creed: 'Let's roll.' In the sacrifice of soldiers, the fierce brotherhood of firefighters, and the bravery and generosity of ordinary citizens, we have glimpsed what a new culture of responsibility could look like." The war, Bush was saying in so many words, had made America conservative. He continued, "We've come to know truths that we will never question: evil is real, and it must be opposed."[35] Here was a new American crusade (a phrase Bush used and then quickly discarded after being told that in parts of the Islamic world, the word *crusade* referred to medieval Christians' attempts to defeat the forces of Islam).

The Bush administration focused its most heated rhetoric on Iraq. President Bush, Vice President Cheney, and National Security

Advisor Condoleezza Rice repeatedly claimed that the brutal Iraqi dictator had weapons of mass destruction and that he meant to use those weapons against the American people. Saddam, they warned, was conspiring with al-Qaeda, and Iraq's weapons of mass destruction could be turned over to Osama bin Laden. Rice put the case bluntly: "The problem here is that there will always be some uncertainty about how quickly he [Saddam] can acquire nuclear weapons. But we don't want the smoking gun to be a mushroom cloud."[36] Conservative mass media outlets, the multitudinous offspring of Bill Buckley's 1950s brain child, including FOX television news and radio megastar Rush Limbaugh, echoed the message of the dire threat Iraq presented in ever more alarming registers. Only through "regime change," said President Bush could the destruction of the American people be averted.

An influential group of intellectual policymakers, known collectively as neoconservatives, urged the president forward. Some of these neoconservatives had been affiliated, in the pre–Ronald Reagan era, with the Democratic Party, and most, by and large, were moderate on social matters. But on foreign policy issues they were resolutely in the camp of hard-liners. The neo-cons rejected liberals' post-Vietnam hesitation in using military force to pursue American interests. They believed that the United States faced implacable ideological enemies who presented an existential threat to the American people. Liberals refused to recognize the evil that ruled the hearts of America's enemies. These neo-cons insisted that the United States had the right to act unilaterally against any and all international threats, and, even more, that the United States had a world-historical mission to spread the virtues of liberty.

The most passionate neo-con advocate of these policies was also the best placed: Paul Wolfowitz was the assistant secretary of defense. Back in 1997, he had joined the Project for a New American Century, founded by leading neo-cons William Kristol and Robert Kagen. They had formed the Project in response to President Bill Clinton's cautious, multilateral foreign policy stance. They championed a far more aggressive use of America's massive military power to eliminate American enemies and to spread American ideals across the planet.

At the advent of the twenty-first century, Iraq was at the top of their enemies list. Long before 9/11, Wolfowitz and like-minded men had argued that removing Saddam Hussein from Iraq would quickly lead to the democratization of that country. Once people in other nations in the Middle East saw the virtue of the new Iraqi democracy, they too would choose the path of freedom and democracy.

President Bush was entranced by this vision. Here, he hoped, was an opportunity to remake the Middle East, safeguard Israel, and produce an American peace across the globe. That his father had failed to remake Iraq after the 1991 Gulf War was further reason to push forward to conclude unfinished business. It was compassionate conservatism on a global scale. A few conservatives in the mold of Robert Taft were horrified by the president's embrace of the neo-con vision. Like Taft, they believed that the United States should take any measure necessary to safeguard the United States. If—and they wanted more evidence—Iraq was a danger, it should be neutralized. But the old-line conservatives could not imagine how the United States could transform Iraqi society into a democracy, nor did they believe it should. Had not Bush himself said during the 2000 election campaign that the United States should not be in the business of nation building? Cultural traditions, the bedrock of social stability, were long in the making. That was a core conservative belief, they thundered. Within the Bush administration these old conservative voices were ignored.

Conservatism, as a foreign policy approach, provided no clear direction to most specific policy decisions. But at least since the mid-1950s, most conservatives had embraced a shared understanding of the role of the United States in the world. The United States was an exceptional country. Those who opposed it opposed the world-historical virtues for which it stood, and thus America's enemies were enemies of freedom, democracy, and liberty. Powerful members of the Bush administration, most of all muscular conservatives such as Vice President Dick Cheney and Secretary of Defense Donald Rumsfeld, did not necessarily agree with the neo-cons that the Middle East could—or even should—be transformed into a land of happy democracies. But they did believe that the United States had the unilateral right to exercise its military might to destroy threats to its national security and to expand American economic and political power where and when it could. So while the neo-con ideologues and the more hard-headed—and hard-hearted—conservative warhawks, especially Vice President Cheney, did not share the exact same foreign policy vision, both factions wanted to take out Saddam Hussein and establish a new government in Iraq. President Bush never saw any need to sort out the differences that underlay his different advisers' motives and understandings; he simply embraced them all. So did most of the Americans who voted for him. In March 2003, President Bush went to war against Saddam Hussein.

The war went well. The army of Iraq was quickly destroyed, and Saddam was deposed. In a few weeks time the United States was in control of the nation of Iraq. But the neo-cons and the Bush administration had been wrong about the Iraqi people. Vice President Cheney, using rhetoric drawn from the neo-cons in the Defense Department, had assured the American people that Iraqis would welcome the United States military as liberators and that Iraq would quickly become a beacon of democracy in the Middle East. Instead, Iraq became a battleground, with Iraqi Shiites and Iraqi Sunnis at each others' throats. Iraqis of many persuasions looked at the United States not as liberator but as conqueror. Iraqis, even as they fought each other, began to wage a war of liberation against the United States. Lured to the insurgency was an array of other non-Iraqi Islamic fighters, including elements of al-Qaeda. Iran, a Shiite regime, supported the Iraqi Shiites fighting the United States. Americans causalities mounted. Edmund Burke, the great conservative, would not have been surprised by the deadly cultural and religious terror unleashed by the American conquest, but President Bush was dumbfounded.

Still, as the 2004 election approached, Bush told the American people that they must stay the course. Though no weapons of mass destruction had been found in Iraq and no ties had been discovered linking Saddam Hussein to al-Qaeda or any terrorist acts against the United States, Bush insisted that the Iraq war was justified. In one of his rare press conference appearances, he read a prepared statement: "Above all, the defeat of violence and terror in Iraq is vital to the defeat of violence and terror elsewhere; and vital, therefore, to the safety of the American people. Now is the time, and Iraq is the place, in which the enemies of the civilized world are testing the will of the civilized world. We must not waver." In response to a reporter's skeptical question calling into doubt the rationale for the war, Bush was blunt: "Iraq *is* a part of the war on terror. . . . And it's essential we win this battle in the war on terror. By winning this battle, it will make other victories more certain in the war against the terrorists."[37]

Throughout the 2004 campaign, the Iraq war dominated the political debates. The Bush administration, led by Vice President Cheney, continued to argue that the war was necessary to protect the American people from terrorists and that the anti-American insurgents in Iraq were themselves terrorists dominated by al-Qaeda. That the war in Afghanistan continued to fester, that the Taliban was growing in strength, and that Osama bin Laden had not been killed or captured was largely ignored. President Bush, his campaign repeatedly stated, kept the United States safe; better to fight the terrorists in Iraq than in the United States. Bush's Democratic opponent, the liberal Massachusetts Senator John Kerry, tried to make the deadly, "preemptive" war justified by the Bush administration on false and misleading information his major campaign issue. But Kerry failed to make his case.

Kerry was hampered by three major problems. First, the Bush campaign derided Kerry as just another Massachusetts tax-and-spend liberal. Despite the Clinton-Gore record, the label still stung. Second, Kerry's opposition to the Iraq war was mocked as typical liberal "flip-flopping." Kerry, said the Bush campaign, voted to fund the Iraq war, but now when the going had gotten tough, he wanted "to cut and run." The Bush campaign argued that President Bush was unwavering in his beliefs but that Kerry, the liberal, had no clear standards or beliefs. Finally, Kerry was perceived by some voters, helped by the Bush campaign, as a "limousine liberal" whose personal fortune and lifestyle (he spoke French) distanced him from the problems and concerns of everyday Americans. Somewhat bizarrely, conservative supporters of Bush also were able to turn Kerry's Vietnam War experiences, which he featured in his campaign, against him. Kerry, unlike most of his peers at Yale, had volunteered for naval service during the war and had seen major combat. He had won the Silver Star and received three Purple Hearts for his battlefield wounds. Later, however, after returning home from the war, Kerry had thrown himself into the antiwar movement and had helped to lead Vietnam Veterans against the War. A series of brutal and misleading ads raised doubts about Kerry's valor and chastised him for protesting the war. Though Kerry supporters saw his war service and then antiwar activism as evidence of his powerful moral conscience and his ability to change his views based on changing circumstances, conservatives, and some less ideological Americans, were appalled by Kerry's adaptability. The ads chipped away at Kerry's support.

On election day 2004, a narrow majority of American voters gave Bush their support. Bush strengthened conservatives' hold on the South and the West. Still, Kerry won the West Coast, all of the Northeast, and all of the Great Lakes states except Indiana. Republicans also picked up three seats in the House and four Senate seats. Bush's leadership in the War on Terror figured prominently in his victory. Despite the evident failures in policy and the false justifications of the preemptive war in Iraq, a majority of voters preferred the hard-line security measures proffered by President Bush and American conservatives.

Bush's reelection was the highpoint of his presidency. One debacle after another followed that victory. His first failure came after he tried to use his three million–vote majority to push Congress to end the Social Security system created by Franklin Roosevelt's New Deal. Bush wanted to begin privatizing the system and end government control of America's major old-age pension system. Individual American should, he insisted, be allowed to invest their own money as they saw fit to create their own pensions. While fellow conservatives rallied around Bush's proposal to end liberalism's most enduring program, few others did. Bush expended a great deal of his political capital in a losing fight.

A few months after Bush made his case against the Social Security system, Hurricane Katrina hit the Gulf States. The levees that protected New Orleans were breeched by the storm surge, and the city flooded. Nearly two thousand Americans, most of them poor and African American, were killed, and hundreds of thousands of people were left homeless. The Bush administration responded miserably to the horror. Michael Brown, the Bush appointee in charge of the Federal Emergency Management Agency, turned out to be an incompetent. Like several other high-level Bush appointees, he had received his job because of his loyalty to Bush and the conservative cause, not because he had the requisite skills and devotion to government service to do his job well. Despite Brown's clear failure, President Bush showed the same kind of unwavering faith in his people and principles that he was showing in the Iraq war. He went on record commending Michael Brown: "Brownie, you're doing a heckuva job."[38] Americans were not pleased by what they watched on their television sets, and some, at least, began to wonder if conservatives' antigovernment rhetoric and policies had not gone too far. Sometimes, such as when a hurricane struck, and despite the fabled words of Ronald Reagan, a strong and competent government was not a problem; it was the solution.

Throughout 2005, 2006, 2007, and 2008 the Iraq war ravaged on. Vice President Cheney had once said that the war would cost Americans next to nothing: American troops would be welcomed, and Iraqi oil revenues would pay for the reconstruction of Iraqi's broken nation. He was wrong. The total direct and indirect American costs of this war of choice totaled well over a trillion dollars by the end of 2008. More than 4,200 Americans had died, and more than ten times that many had been wounded by the end of 2008. Iraq had no weapons of mass destruction, and its government had not assisted al-Qaeda. Nonetheless, Iraqis paid a brutal price for their inability to rid themselves of Saddam Hussein; an estimated one hundred thousand Iraqi men, women, and children died violent deaths as a result of the American invasion and occupation.

Americans watched the carnage go on year after year. They mourned the toll the war took on America's servicemen and women. And they came to understand that the war had been based on lies. By 2008, a majority of Americans had lost faith in their president's decision to wage a preventive/preemptive war on their behalf in a country that had, in fact, represented a limited threat to the national security. A majority had also become embarrassed and even disgusted by the harsh measures the Bush administration had taken against "enemy combatants" and men suspected of being terrorists. These measures included waterboarding, "enhanced" interrogation, and indefinite captivity without any rights or recourse. Conservatives' hard line on "evildoers," most Americans decided, had taken the United States in the wrong direction.

Then, with the Bush administration focused on the War on Terror, came the hardest blow of all. America's economy had been based for some three decades, through both Democratic and Republican administrations, on the conservative principle of deregulation and belief in the power of the unrestrained free market to create jobs and prosperity. President Jimmy Carter had begun the deregulatory turn; Reagan had propelled it forward, focusing on the deregulation of the financial sector. Every president thereafter followed this conservative economic policy of reducing government discipline of the private sector. New Democrat Bill Clinton had certainly supported environmental and safety regulations, but he, too, had been an enthusiastic supporter of a deregulated financial sector. Bush was a true believer— but his administration did little more than follow the long-term conservative trajectory begun in the late 1970s.

Beginning in late 2007, things began to go wrong with America's exuberant financial system. The core trouble occurred in the home mortgage industry, which had become an unregulated free-for-all. Myriad players, ranging from long-established banks to fly-by-night financial service businesses, used a mind-numbing array of mortgage "instruments," from traditional thirty-year mortgages to "sub-prime" mortgages (a fancy name for high-cost loans to people with bad or even no creditworthiness), to offer most any adult who could sign his or her name money to buy property. Strangest of all, in retrospect, these individual loans were then bundled together, often with little regard for the actual riskiness of the various underlying mortgages, into huge public offerings, which were owned and traded by the world's largest banks, pension funds, mutual funds, and even governments, often on highly leveraged terms. Buyers of these multiplying mortgage "instruments" believed that even if individual mortgages went bad, the foreclosed properties upon which the mortgages had been made would have sufficient value to keep anyone from actually losing money. In other words, as long as home prices kept rising, the system would work.

Prices did not keep rising. Like other capitalist bubbles before it—such as the 1929 stock market crash—prices had run too far ahead of underlying value. In this case, the inflated price of homes exceeded people's ability to pay for the property, even with the fanciful mortgages America's financial industry had created. Suddenly, too many people wanted out of their expensive homes, but they could not sell them for enough money to pay off their mortgages. So, as these "underwater" people stopped paying off their mortgages, the people who owned those mortgages also started losing money, and they could not sell the foreclosed properties for enough money to avoid losing their investment. Lots of people and businesses were suddenly losing lots of money. And since those individual mortgages had been bundled together and sold to major banks and pension funds and even governments, critical institutions in the United States and around the world began to go broke. The Bush administration had not created this mess, but it had done nothing to restrain or regulate it, either.[39]

As had happened in 1929, a relatively unrestrained and unregulated capitalism had created a catastrophe. The economy began to contract, people lost their homes, people lost their jobs, and many of America's great banks and corporations collapsed or fell into bankruptcy. Conservatives had long argued that the free market best disciplined the American people: by rewarding hard work, good ideas, and smart economic risks, the free market produced national prosperity and individual fortunes. By the summer of 2008, Americans began to reconsider their long adventure in unregulated free market economics. As the economy tumbled, the conservative economic principles heralded by conservative leaders from Robert Taft through George W. Bush lost much of their creditworthiness in the political marketplace. The liberal economist Robert Kuttner did his best to write the obituary for conservative economics: "The current carnage on Wall Street, with dire spillover effects on Main Street, is the result of a failed ideology—the idea that financial markets could regulate themselves. Serial deregulation fed on itself. . . . [T]he public should never again forget that this needless collapse was brought to us by free-market extremists."[40] According to the Gallup Poll, on election day 2008, the lame-duck President George Bush enjoyed an approval rating of just 20 percent of the American people.

An extraordinary, if unlikely, liberal politician was the beneficiary of the implosion of the Bush presidency and the debacle of modern American political conservatism. Barack Hussein Obama, the half-black and half-white, very junior senator from Illinois, had run his entire campaign for the presidency attacking the conservative principles of George W. Bush. His campaign had first gained traction in 2007 based on Obama's long-standing and unequivocal opposition to the preemptive war in Iraq. Obama insisted that America was safer when it acted in concert with other nations and not unilaterally. He insisted that diplomacy, not bellicosity, was the answer to America's international problems. Iraq, he said, was the wrong war, at the wrong time, for the wrong reasons. By mid-2008, Obama's stand, which he had held since 2002, was shared by a majority of Americans. His outspoken leadership, backed by his remarkable eloquence on the issue, enraptured liberals and increasing numbers of political moderates.

Obama had been equally blunt in his critique of the deregulatory economic principles of modern conservatism. In early 2008 in New York City, the heart of America's financial system, Obama demanded a return to a more disciplined approach to free market regulation. He blasted the Bush administration: "Our free market was never meant to be a free license to take whatever you can get, however you can get it. . . . Unfortunately, instead of establishing a 21st century regulatory framework, we simply dismantled the old one—aided by a legal but corrupt bargain in which campaign money all too often shaped policy and watered down oversight."[41]

In Obama's campaign stump speech, his words echoed those of Franklin Roosevelt. In 1933, with the Great Depression in full fury, Roosevelt had condemned the quasi-laissez-faire economics that had long ruled the United States: "The money changers have fled from their high seats in the temple of our civilization. We may now restore that temple to the ancient truths. The measure of the restoration lies in the extent to which we apply social values more noble than mere monetary profit."[42] In October 2008, with more than 750,000 jobs already lost that year and most of America's largest banks crashing,

Obama told the American people that it was time for change: "We need policies that grow our economy from the bottom up, so that every American, everywhere has the chance to succeed. Not just the person who owns the factory but the men and women working on the factory floor. Not just the CEO, but the secretary and the janitor. If we've learned anything from this economic crisis, it's that we're all connected; we're all in this together. We'll rise and fall as one nation, as one people."[43]

Obama's self-described conservative Republican opponent for the presidency, Arizona Senator John McCain, and his running mate, the folksy, social conservative Alaska Governor Sarah Palin, blasted Obama as a socialist. Later, conservative evangelical and onetime presidential aspirant Mike Huckabee accused Obama of following in the footsteps of "Lenin and Stalin." And former conservative Republican Speaker of the House Newt Gingrich looked at Obama's economic plans and warned the American people that an Obama presidency had all the makings of a "dictatorship."[44] It was Roosevelt redux; all these charges had been made against FDR and his New Deal. And as was true in the Roosevelt campaign in 1932, a majority of the American electorate was no longer listening to such charges.

Obama called himself a progressive, not a liberal. And unlike most of the liberal politicians who had preceded him—though not Franklin Roosevelt or "new" Democrat Bill Clinton—he made clear that his Christian beliefs played a fundamental role in his life. He showcased his lovely family before American voters, and, like George W. Bush, he admitted to past personal failings, if only to foreground the moral life and strong character he had developed over time. So, Obama was not an old-fashioned liberal, though as an African American candidate he was the recipient of liberals' greatest civil rights triumph, the end of legal racial discrimination.

Even if Obama did not advertise himself as a liberal, his policies overwhelmingly were. He called for more government regulation of the economy to protect Americans against the fierce insecurities and depredations of the capitalist system. He rejected those who called on traditional values to castigate gay Americans and sneer at feminists. He spoke freely of a fully inclusive social compact and championed equality over individual liberty. Even as he spoke of his spiritual beliefs, he called for a reliance on scientific expertise and not religious orthodoxies in making public policy. Finally, he called for an end to the bellicose, unilateral foreign policy approach that had long characterized modern American conservatism. Obama promised to reach out to the rest of the world with an open hand, not a mailed fist.

Obama defeated his conservative Republican opponent John McCain for the presidency on November 4, 2008. No one called for a recount this time. Barack Obama won 365 electoral votes to McCain's 173, holding the Northeast, the Pacific Coast, and the Great Lakes states, including Ohio. But Obama also cracked conservatives' long hold on the South, winning Florida, Virginia, and North Carolina. And in the West he added New Mexico, Colorado, and Nevada. The House and the Senate also went strongly Democratic, creating a liberal-moderate majority in Congress.

George W. Bush had given modern conservatism a two-term presidency. But Bush's military, international, domestic, and economic failures dealt the modern conservative movement a mighty blow. Some conservatives tried to explain away the 2008 defeat, arguing that Bush had not been a true conservative. They had a weak argument. Bush's policy failures were conservative failures. In 2009, liberals, after many years out of power, would have their chance, again, to craft a political order. Conservatives, as many of them admitted publicly, could only hope that the liberal Obama presidency would fail so that they could, someday soon, try again. The modern conservative movement had fallen.

CONCLUSION

WHEN ROBERT TAFT DIED IN 1953, he feared that Americans had lost their way. He believed he was fighting a losing, rear-guard action against a modern liberal colossus. While he had seen some New Deal economic measures beaten back, he had been anguished by his party's—the Republican Party's—capitulation to the welfare state with its comprehensive government-mandated social provision programs, hydra-like economic regulations, and egalitarian ethos. He had done his best to take on liberals' frontline troops—organized labor with their demand for economic equity and government-insured security. But at his death, more than 35 percent of private sector employees were union members. Ironically, that very year would be the highpoint for organized labor in the United States, in part thanks to Taft's legislative battles.

William Buckley had picked up Taft's gauntlet and run with it in a new direction. Buckley believed that conservatives needed to do more than fight legislative battles; they needed to create a new political culture. Championed by erudite and witty men such as himself, he imagined, conservative ideas would do public battle with the tired and morally adrift liberalism the New Deal had bequeathed to the American people. By demonstrating that liberalism was cousin to socialism and atheistic communism, he believed he could move Americans to acknowledge the moral and spiritual superiority of conservative principles. Buckley saw himself as a rebellious voice in the wilderness, even in the late 1950s. But, he knew, too, that he had established a conservative beachhead in America's public life. In his graying years, he participated in making that conservative public mainstream and massively powerful.

Barry Goldwater was conservatism's John the Baptist figure. His 1964 presidential campaign helped coalesce the disparate elements that would constitute the modern conservative electorate. He brought together Taftian economic conservatives with Buckley's intellectual and religiously driven legions. But even more significant, he brought southern segregationist whites and fierce anticommunists to the Republican Party. After Goldwater, race politics would, for many decades, be a fundamental aspect of the conservative movement. Goldwater helped to create a mass electoral bloc dedicated to the conservative cause and working through the Republican Party. Goldwater was swamped by the New Deal electoral coalition in 1964, and, as a result, many pundits predicted the end of modern conservatism. In fact, the exuberant, celebratory liberal victory of 1964 would be the last of its kind for more than forty-four years.

Phyllis Schlafly helped bring back conservatism from its political dead end. Building on many Americans' disdain and distrust of the cultural liberalism that had swept the United States, she energized a new generation of conservative activists, many of them women. Whereas Richard Nixon had mobilized voters by drawing on Americans' discomfort with the many protest movements of the 1960s and the general breakdown in law and order, Schlafly went further and contributed a less time-bound weapon to the conservative political arsenal. She argued that liberals' attempt to upend age-old traditional values, especially those related to gender roles and sexuality, would destroy the moral fiber of the American way of life. Millions heeded her call, and those of other religious traditionalists. William Buckley had insisted that conservatism was a moral and religious persuasion as much as it was an economic approach to policymaking. Schlafly, a great publicist in her own right, made those religious and moral claims politically supercharged. She made sure that the politics of gender and sexuality became central to the conservative movement.

In 1980, Ronald Reagan was the beneficiary of all of these conservative activists and of the electorate they had stirred. A masterful politician, he brought an unmatched charisma to the conservative movement. Reagan had been thinking and talking about conservative ideas, ranging from an uncompromising anticommunism to a zealous faith in the free market system, for many years by time he ran for the presidency in 1980. He communicated those ideas, at a time when liberalism had been discredited in the eyes of many Americans, with a simple grace and certainty that won conservatism legions of new converts. Mobilizing broad swathes of racially minded southern whites, evangelical whites, proponents of an unbridled free market system, dedicated anticommunists, and social conservatives of all kinds, Reagan won the presidency. As president, he fulfilled many conservatives' highest hopes by cutting taxes, deregulating the economy, and pushing hard to reverse the liberal and secular trends that had for so long dominated American society. Reagan became conservatives' great icon.

George W. Bush would have a very hard time living up to the Reagan legacy. But he tried. He built on the Reagan coalition to win the presidency in the contested election of 2000. As president, he too cut taxes and deregulated the economy. Far more than Reagan, he reached out to religious traditionalists and tried to instill a religious sensibility into both his domestic and international policymaking, most boldly by declaring a war on evil in the aftermath of the 9/11 terrorist attacks. But Bush will be remembered more for his failures than his successes. His antigovernment ideology failed the American people during the Hurricane Katrina tragedy, and the economic conservative principles to which he adhered exploded in the last years of his presidency, sending the United States and much of the world into an economic tailspin. And Bush's war on evil turned out far differently than he had promised, disillusioning Americans and leaving conservative foreign policy precepts in tatters. Bush had inherited a vast and powerful conservative movement. When he left office, the liberal Barack Obama was president. The remnant of the conservative movement found itself without sure direction or answers to the problems that the long conservative ascendency had bequeathed to the American people— harrowing economic inequity, a devastated industrial base, ecological dangers, massive government debt, a broken health-care system, a failing social-safety net, and diminished international power.

Conservatives had, however, changed the course of American history. They had produced a new disciplinary order in the United States. Conservatives had insisted that the free market and not government economic control was the best road, not just to prosperity but also to a morally sound independent citizenry. Government welfare and government restrictions on the marketplace, they argued, produced dependency and shackled the entrepreneurial creativity of America's most productive individuals and businesses. While that piece of wisdom took a beating in the early years of the twenty-first century, conservative economic principles had played a vital role in the economic resurgence the United States had enjoyed in the late twentieth century. Even liberals had come to pay greater respect to the need to reward private sector creativity, to avoid measures that fostered economic dependency, and to exercise restraint in regulating and taxing free market productivity.

Conservatives' faith in traditional social hierarchies did not, over time, convert liberals. Conservatives from Taft's era onward had argued that long-standing cultural precepts should be honored for the social stability they produced and for the religious beliefs they often reflected. As a result, conservatives, even those as personally tolerant as William Buckley and Ronald Reagan, had been indifferent or even hostile to the many movements in the United States for equality. Most conservatives rejected the civil rights movement and for many years gladly allied themselves with racial segregationists. More outspokenly, they opposed the women's rights movement, and many influential conservatives insisted that hierarchical gender roles, in which women were subordinate to men, were religiously mandated. As was true of racism, over time, ever fewer Americans accepted the onetime conservative verity that a gender hierarchy is an appropriate and necessary social instrument in a nation dedicated to equal rights. In the early twenty-first century, conservatives' fear that ending the long strictures against homosexuality would lead to social devastation still had political salience for some Americans, especially the elderly. But this traditional social hierarchy, too, was even then losing its hold on the moral imagination of a majority of Americans, especially the young. Over time, conservatives' opposition to equality for a majority of Americans—women, people of color, and homosexuals—had placed them on the wrong side of the grand sweep of American history.

Conservatives' foreign policy record was a mixed and complicated one. The only clear line that connects the main conservative figures from the time of Robert Taft through the presidency of George W. Bush was a belief in and reliance on unilateralism and a fierce opposition to nations perceived as evil. Robert Taft's belief that the United States should avoid intervening militarily in other nations' affairs and be generally cautious of trying to steer other nations to American beliefs stands in almost direct opposition to the Bush doctrine of pre-emptive war. And certainly some conservatives rejected Bush's call to arms in Iraq on those very terms. Scholars and pundits have come to call the Taftian stance paleoconservatism and the Bush approach neo-conservatism. But all conservatives since Taft's time have supported creating massive American military might and the use of that power to further American principles and interests in the world. Bellicosity and not diplomacy have been the hallmark of conservatives' approach to managing global tensions. World order, they insist, must be made by American power. And unlike liberals who tend to see nations as rational actors seeking to maximize their own interests, a majority of conservatives have seen a world divided between good and evil. The United States, as the singularly vital representative of that good, conservatives from Barry Goldwater to George Bush have argued, must stand strong and uncompromising in the face of that evil. For decades, the Soviet Union was that evil presence; in more recent time, according to President Bush and his allies, terrorists and their supporters, as well as rogue nations such as North Korea, have come to embody evil in the world. In a world in which new powers such as China, India, and the European Union figure so prominently, the bipolar model—us versus them—that has figured the conservative political imaginary seems increasingly ill-suited to the world the American people must navigate.

Conservatives have offered Americans a disciplinary order that promises domestic tranquillity, peace through strength, and national prosperity. This conservative political movement has had many champions and, herein, I have selected a key handful to stand for the many who have organized, debated, preached, and fought to make conservatism the common sense of the American people. As I write these last sentences, the conservative political movement, some seventy years in the making, is in disarray, waiting for new champions or, perhaps, simply changing circumstances.

Contemporary conservatism is not moribund. Conservatives are not without power and presence in American life. The conservative counterpublic that William Buckley championed remains vibrant and influential; conservative media figures such as Rush Limbaugh and Glenn Beck remain household names, and institutional beachheads such as Fox News ensure that a conservative worldview is broadcast widely. Congressional conservatives completely control the Republican Party on Capitol Hill and, in the Taftian tradition, they bluntly refuse to go along with the neo–New Deal policies of the Obama administration, raising roadblocks everywhere they can. Still, the way forward for the conservative movement remains uncertain. Maybe modern conservatism—born in the fight against the New Deal; strengthened in the anticommunist struggle; its ranks greatly expanded by those Americans who opposed the claims made by people of color, feminists, and gay activists who demanded equal rights; and provided intellectual legitimacy in the 1970s by the failures of liberal economic policy—has outlasted its historic purpose in Americans' continuing political struggle to find social order and individual meaning in the world's most dynamic and diverse nation.

NOTES

INTRODUCTION

1. Franklin Roosevelt, acceptance speech, Democratic National Convention, Philadelphia, June 27, 1936, available at http://millercenter.virginia.edu/scripps/diglibrary/prezspeeches/roosevelt/fdr_1936_0627.html.

2. *The Papers of Robert A. Taft*, vol. 1, *1889–1938*, ed. Clarence E. Wunderlin Jr. (Kent, Ohio: Kent State University Press, 1997), 506.

3. Franklin Roosevelt's statement on signing the Social Security Act, August 14, 1935, Franklin Roosevelt Museum and Library, http://docs.fdr library.marist.edu/odssast.html.

4. William F. Buckley Jr. and L. Brent Bozell, *McCarthy and His Enemies: The Record and Its Meaning* (Chicago: Henry Regnery, 1954), 335.

5. Taft's sentiment has endured as a part of his legacy in conservative Republican circles; the quoted passage appears on Rebuild the Party, http://rebuildtheparty.ning.com/profile/MrRepublican.

ONE
Robert Taft: The Gray Men of Modern Conservatism and the Rights of Property

1. Clinton Rossiter, review of *The Conservative Mind*, by Russell Kirk, *American Political Science Review* 47, no. 3 (September 1953): 869.

2. *The Papers of Robert A. Taft*, vol. 1, *1889–1938*, ed. Clarence E. Wunderlin Jr. (Kent, Ohio: Kent State University Press, 1997), xxxviii. Taft has been well served by scholars; James T. Patterson, author of several major works in recent American history, published a definitive biography of Taft, *Mr. Republican: A Biography of Robert A. Taft* (Boston: Houghton Mifflin, 1972), and Clarence E. Wunderlin Jr. prepared a superb four-volume edition of Taft's papers, as well as a pithy analysis of his foreign policy views, *Robert A. Taft: Ideas, Traditions, and Party in U.S. Foreign Policy* (Lanham, Md.: Rowman and Littlefield, 2005). For an astute review of Wunderlin's monograph and volume 3 of the Taft papers, see George Fujii, "Isolating the Principles behind 'Mr. Republican,'" H-Diplo, December 2005, http://h-net.msu.edu/cgi-bin/logbrowse.pl?trx=vx&list=h-iplo&month=0601&week=a&msg=nwcPsDlJhfeXbFd6oFbZRg&user=&pw=.

3. *Papers of Taft*, 1:xlv.

4. Excerpted from Charles Beard's "Framing the Constitution," in *American Government: Readings and Cases*, ed. Peter Woll, 11th ed. (New York: Harper Collins, 1993); originally published in Charles Beard, *The Supreme Court and the Constitution* (1912), available at http://www.cooperativeindividualism.org/beard_constitution.html.

5. Robin Einhorn, *American Taxation, American Slavery* (Chicago: University of Chicago Press, 2006), 214.

6. James Madison wrote this in 1792, quoted in Gary J. Kornblith and John M. Murrin, "The Dilemmas of Ruling Elites in Revolutionary America," in *Ruling America*, ed. Steve Fraser and Gary Gerstle (Cambridge, Mass.: Harvard University Press, 2005), 53.

7. Senator John G. Tower, the first Republican elected to the U.S. Senate from Texas since Reconstruction, makes the case for Jefferson as a conservative in his surprisingly erudite monograph, *A Program for Conservatives* (New York: McFadden Books, 1962), 12. Tower was a professor of political science before becoming a senator.

8. *Papers of Taft*, 1:554.

9. Roosevelt quoted in David M. Kennedy, *Freedom from Fear: The American People in Depression and War, 1929–1945* (New York: Oxford University Press, 1999), 131.

10. Franklin D. Roosevelt, inaugural address, March 4, 1933, in *The Public Papers and Addresses of Franklin D. Roosevelt*, vol. 2, *The Year of Crisis, 1933*, ed. Samuel Rosenman (New York: Random House, 1938), 14–15.

11. Franklin Roosevelt, acceptance speech, Democratic National Convention, Philadelphia, June 27, 1936, available at http://millercenter.virginia.edu/scripps/diglibrary/prezspeeches/roosevelt/fdr_1936_0627.html.

12. *Papers of Taft*, 1:506.

13. *The Papers of Robert A. Taft*, vol. 2, *1939–1944*, ed. Clarence E. Wunderlin Jr. (Kent, Ohio: Kent State University Press, 2001), 16.

14. Alfred P. Sloan to John J. Raskob, July 24, 1934, John J. Raskob Papers, Hagley Library, Wilmington, Del., folder 61B.

15. S. M. DuBrul to Donaldson Brown, June 19, 1934, John J. Raskob Papers, folder 61B.

16. All of this material is drawn from John J. Raskob Papers, folder 61B.

17. Smith quoted in George Wolfskill, *The Revolt of the Conservatives: A History of the American Liberty League, 1934–1940* (Boston: Houghton Mifflin, 1962), 132.

18. Franklin D. Roosevelt, address at Madison Square Garden, New York City, October 31, 1936, in *The Public Papers and Addresses of Franklin D. Roosevelt*, ed. Samuel Rosenman (New York: Random House, 1938), 5:568–69.

19. Godfrey Hodgson, "The Foreign Policy Establishment," in *Ruling America*, ed. Steve Fraser and Gary Gerstle (Cambridge, Mass.: Harvard University Press, 2005), 223; for this quote and other Teddy Roosevelt exemplars, see http://www.theodoreroosevelt.org/life/Quotes.htm.

20. Alan Brinkley, *The End of Reform* (New York: Knopf, 1995).

21. Winston Churchill, "We Shall Fight on the Beaches," June 4, 1940, Churchill Centre, http://www.winstonchurchill.org/learn/speeches/speeches-of-winston-churchill/128-we-shall-fight-on-the-beaches#.

22. George Washington, Farewell Address (1796), Avalon Project, http://avalon.law.yale.edu/18th_century/washing.asp.

23. Taft quoted in Patterson, *Mr. Republican*, 198.

24. Justus D. Doenecke, *Storm on the Horizon: The Challenge to American Intervention, 1939–1941* (New York: Rowman Littlefield, 2000).

25. Randolph Bourne, *War and the Intellectuals* (Indianapolis, Ind.: Hackett Publishing, 1999), 84.

26. Taft quoted in Wunderlin, *Robert A. Taft*, 49.

27. *Papers of Taft*, 2:127.

28. Cowles quoted in *Papers of Taft*, 2:128.

29. Taft quoted in Patterson, *Mr. Republican*, 229.

30. Roosevelt quoted in David M. Kennedy, *Freedom from Fear* (New York: Oxford University Press, 1999), 783.

31. Taft quoted in Patterson, *Mr. Republican*, 269.

32. *Papers of Taft*, 2:613.

33. All quotes are taken from Patterson, *Mr. Republican*, 274–75.

34. Nelson Lichtenstein, *State of the Union* (Princeton, N.J.: Princeton University Press, 2002), 102.

35. Ibid.,100–101.

36. Quoted in Nelson Lichtenstein, *Walter Reuther: The Most Dangerous Man in Detroit* (Urbana: University of Illinois Press, 1997), 231.

37. *The Papers of Robert A. Taft*, vol. 3, *1945–1948*, ed. Clarence Wunderlin Jr. (Kent, Ohio: Kent State University Press, 1997), 172.

38. Ibid., 175.

39. The quote is taken directly from Patterson, *Mr. Republican*, 337.

40. Taft quoted in ibid., 249.

41. Ibid., 250–51.

42. I am following Patterson's analysis here; see chapter 23, "Taft-Hartley," in *Mr. Republican*, 335–66.

43. Elizabeth Fones-Wolf, *Selling Free Enterprise* (Urbana: University of Illinois Press, 1994), 43.

44. Lichtenstein, *State of the Union*, 115.

45. *Papers of Taft*, 3:385.

46. Alice Roosevelt Longworth is usually credited with the cutting remark, though the pundit William Safire complicates the tale in *Safire's Political Dictionary* (New York: Oxford University Press, 2008), 414–15.

47. David Farber, *Sloan Rules: Alfred P. Sloan and the Triumph of General Motors* (Chicago: University of Chicago Press, 2002), 240.

TWO

William Buckley: Building the Conservative Political Culture

1. William Buckley, *God and Man at Yale* (Chicago: Henry Regnery, 1951), xvi.

2. Ibid., xvii.

3. Ibid., 226.

4. Gannon quoted in Edward A. Purcell Jr., *The Crisis of Democratic Theory* (Lexington: University Press of Kentucky, 1973), 241.

5. Purcell, *Crisis of Democratic Theory*, 3.

6. Niebuhr quoted in ibid., 247.

7. Buckley, *God and Man at Yale*, 148.

8. Ibid., 151.

9. Abraham Lincoln, second inaugural address, March 4, 1865, Avalon Project, http://avalon.law.yale.edu/19th_century/lincoln2.asp.

10. A long list of such quotes is available at the Watchful Eye Web site, http://www.watchfuleye.com/Mencken.html. Mencken, I should note, was not a liberal. He was, rather, a foe of the folk—a scornful critic of mass culture and the traditional beliefs of the masses. In the United States in the 1920s, many intellectuals on both the left and the right shared a fierce concern about the public's ability to exercise reasoned judgment in the political realm. Walter Lippmann voiced those concerns most emphatically in the public sphere.

11. From an essay Bryan wrote in June 1925, excerpted in Jeffrey P. Moran, *The Scopes Trial* (Boston: Bedford/St. Martin's, 2002), 190–91.

12. Bryan also feared that Darwin's theory of evolution pointed toward a "survival of the fittest" credo that ran counter to his Christian belief that people should help one another. See Michael Kazin, *A Godly Hero: The Life of William Jennings Bryan* (New York: Knopf, 2006).

13. From a 1956 essay by Buckley quoted in the superb biography by John B. Judis, *William F. Buckley, Jr.: Patron Saint of the Conservatives* (New

York: Simon and Schuster, 1988), 217. I am indebted to Judis throughout this chapter for the narrative of Buckley's life.

14. J. Gresham Machen, *Christianity and Liberalism* (1923), http://www.biblebelievers.com/machen/machen_introduction.html. For more on Machen, see D. G. Hart, *Defending the Faith: J. Gresham Machen and the Crisis of Conservative Protestantism in Modern America* (Phillipsburg, N.J.: P & R Publishing, 2003).

15. Leo P. Ribuffo, *The Old Christian Right: The Protestant Far Right from the Great Depression to the Cold War* (Philadelphia: Temple University Press, 1983).

16. Ibid., 80.

17. Winrod quoted in ibid., 104.

18. Winrod and Smith quoted in "They Hate Ike," *Time*, May 5, 1952, http://www.time.com/time/magazine/article/0,9171,820744-1,00.html. For an overview of Smith's life, see Glen Jeansonne, *Gerald L. K. Smith: Minister of Hate* (New Haven, Conn.: Yale University Press, 1988).

19. Ribuffo, *Old Christian Right*, 244–45.

20. Judis, *William F. Buckley, Jr.*, 27.

21. Quoted in William R. Hutchison, *Religious Pluralism in America: The Contentious History of a Founding Ideal* (New Haven, Conn.: Yale University Press, 2003), chap. 8.

22. Quoted in ibid.

23. Harry Truman, "The Truman Doctrine," March 12, 1947, American Rhetoric, http://www.americanrhetoric.com/speeches/harrystrumantruman doctrine.html.

24. Richard Gid Powers, *Not without Honor: The History of American Anticommunism* (New York: Free Press, 1995), 205.

25. Ibid., 235.

26. William F. Buckley Jr. and L. Brent Bozell, *McCarthy and His Enemies: The Record and Its Meaning* (Chicago: Henry Regnery, 1954), 302.

27. Sheen quoted in Thomas C. Reeves, *America's Bishop: The Life and Times of Fulton J. Sheen* (San Francisco: Encounter Books, 2001), 87–88.

28. Ibid., 105.

29. The place of Catholics in the anticommunist cause is efficiently summarized in Patrick Allitt, *Religion in America since 1945: A History* (New York: Columbia University Press, 2003), 22–24.

30. Dean Acheson quoted in Powers, *Not without Honor*, 228.

31. McCarthy quoted in ibid., 242.

32. Buckley and Bozell, *McCarthy and His Enemies*, 153.

33. Ibid., 311.

34. Ibid., 323.

35. Ibid., 334.

36. Ibid., 335.

37. Quoted in Judis, *William F. Buckley, Jr.*, 110.

38. The quote, as well as the short history of the *Freeman*, is cited from the canonical, conservative history by George H. Nash, *The Conservative Intellectual Movement in America since 1945* (New York: Basic Books, 1976), 17.

39. Quoted in Judis, *William F. Buckley, Jr.*, 119.

40. Judis, *William F. Buckley, Jr.*, 113.

41. Nash, *Conservative Intellectual Movement in America*, 73–74.

42. Sheen quoted in Reeves, *America's Bishop*, 240.

43. The quote, as well as the general narrative, is taken from Ellen Schrecker, *Many Are the Crimes: McCarthyism in America* (Boston: Little, Brown, 1998), 264.

44. Stevenson quoted in M. J. Heale, *American Anticommunism: Combating the Enemy Within, 1830–1970* (Baltimore: Johns Hopkins University Press, 1990), 182.

45. Judis, *William F. Buckley, Jr.*, 120–21, 140.

46. Quoted in Nash, *Conservative Intellectual Movement in America*, 148.

47. Quoted in Judis, *William F. Buckley, Jr.*, 140.

48. William F. Buckley Jr., "Publisher's Statement," *National Review*, November 19, 1955, http://www.nationalreview.com/flashback/buckley 200406290949.asp.

49. L. Brent Bozell, "Budgetary Elephantiasis," *National Review*, February 2, 1957, 104.

50. "It's Not So Simple," *National Review*, February 2, 1957, 103.

51. William Buckley, "As for the Nonconformists," *National Review*, March 16, 1957, 261.

52. The story of their meeting is provided by Buckley, and the line is quoted in Jennifer Burns, "Godless Capitalism: Ayn Rand and the Conservative Movement," *Modern Intellectual History* 1, no. 3 (2004): 359. Burns provides an incisive account of Rand's battle with the *National Review* crowd.

53. Tonsor quoted in Nash, *Conservative Intellectual Movement in America*, 136. Stephen Tonsor, I should disclose, first taught me how think as a historian does.

54. Whittaker Chambers, "Big Sister Is Watching You," *National Review*, December 28, 1957, 594–96.

55. The quote and much of the overview of Welch and the John Birch Society are drawn from Jonathan M. Schoenwald, "We Are an Action Group: The John Birch Society and the Conservative Movement in the 1960s," in *The Conservative Sixties*, ed. David Farber and Jeff Roche (New York: Peter Lang, 2003). The famous quote is on p. 25.

56. Quoted in ibid., 26.

57. Rusher quoted in John A. Andrew III, *The Other Side of the Sixties: Young Americans for Freedom and the Rise of Conservative Politics* (New Brunswick, N.J.: Rutgers University Press, 1997), 103.

58. The editorial appears in the February 3, 1962, *National Review*; I have taken the quoted material from John Judis's *William F. Buckley, Jr.*, 199. While I have not followed Judis's analysis of Buckley's relationship with the JBS in all regards, I am indebted to it.

59. Quoted in Judis, *William F. Buckley, Jr.*, 138.

60. From the *National Review*, April 6, 1965, 273, but I have taken the quote from *Quotations from Chairman Bill: The Best of Wm. F. Buckley, Jr.* (New Rochelle, N.Y.: Arlington House, 1970), 28.

61. "The Week," *National Review*, January 12, 1957, 27–28.

62. William F. Buckley, Jr., *Up from Liberalism* (New York: McDowell, Obolensky, 1959).

63. "The Sharon Statement" is reprinted in Andrew, *The Other Side of the Sixties*, 221.

64. Rick Perlstein, *Before the Storm: Barry Goldwater and the Unmaking of the American Consensus* (New York: Hill and Wang, 2001), 70.

THREE

*Barry Goldwater: Cowboy Conservatism,
Race Politics, and the Other Sixties*

1. Goldwater made the statement to the *Chicago Tribune* in early 1964; quoted in Rick Perlstein's pathbreaking account of Goldwater's 1964 run for the presidency, *Before the Storm: Barry Goldwater and the Unmaking of the American Consensus* (New York: Hill and Wang, 2001), 254.

2. Robert Alan Goldberg, *Barry Goldwater* (New Haven, Conn.: Yale University Press, 2005), 108.

3. "Beware the Comsymps," *Time*, April 21, 1961, http://www.time.com/time/magazine/article/0,9171,895276,00.html.

4. Lisa McGirr, *Suburban Warriors: The Origins of the New American Right* (Princeton, N.J.: Princeton University Press, 2001).

5. Speech by Joseph McCarthy, Wheeling, W.Va., February 9, 1950, http://historymatters.gmu.edu/d/6456.

6. M. J. Heale, *American Anticommunism: Combating the Enemy Within, 1830–1970* (Baltimore: Johns Hopkins University Press, 1990), 199.

7. Welsh quoted in David H. Bennett, *The Party of Fear* (New York: Vintage, 1990), 319.

8. Quoted in Goldberg, *Barry Goldwater*, 138. I am following Goldberg's analysis of Goldwater and Welch.

9. Daniel Bell, ed., *The Radical Right* (New York: Doubleday, 1963). The first edition of the book stemmed from a conference held at Columbia University in 1954 to ponder McCarthyism.

10. Richard Hofstadter, The Pseudo-Conservative Revolt," in ibid., 76. The essay first appeared in *American Scholar* (Winter 1954–55).

11. Hofstadter, "Pseudo-Conservatism Revisited: A Postscript (1962)," in Bell, ed., *The Radical Right*, 99.

12. Goldwater quoted in Peter Iverson, *Barry Goldwater: Native Arizonan* (Norman: University of Oklahoma Press, 1997), 83, 84.

13. Nelson Lichtenstein, *State of the Union* (Princeton, N.J.: Princeton University Press, 2002), 139.

14. Quoted in Goldberg, *Barry Goldwater*, 122.

15. Ibid., 123.

16. Perlstein, *Before the Storm*, 1–16, 43–68.

17. The analysis here is straight from Perlstein, *Before the Storm*, chap. 3; the quoted passages appear on p. 48.

18. Wannamaker quoted in Laura Jane Gifford, "'Dixie Is No Longer in the Bag': South Carolina Republicans and the Election of 1960," *Journal of Policy History* 19, no. 2 (2007): 214. North Carolina conservative activist Jesse Helms, elected to the Senate as a Republican in 1972, felt similarly about Goldwater in 1960; see Bryan Hardin Thrift, "Jesse Helms, the New Right, and American Freedom" (Ph.D. diss., Boston University, 2005), 103.

19. For the quotes, see the 2004 preface to *The Conscience of a Conservative*, written by Edwin J. Feulner, available at http://www.heritage.org/Research/features/PresidentsEssay/PresEssay2004.pdf. For more on Westbrook Pegler and an important explanation of the role antiunionism played in conservative politics in the 1930s through the 1950s, see the useful article by David Witwer, "Westbrook Pegler and the Anti-union Movement," *Journal of American History* 92, no. 2 (September 2005): 527–52.

20. "Old Guard's New Spokesman," *Time*, May 2, 1960, http://www.time.com/time/magazine/article/0,9171,826352-2,00.html.

21. Barry M. Goldwater, *The Conscience of a Conservative* (New York: Macfadden-Bartell, 1961), 10–11. This edition and publisher replaced the original Victor edition in 1961 after the book proved to be a best seller. It is identical to the 1960 edition.

22. Quoted in Perlstein, *Before the Storm*, 65.

23. Goldwater, *The Conscience of a Conservative*; both quoted passages appear on p. 38.

24. For the decision, see http://usinfo.state.gov/usa/infousa/facts/democrac/33.htm.

25. "Republican Party Platform of 1960," http://www.presidency.ucsb.edu/showplatforms.php?platindex=R1960.

26. Quoted in Perlstein, *Before the Storm*, 95.

27. Theodore White, *The Making of the President, 1964* (New York: Atheneum, 1965), 89.

28. Transcript, John G. Tower Oral History Interview I, 8/8/71, by Joe B. Frantz, Internet Copy, LBJ Library, http://www.lbjlib.utexas.edu/johnson/archives.hom/oralhistory.hom/tower/tower01.pdf.

29. For white Texans' turn to a self-conscious political conservatism, see Jeff Roche, "Cowboy Conservatism," in *The Conservative Sixties*, ed. Jeff Roche and David Farber (New York: Peter Lang, 2003), 79–92.

30. William Leuchtenburg, *The White House Looks South* (Baton Rouge: Louisiana State University Press, 2005), 274.

31. Quoted in ibid., 290–1.

32. Bush quoted in Jon Margolis, *1964: The Last Innocent Year* (New York: William Morrow, 1999), 102.

33. See Perlstein, *Before the Storm*, 196.

34. White, *Making of the President, 1964*, 136.

35. "John E. Grenier," Adams and Reese LLP, http://www.adamsan dreese.com/JohnGrenier.html.

36. Folsom quoted in Dan T. Carter, *The Politics of Rage* (Baton Rouge: Louisiana State University Press, 1995), 86.

37. Wallace quoted in ibid., 95. For Wallace and race in the late 1950s and early 1960s, see chap. 3 of Carter's splendid work.

38. Quoted in ibid., 95.

39. Ibid., 96.

40. William A. Rusher, "Crossroads for the GOP," *National Review*, February 12, 1963, 109–12.

41. Goldwater quoted in Carter, *Politics of Rage*, 218.

42. "Assassination and Funeral of President John F. Kennedy," Museum of Broadcast Communications, http://www.museum.tv/archives/etv/K/ htmlK/kennedyjf/kennedyjf.htm.

43. Kennedy quoted in Taylor Branch, *Parting the Waters* (New York: Simon and Schuster, 1988), 839.

44. "President Lyndon B. Johnson's Address before a Joint Session of Congress," November 27, 1963, Lyndon Baines Johnson Library and Museum, http://www.lbjlib.utexas.edu/johnson/archives.hom/speeches.hom/ 631127.asp.

45. "To: Republican Members of Congress, From: William B. Pendergast, Director Research, August 21, 1963," Republican National Committee, Charles Goodell Papers, New York Public Library, New York City.

46. "June 10, 1964 Civil Rights Filibuster Ended," United States Senate, http://www.senate.gov/artandhistory/history/minute/Civil_Rights_Filibus ter_Ended.htm.

47. Perlstein, *Before the Storm*, 364 (including the Goldwater quotes).

48. Dirksen quoted in ibid., 364–65.

49. Johnson quoted in ibid., 365.

50. I am closely following the account given by John A. Andrew III, *The Other Side of the Sixties* (New Brunswick, N.J.: Rutgers University Press, 1997), 179–91. To hear The Goldwaters and their lyrics, go to http://www2 .nationalreview.com/audio/Side%201.mp3 and http://www2.nationalreview .com/audio/Side%202.mp3.

51. Chandler's editorial quoted in J. Allen Broyles, *The John Birch Society: Anatomy of a Protest* (Boston: Beacon, 1964), 88–89. The three hundred

California chapters of JBS comes from McGirr, *Suburban Warriors*, 63, where she also numbers total JBS membership in the early 1960s at sixty thousand.

52. For a pithy overview of the JBS, see Jonathan Schoenwald, "'We Are an Action Group': The John Birch Society and the Conservative Movement in the 1960s," in *The Conservative Sixties*, ed. David Farber and Jeff Roche (New York: Peter Lang, 2003), 21–36.

53. Fred C. Schwarz, *You Can Trust the Communists (To Be Communists)*, chap. 11, CACC Web site, Books Online, http://www.schwarzreport.org.

54. "Need to Recapture Ideals Cited at Anti-Communist School," *CACC Newsletter*, October 1960, CACC Web site, Newsletter, http://www.schwarzreport.org.

55. Schwarz, *You Can Trust the Communists*, chap. 11.

56. McGirr, *Suburban Warriors*, 60–64.

57. Ibid., 106–7, for the Shuller quote and McIntyre material.

58. McGirr, *Suburban Warriors*, 101–2.

59. John Stormer, *None Dare Call It Treason* (Florissant, Mo.: Liberty Bell Press, 1964), 124.

60. The figures for both books come from McGirr, *Suburban Warriors*, 135.

61. The quoted passages and analysis are from Donald T. Critchlow, *Phyllis Schlafly and Grassroots Conservatism* (Princeton, N.J.: Princeton University Press, 2005), 119–21.

62. Goldwater quoted in White, *Making of the President, 1964*, 126

63. Quoted in ibid., 126.

64. White, *Making of the President, 1964*, 201, 202.

65. Lodge quoted in Perlstein, *Before the Storm*, 374.

66. Barry Goldwater, 1964 acceptance speech, http://www.washingtonpost.com/wp-srv/politics/daily/may98/goldwaterspeech.htm.

67. Both quotes are from Perlstein, *Before the Storm*, 392.

68. Elmo Roper, "The Meaning of San Francisco," *Saturday Review*, August 22, 1964, 17.

69. White, *Making of the President 1964*, 217.

70. Johnson quoted in Margolis, *1964*, 166.

71. Goldwater quoted in Perlstein, *Before the Storm*, 352.

72. Goldberg, *Barry Goldwater*, 141–43; the quoted material is drawn by Goldberg from Goldwater's *Conscience of a Conservative*.

73. Quoted in Goldberg, *Barry Goldwater*, 191–92.

74. The "Daisy Girl" ad is all over the Internet. For good, clean versions go to YouTube (http://www.youtube.com), but beware of parodies or reworked versions.

75. "Anatomy of Triumph," *Time*, November 4, 1964, http://www.time .com/time/magazine/article/0,9171,828299,00.html; and Perlstein, *Before the Storm*, 513–15.

76. All quoted passages and the general analysis are from Stephan Lesher, *George Wallace* (Reading, Mass.: Addison-Wesley, 1994), 308–10.

77. Thurmond quoted in Earl Black and Merle Black, *The Vital South* (Cambridge, Mass.: Harvard University Press, 1992), 152–53.

78. Nunn quoted in Earl Black and Merle Black, *The Rise of Southern Republicans* (Cambridge, Mass.: Harvard University Press, 2002), 81.

79. Quoted in John Judis, *William F. Buckley, Jr.* (New York: Simon and Schuster, 1988), 231.

80. Perlstein, *Before the Storm*, 474; and Nicol C. Rae, *The Decline and Fall of the Liberal Republicans: From 1952 to the Present* (New York: Oxford University Press, 1989), 58.

81. Senator John Tower's description of Goldwater's ideology, quoted in Goldberg, *Barry Goldwater*, 24.

FOUR
Phyllis Schlafly: Domestic Conservatism and Social Order

1. Quoted in Donald Critchlow, *Phyllis Schlafly and Grassroots Conservatism* (Princeton, N.J.: Princeton University Press, 2005), 135. I rely throughout this chapter on Critchlow's richly researched, elegantly written, and sympathetic biography of Schlafly. I am, however, less willing than Critchlow to accept Schlafly's perspective and political framework in my analysis.

2. Ibid., 19–24; the quote appears on 21.

3. Ibid., 27.

4. Quoted in ibid., 47–48, 56. Critchlow emphasizes the "housewife" persona adopted by Schlafly.

5. I am relying on Paula Baker, "The Domestication of Politics: Women and American Political Society, 1780–1920," *American Historical Review* 89, no. 3 (June 1984): 620–47.

6. Smith quoted in Laura McEnaney, "He-Men and Christian Mothers: The America First Movement and the Gendered Meanings of Patriotism and Isolationism," *Diplomatic History* 18, no. 1 (Winter 1994): 55.

7. Michelle Nickerson, "Moral Mothers and Goldwater Girls," in *The Conservative Sixties*, ed. David Farber and Jeff Roche (New York: Peter Lang, 2003), 51–62.

8. Quoted in Critchlow, *Phyllis Schlafly*, 78.

9. Based on David L. O'Conner, "The Cardinal Mindszenty Foundation: American Catholic Anti-Communism and Its Limits," *American Communist History* 5, no. 1 (2006): 37–66; the quote by O'Gara in the previous paragraph is on p. 47. Critchlow, in *Phyllis Schlafly*, provides excellent detail about Schlafly's role but only limited comment on the controversy it generated within the American Catholic Church hierarchy; see chap. 3 and pp. 104–6. Regarding the McCarthyite label, I use it to underline that for Schlafly, as for Buckley, such a label was a badge of honor, not an undermining slur.

10. Quotes about Schlafly in Carol Felsenthal, *The Biography of Phyllis Schlafly: The Sweetheart of the Silent Majority* (Chicago: Regnery Gateway, 1981), 125–28. The author of this balanced early biography does her best to explore how Schlafly combined her home life with her political work. Like Critchlow, however, she gives little information on how much household help and child-care assistance Mrs. Schlafly had either from family or staff, especially when she was traveling, as she often did. The evidence does suggest that Schlafly had an incredible capacity to juggle successfully family and work.

11. Critchlow, *Phyllis Schlafly*, 111.

12. Quoted in ibid., 115.

13. Quoted in ibid., 139.

14. "This President Thing," *Time*, June 14, 1963, http://www.time.com/time/magazine/article/0,9171,874809-2,00.html.

15. Phyllis Schlafly, *A Choice Not an Echo* (Alton, Ill.: Pere Marquette Press, 1964), 25.

16. Ibid., 45.

17. Ibid., 106.

18. Quoted in Critchlow, *Phyllis Schlafly*, 123.

19. Schlafly, *A Choice Not an Echo*, 90.

20. Catherine E. Rymph, *Republican Women* (Chapel Hill: University of North Carolina Press, 2006), 175–76.

21. Phyllis Schlafly and Chester Ward, *The Gravediggers* (Alton, Ill.: Pere Marquette Press, 1964), 5.

22. Ibid., 31–32.

23. Ibid., 114, 11.

24. "Books by Phyllis Schlafly," on the Eagle Forum Web site gives the figure of two million; http://www.eagleforum.org/misc/ps-books.shtml.

25. Nicol C. Rae, *The Decline and Fall of the Liberal Republicans* (New York: Oxford University Press, 1989), 81.

26. Quoted in Rymph, *Republican Women*, 177.

27. Young Republicans of California, *Wire: Convention Special* 1, no. 3, July 14, 1964, in author's possession.

28. Warren Weaver, "GOP Women Face Right-Wing Test: Meet This Week to Elect a New Head in Bitter Fight," *New York Times*, April 30, 1967, 69; "The Making of a President," *Time*, May 12, 1967, http://www.time.com/time/magazine/article/0,9171,843720,00.html.

29. Quoted in Critchlow, *Phyllis Schlafly*, 149.

30. Quoted in Rymph, *Republican Women*, 183–84.

31. Betty Friedan, *The Feminine Mystique* (New York: Dell, 1963), 11, 325.

32. Drawn from Ruth Rosen, *The World Split Open* (New York: Penguin, 2000), 159–61.

33. The wording of the ERA is widely available on the web; e.g., http://equalrightsamendment.org/overview/htm.

34. This and all of the preceding quotes are from Phyllis Schlafly, "What's Wrong with 'Equal Rights' for Women?" *Phyllis Schlafly Report* 5, no. 7 (February 1972); the article is reprinted in William Chafe, Harvard Sitkoff, and Beth Bailey, eds., *History of Our Time* (New York: Oxford University Press, 2008), 187–96.

35. Critchlow, *Phyllis Schlafly*, 218.

36. Donald Mathew and Jane Sherron De Hart, *Sex, Gender and the Politics of ERA* (New York: Oxford University Press, 1990); all quotes from Ervin are drawn from pp. 36–41.

37. Ibid., 51.

38. Drawn from Felsenthal, *The Biography of Phyllis Schlafly*, chap. 17, "How She Did It."

39. Felsenthal, *Biography of Phyllis Schlafly*, 260.

40. Quoted in Neil J. Young, "'The ERA Is a Moral Issue': The Mormon Church, LDS Women, and the Defeat of the Equal Rights Amendment," *American Quarterly* 59, no. 3 (2007): 627.

41. Quoted in Young, "'The ERA Is a Moral Issue,'" 630.

42. An excerpt from Ezra Taft Benson, *General Conference Report*, October 1967, "Mormon Racism in Perspective," http://www.lds-mormon.com/racism.shtml.

43. Young, "'The ERA Is a Moral Issue,'" 628.

44. I am indebted here to the work of Idaho historian Rosemary Wimberly and base a part of this analysis on her unpublished, carefully documented paper "Women and Men on the Right: The Equal Rights Amendment and Anti-Feminism in the Cold War West." For the motives of Mormon women, see Young, "'The ERA Is a Moral Issue.'"

45. The quote is from 1980; http://shs.westport.k12.ct.us/jwb/Women/Power/Falwell.htm.

46. John D'Emilio and Estelle Friedman, *Intimate Matters: A History of Sexuality in America* (New York: Harper and Row, 1988), 316.

47. Jeffrey Moran, *Teaching Sex: The Shaping of Adolescence in the 20th Century* (Cambridge, Mass.: Harvard University Press, 2000), chap. 6.

48. All quoted in D'Emilio and Friedman, *Intimate Matters*, 346–47.

49. "About Focus on the Family," Focus on the Family, http://www.focusonthefamily.com/about_us.aspx.

50. "Vision Statement," Concerned Women for America, http://www.cwfa.org/about.asp.

FIVE

Ronald Reagan: The Conservative Hero

1. For an entertaining and scholarly version of this one-dimensional critique, see Michael Paul Rogin, *Ronald Reagan, the Movie* (Berkeley: University of California Press, 1987); the quoted passage is on p. 3. Reagan seems to have heard about Rogin's attack or at least a similar one; exasperated, he

complained to a friend about poorly informed biographers: "One has proclaimed that I'm only reading lines I spoke in a movie" (quoted in John Paul Diggins, *Ronald Reagan* [New York: Norton, 2007], 307).

2. Judith Stein, *Running Steel, Running America* (Chapel Hill: University of North Carolina Press, 1998), 195.

3. In recounting the details of Ronald Reagan's life, I rely on several biographies. Reagan has been lucky in having several extraordinary authors write accounts of his life. Lou Cannon, who began covering Reagan as a journalist in California, is the best at exploring his personal journey; see, in particular, *President Reagan: The Role of a Lifetime* (New York: Simon and Shuster, 1991). And while historians, as well as other critics, have expressed serious reservations about his methodology, for a spectacular exploration of Reagan's inner life and character no one exceeds Edmund Morris in *Dutch: a Memoir of Ronald Reagan* (New York: Random House, 1999); and for the best intellectual biography of Reagan—and for the best defense of an intellectual Reagan—read Diggins, *Ronald Reagan*.

4. Ronald W. Reagan, *An American Life* (New York: Simon and Schuster, 1990), 105.

5. Quoted in Rogin, *Ronald Reagan, the Movie*, 27.

6. Robert Collins, *Transforming America* (New York: Columbia University Press, 2007), 35.

7. Quoted in Diggins, *Ronald Reagan*, 85–86.

8. Quoted in Rogin, *Ronald Reagan, the Movie*, 31–32.

9. Diggins, *Ronald Reagan*, 107–15.

10. The "senior partner" quip is quoted in Cannon, *President Reagan*, 92; Cannon discusses Reagan and taxes on 90–92.

11. Richard Corliss, "His Days in Hollywood," *Time*, June 14, 2004, 61.

12. Reagan, *An American Life*, 129.

13. All quotations from Ronald Reagan, "A Time for Choosing," address on behalf of Senator Barry Goldwater, October 27, 1964, are from the version available on the Reagan Presidential Library Web site, http://ronaldreagan library.com, in the speeches section.

14. Cannon, *President Reagan*, 44.

15. Gerard J. De Groot, "Ronald Reagan and Student Unrest in California, 1966–1970," *Pacific Historical Review* 65, no. 1 (February 1996): 107–29.

16. Quoted in ibid., 110.

17. Quoted in ibid., 109n.7.

18. Quoted in ibid., 111.

19. "Ronald for Real," *Time*, October 7, 1966. This cover story on Reagan, predicting his win in California, explores his campaign.

20. Quoted in De Groot, "Ronald Reagan and Student Unrest," 115.

21. De Groot, "Ronald Reagan and Student Unrest," 115; see also David Farber, *Chicago '68* (Chicago: University of Chicago Press, 1988).

22. Quoted in Collins, *Transforming America*, 43.

23. Lou Cannon, *Governor Reagan: His Rise to Power* (New York: Public Affairs, 2003), 208–14.

24. A picture of the banner with the English-language taunt appears in Ian Nathan, "Escape from Tehran," *Empire*, April 2008, 87.

25. Jimmy Carter, State of the Union address, January 23, 1980, Jimmy Carter Library,http://www.jimmycarterlibrary.org/documents/speeches/su80 jec.phtml.

26. Bruce Schulman, *The Seventies: The Great Shift in American Culture, Society, and Politics* (Cambridge, Mass.: Da Capo Press, 2001), 198.

27. John S. Saloma III, *Ominous Politics: The New Conservative Labyrinth* (New York: Hill and Wang, 1984).

28. Patrick Allitt, *Religion in American since 1945: A History* (New York: Columbia University Press, 2003), 152.

29. Quoted in John Micklethwait and Adrian Woolridge, *The Right Nation* (New York: Penguin, 2004), 84.

30. James Patterson, *Restless Giant* (New York: Oxford University Press, 2005), 144.

31. Schulman, *The Seventies*, 194.

32. Joseph Crespino, "Did David Brooks Tell the Whole Story about Reagan's Neshoba County Fair Visit?" November 12, 2007, History News Network, http://hnn.us/articles/44535.html.

33. This argument is made at length by Matthew Lassiter, *The Silent Majority* (Princeton, N.J.: Princeton University Press, 2006).

34. Reagan and Carter quoted in Andrew Busch, *Reagan's Victory: The Presidential Election of 1980 and the Rise of the Right* (Lawrence: University Press of Kansas, 2005), 117.

35. Busch, *Reagan's Victory*, 125–28.

36. Ibid., 174.

37. Ronald Reagan, "Intent to Run for President," New York, N.Y., November 13, 1979, Reagan Presidential Library Web site, http://ronaldreagan library.com, in the speeches section.

38. Collins, *Transforming America*, 59–67.

39. W. Elliot Brownlee and C. Eugene Steuerle, "Taxation," in *The Reagan Presidency: Pragmatic Conservatism and Its Legacies*, ed. W. Elliot Brownlee and Hugh Davis Graham (Lawrence: University Press of Kansas, 2003), 160.

40. Recounted in Collins, *Transforming America*, 71.

41. Will quoted in Cannon, *President Reagan*, 21.

42. Reagan quoted in Collins, *Transforming America*, 70.

43. Quoted in Chester Pach, "Sticking to His Guns: Reagan and National Security," in *The Reagan Presidency: Pragmatic Conservatism and Its Legacies*, ed. W. Elliot Brownlee and Hugh Davis Graham (Lawrence: University Press of Kansas, 2003), 86.

44. Quoted in ibid., 90.

45. Quoted in Samuel F. Wells Jr., "Reagan, Euromissiles, and Europe," in *The Reagan Presidency: Pragmatic Conservatism and Its Legacies*, ed. W. Elliot Brownlee and Hugh Davis Graham (Lawrence: University Press of Kansas, 2003), 134.

46. All quotes are from Diggins, *Ronald Reagan*, 221–22.

47. Kirkpatrick quoted in James Mann, *Rise of the Vulcans* (New York: Penguin, 2004), 92.

48. Reagan quoted in Bob Woodward, *Veil* (New York: Simon and Schuster 1987), 299.

49. Quoted in ibid., 263.

50. Woodward, *Veil*, 254.

51. Quoted in Allitt, *Religion in America since 1945*, 155.

52. Ronald Reagan, "Address to National Association of Evangelicals," March 8, 1983, in *Reagan as President*, ed. Paul Boyer (Chicago: Ivan Dee, 1990), 167.

53. Donald Critchlow, "Mobilizing Women: The 'Social' Issues," in *The Reagan Presidency: Pragmatic Conservatism and Its Legacies*, ed. W. Elliot Brownlee and Hugh Davis Graham (Lawrence: University Press of Kansas, 2003), 302–6.

54. Stephen Skowronek, *The Politics Presidents Make: Leadership from John Adams to Bill Clinton* (Cambridge, Mass.: Harvard University Press, 1997), 37–39.

55. Adams quoted in Joseph J. Ellis, *Founding Brothers* (New York: Vintage, 2000), 125.

SIX
George W. Bush: The Conservative Calling and the Great Crack-up

1. William Jefferson Clinton, State of the Union address, January 23, 1996, http://clinton2.nara.gov/WH/New/other/sotu.html.

2. George W. Bush, Bush for President announcement, June 12, 1999, Cedar Rapids, Iowa, http://www.4president.org/speeches/bush2000announcement.html.

3. Lois Romano and George Lardner Jr., "Following His Father's Path— Step by Step by Step," *Washington Post*, July 27, 1999.

4. "Midland's Community Bible Study," *Frontline*, "The Jesus Factor," http://www.pbs.org/wgbh/pages/frontline/shows/jesus/president/cbs.html.

5. Shown on *Frontline*, "The Jesus Factor."

6. This account, as well as the quoted material, is from Patricia Kilday Hart, "Not So Great in '78," *Texas Monthly*, June 1999, http://www.texas monthly.com/1999-06-01/feature5.php.

7. Richard Woodbury, "A Cowpoke for Governor," *Time*, March 19, 1990, http://www.time.com/time/magazine/article/0,9171,969600-1,00.html. The two Williams quotes are also from this article.

8. Quoted in Lou Dubose, Jan Reid, and Carl Cannon, *Boy Genius: Karl Rove, the Brain behind the Remarkable Political Triumph of George W. Bush* (New York: PublicAffairs, 2003), 58.

9. Ann Richards, Democratic National Convention keynote address, Atlanta, July 19, 1988, http://www.americanrhetoric.com/speeches/ann richards1988dnc.htm.

10. "An Eloquent George Bush?" http://youtube.com.

11. Quoted in Dubose, Reid, and Cannon, *Boy Genius*, 73.

12. "1998 Texas GOP Convention Film," http://youtube.com.

13. Robert Draper, *Dead Certain: The Presidency of George W. Bush* (New York: Free Press, 2007), 54.

14. Patrick J. Buchanan, address to the Republican National Convention, Houston, August 17, 1992, http://www.americanrhetoric.com/speeches/patrickbuchanan1992rnc.htm.

15. George W. Bush, acceptance speech, Republican National Convention, Philadelphia, August 3, 2000, http://www.gwu.edu/~action/bush 080300.html.

16. Brent Staples, "Editorial Observer: The Republican Party's Exercise in Minstrelsy," *New York Times*, August 2, 2000.

17. Bush did not have a perfect record on the race issue. During the South Carolina primary, in Bush's battle with Senator John McCain for the Republican nomination, Bush supporters did launch a racist-oriented attack on McCain, plastering images of what they called his "black" baby around the state. McCain and his wife had adopted a dark-skinned baby girl from Bangladesh. Bush did not blast his supporters for this tactic, and he also ducked the racially charged Confederate flag issue in the state by saying that he would leave that matter to the people of South Carolina.

18. George W. Bush, acceptance speech, Republican National Convention, Philadelphia, August 3, 2000, http://www.gwu.edu/~action/bush 080300.html.

19. The third Gore-Bush presidential debate, October 17, 2000, transcript, http://www.debates.org/pages/trans2000c.html.

20. "How Groups Voted in 2000," Roper Center Public Opinion Archives, http://www.ropercenter.uconn.edu/elections/how_groups_voted/ voted_00.html; "Religion and the Presidential Vote," December 6, 2004, Pew Research Center for the People and the Press, http://people-press.org/ commentary/?analysisid=103.

21. President George Bush, "Remarks on Signing the Economic Growth and Tax Relief Reconciliation Act of 2001," June 7, 2001, American Presidency Project, http://www.presidency.ucsb.edu/ws/index.php?pid=45820.

22. A useful federal budget deficit chart can be found at the Congressional Budget Office Web site, http://www.cbo.gov/budget/data/historical.pdf.

23. Quoted in Mark A. Peterson, "Bush and Interest Groups," in *The George W. Bush Presidency*, ed. Colin Campbell and Bert A. Rockman (Washington, D.C.: CQ Press, 2004), 248.

24. Christopher Lee, "Bush Choice for Family-Planning Post Criticized," *Washington Post*, November 17, 2006.

25. "President George W. Bush's Address on Stem Cell Research," August 9, 2001, Inside Politics, CNN, http://archives.cnn.com/2001/ALLPOLITICS/ 08/09/bush.transcript/.

26. Quoted in Draper, *Dead Certain*, 151–52.

27. President George W. Bush, "Remarks at the National Day of Prayer and Remembrance," September 14, 2001, Episcopal National Cathedral, Washington, D.C., http://www.americanrhetoric.com/speeches/gwbush911 prayer&memorialaddress.htm.

28. Franklin Roosevelt, Pearl Harbor address to the nation, December 8, 1941, http://www.americanrhetoric.com/speeches/fdrpearlharbor.htm; John F. Kennedy, inaugural address, January 20, 1961, http://www.american rhetoric.com/speeches/jfkinaugural.htm.

29. Peter Singer, *The President of Good and Evil* (New York: Dutton, 2004), 2.

30. George W. Bush, commencement address, June 1, 2002, United States Military Academy, West Point, New York, http://teachingamerican history.org/library/index.asp?document=916.

31. Quoted in *What They Think of US*, ed. David Farber (Princeton, N.J.: Princeton University Press, 2007), 37.

32. Quoted in ibid., 131.

33. "President Bush: Job Ratings," PollingReport.com, http://www .pollingreport.com/BushJob1.htm.

34. President George W. Bush, 2002 State of the Union address, January 29, 2002, American Rhetoric, http://www.americanrhetoric.com/speeches/ stateoftheunion2002.htm.

35. Ibid.

36. Quoted in "Top Bush Officials Push Case against Saddam," September 8, 2002, http://cnn.com/insidepolitics, http://archives.cnn.com/2002/ ALLPOLITICS/09/08/iraq.debate/.

37. George W. Bush, prime-time press conference on Iraq war, April 13, 2004, http://www.americanrhetoric.com/speeches/wariniraq/gwbushiraq 41304.htm.

38. For evidence of the shadow Bush's infamous comment placed on the Republican Party and the conservative movement, more generally, see "New Hurricane Brings Opportunity and Risk for Republicans," *New York Times*, August 29, 2008, http://www.nytimes.com/2008/08/29/world/ americas/29iht-2katrina.1.15740950.html.

39. Further complicating and greatly exacerbating the crisis were a number of more exotic unregulated financial instruments, especially credit

default swaps, devised in the 1990s. Credit default swaps were supposed to be a form of insurance for some of the riskier securities held by banks and other large institutions. However, because there was no real government oversight of credit default swaps, these financial instruments were often undercapitalized in the event of a major default. The massive insurance company AIG, for example, was unable to meet its credit default swaps obligations as bundled mortgages began to lose their value and as a result was certain to fail without the infusion of massive amounts of government money, bringing down with it many other linked companies in the financial system.

40. Robert Kuttner, "Seven Deadly Sins of Deregulation—and Three Necessary Reforms," *American Prospect*, September 17, 2008, http://www.prospect.org/cs/articles?article=seven_deadly_sins_of_deregulation_and_three_necessary_reforms.

41. Quoted in James Ridgeway, "It's the Deregulation, Stupid," March 28, 2008, *Mother Jones*, http://www.motherjones.com/politics/2008/03/its-deregulation-stupid.

42. Franklin Roosevelt, first inaugural address, March 4, 1933, Avalon Project, http://avalon.law.yale.edu/20th_century/froos1.asp.

43. "Analyzing Obama's Stump Speech," *New York Times*, December 1, 2008, http://elections.nytimes.com/2008/president/candidates/stump-speeches/obama.html.

44. All quoted in Bob Herbert, "Out of Touch," *New York Times*, May 1, 2009.

INDEX